Praise for *Desert Wisdom*

"If you talk with your friends while in the midst of reading Desert Wisdom they will probably suspect you've fallen in love. And they will be right, for Neil Douglas-Klotz has provided, for the modern reader, a way into one of the planet's most powerful experiences of an ecstatic and mystical love—the way of the native Middle Eastern wisdom traditions. In particular, Douglas-Klotz's translations of some of the sayings of Jesus are the most radical, penetrating, and exhilarating I have ever read. Desert Wisdom is a passageway for anyone wishing to contact the numinous and creative energy capable of transforming our time into a new millennium of peace and wisdom."

—**Brian Swimme**, Co-author, with Thomas Berry, of *The Universe Story*

"In Desert Wisdom, Neil Douglas-Klotz continues in the same radical spirit as his work translating the "Our Father" prayer in *Prayers of the Cosmos.* He opens our eyes anew to the mystical truths and sacred depths of scriptural and non-scriptural passages that have become so overly familiar in their superficial translations that they can no longer move our hearts. He moves us from the letter that kills to the spirit that gives life and he assists in today's all important task to undergo deep ecumenism, that is, the eliciting of wisdom from our traditional religious sources. This is a prophetic and mystical accomplishment of the first order!

—**Matthew Fox**, author of *Original Blessing* and *The Reinvention of Work*

"Read this book aloud. Let the sounds wrap around your heart. These are translations so unhampered by reduction, stiffness and religiosity that the modern window opens quiet on the ancient garden."

—**Carolyn McVickar Edwards**, Author of *The Storyteller's Goddess*

"In these troubled and heated spiritual times, Mr. Douglas-Klotz's **Desert Wisdom** comes along like a refreshing breeze of cool, arid air. Mr. Douglas-Klotz has not only collected some of the finest words that are spiritual, humorous and thought-provoking, but he has managed to translate them from their original Semitic tongues into beautiful prose and poetry. Middle Eastern enchantment for the soul. Bravo!

—**Fred Alan Wolf,** Ph.D., American Book Award-winning author of *Taking the Quantum Leap* and *The Dreaming Universe*

"Neil Douglas-Klotz is a Master of Sacred Dance. He takes us into the domain of the Nazarene Lord of the Dance via the Aramaic rhythms and cadences that still to this day have the power to raise us to heaven."

—**Rabbi Zalman M. Schachter**, Aleph Alliance for Jewish Renewal, Author of *Paradigm Shift, Spiritual Intimacy*

"Desert Wisdom opens a new window on the ancient texts of the Middle East through which we can view their insights from a fresh perspective. Douglas-Klotz has the rare ability to approach a diversity of traditions with respect and sensitivity. This helps us to honor their commonalities rather than focus on their divisions. An important book in this time when peace in that region once again has become a fragile possibility."

—**Starhawk,** author of *The Spiral Dance* and *The Fifth Sacred Thing*

"This collection, entitled **Desert Wisdom**, was written with pure intentions and intricate detail by Neil Douglas-Klotz. It is undoubtedly a landmark book, the beginning of a major movement in the Western world to understand the holy words. It is a comprehension of the teachings of various prophets, especially those in the Holy Qur'an, which have led the development of a great school called Sufism (the school of understanding). The best and only solution to many national and international problems is understanding and recognizing the deeper meanings behind these words. However, in order to appreciate and learn from this book, one must free oneself from cultural and regional prejudices, as the author is exempt from both."

—**Shah Nazar Ali Kianfar**, Ph.D.,
Co-founder, International Association of Sufism

"**Desert Wisdom** is a soulful book which demands a change of consciousness. I admire Neil Douglas-Klotz's courage in confronting our Western world's one-sided views with the deeply mystical practices and teachings of Native Middle Eastern peoples. What a rich, spiritual gift we have in the ancient wisdom of that region of our planet. For those who wish to deepen our sense of interconnectedness, Neil's beautiful, poetic translations are like melodic chants inviting us to breathe with and take our place in the cosmos. **Desert Wisdom** is a sound spiritual guide for our postmodern times."

—**Marlene DeNardo,** S.N.D., former co-chair,
University of Creation Spirituality, Oakland, California

"This book weaves ancient sacred messages by the golden thread of unity, revealing clearly the one spiritual reality behind all existence. Open the book anywhere, and you will discover delightful inner openings and insights. You may even hear a silent dialogue between the sacred soul and its shadow. A most timely and useful contribution to all religious and spiritual studies.

—**Shaykh Fadhlalla Haeri,** Founder,
The Academy of Self Knowledge, South Africa,
author of *The Thoughtful Guide to Sufism* and *Son of Karbala*

Desert Wisdom

Neil Douglas-Klotz, Ph.D. (Saadi Shakur Chishti) is a world-renowned scholar in religious studies, spirituality and psychology. Living in Edinburgh, Scotland, he directs the Edinburgh Institute for Advanced Learning (www.eial.org) and for many years was cochair of the Mysticism Group of the American Academy of Religion. He is also cofounder of the international network of the Dances of Universal Peace. A frequent speaker and workshop leader, he is the author of several books, including *Prayers of the Cosmos, The Hidden Gospel, The Genesis Meditations, The Sufi Book of Life, Blessings of the Cosmos* and *The Tent of Abraham* (with Rabbi Arthur Waskow and Sr. Joan Chittister). Known also for this citizen diplomacy work, in 2004, he cofounded the Edinburgh International Festival of Middle Eastern Spirituality and Peace (www.mesp.org.uk). In 2005 he was awarded the Kessler-Keener Foundation Peacemaker of the Year award for his work in Middle Eastern peacemaking.

Desert Wisdom

A Nomad's Guide
to Life's Big Questions
from the Heart of the Native Middle East

Translations, Commentaries and Meditations
by Neil Douglas-Klotz

Published by ARC Books, a project of the
Abwoon Resource Center/ Shalem Center, 881 High Street, Suite 206,
Worthington, OH 43085 USA. Website:
www.abwoon.com

ISBN: 1456516477
ISBN-13: 9781456516475
Library of Congress Control Number: 2011900252

For my father and mother,
Verner H. Klotz and Frieda Reipke Klotz,
my first spiritual teachers,
who introduced me to the
three 'Holy C's':
Chiropractic, Carson (Rachel) and Cayce (Edgar)

Contents

Quick-Start Guide

Modern Life is for Nomads: Through the internet and mass media, we know more and more about what happens all over the planet. At the same time, we may feel more helpless to do anything about it—rootless and unconnected. There seems to be no certainty, except for the certainty of change.

Ancient Middle Eastern peoples knew much about change, being nomads. The essence of their spirituality arose before settlement and civilization. They became experts in things like hospitality, interdependence and connection to the natural world. Within all the perpetual changes of life, they intuited and visioned stories and wisdom about what connects everything—an underlying and overarching Unity. This book shares some of that wisdom.

Start Making Sense (of Your Self): This is a source book of inspiration, spiritual practice and guidance. You don't need to read it straight through from beginning to end. It won't necessarily make more sense. Instead of offering easy answers (the strong suit of contemporary self-help books), **Desert Wisdom** offers better questions, questions to explore your self, the challenges you face in life and your deeper place in community with others. Better answers take time to surface, just as a plant takes time to grow. Like the internet, you can jump into the **Desert Wisdom** experience many different ways. Here are a few of them:

The Big Questions: I've organized the book by three areas of search that have united human experience since we began to form thoughts and words:

1. **Diversity:** Why am I here? What is my purpose in life?

2. **Interiority:** Who am I? What is the "self"?

3. **Communion:** How do I relate to other people, nature and my surroundings? How do I love and how do I die?

Within the big questions, the thirteen chapters of the book explore more questions and themes that relate to them. In the heading of each page, you'll find these themes and questions. This makes it possible to:

Open Anywhere: The Middle East also has a long tradition of using sacred writings as an oracle in order to assist you to hear the voice of your own guidance. So you can also simply place one hand gently over your heart and breathe a few breaths. Try asking to be led to the wisdom you need for the present moment, and then open to any page you find.

Read Your Way Out: Read the selections before and after the one to which you've opened. Maybe these also relate to the question in your heart. If you're searching this way, this is not the time to get side-tracked by the historical or textual notes. How do the voices to which you've been led speak to where you are *now*? Chances are you'll find a meditation somewhere near the pages you've found. This enables you to:

Have Your Own Experience: Along with the writings themselves, I have included short meditations typical of Middle Eastern spirituality to help you explore the questions. The meditations use simple abilities common to all human beings: the awareness of our breathing, the feeling of internal sound, the ability to visualize and the sensation of our own voice.

A Native Middle Eastern Search Engine: Rather than divide the book by religious or spiritual tradition, I have gathered voices from various Middle Eastern eras to comment on the same questions. This creates a harmony of voices in which you can also hear the unique quality of each voice. The book sets each voice in its ecological or "home" context: the Middle Eastern environmental region, which generated the overall worldview which all these voices share.

Historically, some Middle Eastern voices (or interpretations of them) have been very influential in the development of Western culture. To acknowledge this, each chapter contains interpretive selections from Genesis of the Hebrew scriptures and from the words of Jesus, viewed in the Syriac Aramaic version, which most closely conveys his native language and thought. However, these Biblical voices, overly familiar to some, are translated as poetry with the multiple, possible meanings of the Hebrew or Aramaic layered into the verse or story.

Entering a Different World, and Worldview: Following in the footsteps of previous translators in the ethno-poetic world, I have attempted to translate the way a sacred or ritual text may have been "heard" originally. This means leaving behind Western cosmology and psychology for a primarily ancient Semitic one. Here you can enter a world in which mind, body and spirit are not separate, in which "outer" and "inner" are always connected, and in which the relationship between humans, nature and the "sacred" is still interwoven.

Many Voices, Layered Meaning: To come closer to this world, many of the selections use multiple, layered translation-interpretations of the same passage, rather than a single one. This is part of a long tradition of Middle Eastern mystical interpretation, which is described in the preface and introduction. This tradition (called *midrash* in the Jewish tradition and *ta'wil* in the Islamic) asks you to wrestle with and meditate on various possible meanings of a saying in order to relate it to your own everyday life.

At the end of the book, you will find **Textual Notes** for each chapter that explore the basis for each translation-interpretation and provide additional commentary with links to other research.

Forage for Wisdom: Do you already know the spiritual tradition or type of meditation you're looking for? If so, two additional indexes allow you to search the book by tradition/ textual strand or by the type of meditation, depending on your interest and inspiration.

Explore the Bigger Picture: The two **Prefaces** (new and old) describe what I feel to be the overall importance of the Middle East in the Western psyche.

The **Introduction** describes how I chose and organized the selections for the book and speaks in more detail about the translation style and methods.

The **Appendix** relates the book's purpose to the ongoing search for peace in the Middle East and relates a peace plan first proposed by the American Sufi Murshid Samuel L. Lewis in the 1950's.

Begin Now: At this point, you are ready to search and use **Desert Wisdom**. You don't need to read all the context now. If you are familiar with other types of meditation and are ready for a direct experience with another world—one familiar and yet foreign—why not skip the rest of the introductory material and go directly to the first section, **Voices of Diversity**? Or close again and open anywhere!

Preface to the Second Edition

Each time the Middle East surfaces in modern Western consciousness, it does so with increasing urgency.

Sixteen years ago, when I first published *Desert Wisdom*, it was already clear that the "Middle" or "Near" East represented more in modern Western culture than simply a vague geographical concept that embraces a conglomeration of conflicting religions, states and political problems. The Middle East had become a symbolic, and actual, source of energy—from the petrol at our fuel pumps to the despair-inducing headlines to the mythic ground out of which various religions and sects continually mine the spiritual energy to keep themselves going.

Over the past several generations, various solutions to the "problems" of the Middle East have been proposed. Some voices have declared all-out cultural war on the area and its peoples, the so-called "clash of civilizations" approach. Other voices (political and military) have intervened forcibly in the affairs of various Middle Eastern countries—countries which, after all, were simply the creations of the Western powers themselves after World War I. Still others have declared religion itself to be the problem and proposed a new heaven on earth based on the complete de-spiritualization and secularization of the cosmos.

In 1995, I waded into this conflicted arena with an attempt to show the common ground of Middle Eastern visionary voices on the basis of ecology, that is, a shared home based on environment (northern extension of the "Great Rift Valley") and cosmology (shared stories of origin and destination, primarily in Semitic language). In 1995, ardent religionists unwilling to find common ground with "other" religions accused me of glossing over differences between religions. Simultaneously, ardent secularists who felt that scientific cosmology would be the "gospel" of the modern age accused me of attempting to redeem the energy in what was (or should be) a dead institution (religion). On a practical level, most bookstores refused to stock the book because they had nowhere to shelve it. In 1995, the "Religion" section in most stores still included only Christianity, or at a stretch, Judaism. "Native Traditions" included only indigenous spiritualities of everywhere *except* the Middle East. If a book concerned Middle Eastern spirituality, it had to be about organized religion, so a book that talked about a "native Middle Eastern tradition" often ended up stacked on the floor (a circumstance I witnessed several times when I showed up for a bookstore reading).

The "problem" of the Middle East—in politics, religion, psychology (and book publishing) has not vanished, nor does it promise to do so anytime soon. At the same time, I believe that the arguments for the approach of *Desert Wisdom* remain as strong today as when I began the book almost twenty years ago. The key features of this approach are:

Ecology: All human religious and spiritual experiences arise from an embodied relationship with the environment and nature. These *natural* experiences produce vision, ritual, story and sacred text. Religion organizes or "colonizes" these experiences, increasingly, though often unwittingly, as the province of experts (a clerical, legal, academic or administrative class). Similarly, the natural human impulse to produce music and move in rhythm or dance has gradually been colonized as performing arts—an audience listening to or watching expert professionals, first live, now increasingly virtually.

Vision and Ritual: Vision and ritual go hand in hand. We can understand them on their own terms, not in terms of the later development of written texts, theologies and legal interpretations, organizations, bureaucracies and political hierarchies. I have expanded more on this below.

Big Questions: Vision and ritual naturally arise from questions basic to the human experience: Where do we come from? Where are we going? Who are we? How do we relate to "others"? What is our place in the natural world? How do we "die" and what happens then? All of these questions are posed first in the plural, as a community question, and only progressively over the past two millennia in the singular, as a question for the individual.

In much of my scholarly work since *Desert Wisdom*, I have argued for the primacy of spiritual vision and experience over later cultural developments of them, including institutional theologies. The former cannot be defined by the latter any more than the sense of smell can be defined by Chanel No. 5.

For example, most academic writers on ritual and myth take it for granted that ritual arises out of myth, as an enactment or performance of a previous story. I maintain it was more likely the other way around.

For instance, in many Native Middle Eastern spiritual traditions, the first spiritual practice was said to be "naming." In one of the Genesis stories, the first human being with self-reflexive consciousness breathes with and names its relationship to all other beings. This becomes the first form of sound practice or chant. From this chanting/naming, music arises, which has to do with hearing the overtones of sound resonating with our bodies, and connecting us to nature and the cosmos. Several mystics later called this phenomenon the "symphony of the spheres," but scientists have only recently begun to explore the neuropsychology and psychological acoustics of it.

A deeper, more embodied, empowered sense of sound naturally leads to movement and to group and individual dance. Or, breathing with the natural world in a deeper, more intensely related way can lead to art, which can be both representational as well as abstract. It can also lead to healing, in the way that shamans were able to communicate with the plant world, a phenomenon that survives to the present day in medicines like the Bach Flower remedies. Early ritual, art and healing all arises from somatic (embodied) experiences, either with another being or with the larger cosmos.

Combinations of contemplation, chant, song, art, movement and healing become ritual. People often remember collective rituals by various stories being told around them, but story is the final, narrative, verbal stage of a non-verbal, highly somatic relationship to the cosmos. Stories also help to place these somatic relationships and experiences in relation to the "big questions" mentioned above.

In light of the above, the methods of the Desert Wisdom project remain valid for understanding not only the Middle East, but also ourselves (and what the "Middle East" represents within us).

Retranslation: I have retranslated Middle Eastern wisdom texts from the past five thousand years as visionary experiences, as one might the ritual poetry of other cultures. In this regard I follow in the footsteps of poets like Jerome Rothenberg (1967, 1984, *Technicians of the Sacred)* and Robert Bly (many works, including *Eight Stages of Translation*). In the preface to the first edition of his pioneering work in ethnopoetics, Rothenberg writes:

> PRIMITIVE MEANS COMPLEX
>
> That there are no primitive languages is an axiom of contemporary linguistics where it turns its attention to the

> remote languages of the world. There are no half-formed languages, no underdeveloped or inferior languages.... What is true of language in general is equally true of poetry & of the ritual-systems of which so much poetry is a part. It is a question of energy & intelligence as universal constants &, in any specific case, the direction that energy & intelligence (=imagination) have been given. No people today is newly born. No people has sat in sloth for the thousands of years of its history. Measure everything by the Titan rocket & the transistor radio, & the world is full of primitive peoples. But once change the unit of value to the poem or the dance-event or the dream (all clearly antifactual situations) & it becomes apparent what all those people have been doing all those years with all that time on their hands (punctuation as in original, 1967, p.xxv).

Multi-leveled Versions: In the West, only some Middle Eastern voices have been considered "primitive." Others have been considered, through the lens of Western philosophy and theology, as the only source of truth and civilization. These voices need "re-hearing," allowing the richness of expression originally there to burst the strait-jackets of institutionalization. In the ancient Middle Eastern Semitic languages, the distinction between what we call cosmology—our place in the universe—and psychology—our inner state, did not exist. When cosmology meets psychology, then the way we treat ourselves is the way we treat nature and those around us. And vice versa. The root-and-pattern system of Semitic languages makes possible an approach similar to what is called *midrash* in the Jewish mystical tradition and *ta'wil* in the Islamic one: hearing each statement or story in a multi-leveled way, with all possible meanings of the various Semitic words included.

A Text Organized by the Big Questions: This allows one to neither force nor ignore similarities. The human questions unite us. The diversity of answers is a cause for celebration rather than dismay, or even worse, the colonization of fear into structures of political and religious power.

If any of this is true, then we cannot expect to find common answers to problems or create new rituals from an already fixed text of either an old mythic or a new scientific story. Ancient visions and stories, as well as an increased appreciation of our shared ecological challenges, can help us find our way.

In my view, we need to enter states of somatic awe—"unknowing" rather than knowing—in relationship to the cosmos. We can cultivate such numinous states of awareness through traditional spiritual practices from all parts of the earth. These practices center on abilities common to all human beings, primarily the awareness of breathing, tone/sound and other somatic sensation. They can lead us to unmediated experiences of the "voice" of the universe, as it came through our original human encoding, before it was modified by some unhelpful habits of modern culture. As many stories propose, perhaps we can hear the voice of the Being or Consciousness behind the universe, as it speaks to our problems now.

As we enlarge the awareness of our relationship to each other in a still larger, now sacred cosmos, we can name and re-name these relationships in new, shared ritual. We may discover that old and new forms of music, dance, ceremony and healing arise to weave together new and old stories, creating shared celebrations diverse enough to include all the cultures of the earth and vibrant enough to sustain coming generations.

—Neil Douglas-Klotz, January 2011

Preface to the First Edition

Every part of the earth has evolved crucial insights and wisdom that can offer solutions to the unfolding story of the human species on the earth today. This wisdom came through the mystics, prophets, poets and artists who, by their own willingness to experience a sense of deep communion with the universe, gave voice to enduring meaning and beauty. We need all of this wisdom to meet the ecological, economic, political and spiritual challenges we face today—no one voice has all the answers.

This book aims to convey both wisdom and spiritual practice from the Native Middle Eastern tradition that can help us regain a healthy relationship to the earth and to fulfill our purpose in being here. For similar wisdom, many people have begun to listen seriously to voices of the native traditions of the Americas, Africa and Oceania. Likewise, a voice of wisdom from the Native Middle Eastern tradition is waiting to be heard.

The term "Native Middle Eastern" may seem unusual. By this I mean a spirituality that arises from a particular bioregion, which ranges from northeastern Africa around the Mediterranean Sea to the Anatolian peninsula (present-day Turkey) and extends southeast through the Arabian peninsula and northeast through present-day Iran into the Caucasus Mountains. As evidenced by archeology, this area has been home to human habitation from the earliest times. It is centered roughly around the northern part of what is sometimes called the "Great Rift Valley," a volatile region of faults extending from Lebanon all the way to Mozambique in Africa. The "aftershocks" of this area, geophysical and metaphysical, have resonated throughout the world.

Human beings in this area of the earth evolved unique forms of cosmology, spirituality and psychology over the past eight to ten thousand years that helped to connect them with the natural world and make sense of their lives. This wisdom can be heard not only as separate voices, but also as a harmonious chorus. Just as Native American spirituality presents many varieties of ritual, spiritual practice and tribal organization yet can also be heard as a unified voice, so also the heart of Native Middle Eastern spirituality can offer a perfume that transcends its apparent differences. The fact that this perfume is hard to catch has much to do with the history of relations between the European West and the "Middle" or "Near" East, names themselves chosen by Europeans to describe its relationship to them.

For the past two thousand years, the West has extracted, refined and harnessed the spiritual and philosophical resources of the Middle East to create and fuel much of its modern culture and religion. Foremost among these products were the European versions of Christianity and Judaism, whose prophets were born in the Middle East and spoke Semitic languages. Conflicts between and among the Western versions of these "classical" religions and their various sects, heresies and competing orthodoxies have dominated political and cultural life in the Common Era.

Even the roots of modern science and mathematics arose in the Islamic Middle East and were carried to Europe during its "dark ages." Scientists then fought with religious hierarchies over who would dominate the spiritual and imaginative life of the West. When the politician and the industrialist both entered this battle about three hundred years ago, they irreparably tipped the scales away from a shared worldview of spirit and nature. Without any common vision of purpose, which is the gift of an integrated cosmology and psychology, human life became an ever more divisive fight for resources and wealth.

Over the past century, the West has returned to the Middle East to extract, refine and harness its earth energy resources—oil—as it previously did the Middle East's spiritual resources. In elaborate political chess games after World War I, Western nations carved out countries and engaged in a belated spasm of empire-building to protect their "strategic" interests. Most recently, in various attempts to further peace in the region, the West has not only confronted its own previous interference but also found itself embroiled in conflicts that are deeply rooted in the indigenous spirituality of this region of the earth. After a few hundred years of ignorance, fear and manipulation, how can anyone in the West make sense of the deeper story, embedded in the spirituality that has evolved there?

Like a person awakening from amnesia, the West now turns to the Middle East with vague inklings of the childhood of Judaism and Christianity, with fear and mistrust of the little it really knows of Islam and with virtual ignorance of the varied indigenous spiritualities that were never labeled "classical religions" by the West. As drilling for oil continues, another type of digging continues to unearth ancient manuscripts like the Dead Sea Scrolls and the Nag Hammadi Library, which call into question the previously accepted stories of the origins of Western Christianity, and to a lesser extent, Judaism.

While the desire to secure sources of oil leads the West into increasingly dangerous conflicts in the Middle East, our culture also confronts the overall question of human survival into a postmodern age. How much oil is enough? How much of the earth's resources do we need to feed an addictive lifestyle that is maiming the earth for the next generation of human beings?

On the deepest level, what are we trying to get from the Middle East? What does this region mean for us in the West and for all of humanity at this time? What answers can it contribute to the overall question of human survival on the earth?

To begin to answer these questions, I maintain that Western culture needs to return to the Middle East as a student and partner, not as a teacher and dominator. As the West found in its relations with the former Soviet Union, when cultural stereotypes begin to break down, fear and superstition do also. The "enemy" begins to look more like ourselves. But mere cross-cultural understanding, which seldom extends beyond mental concepts, is not enough. We must begin to experience a part of our collective psyche that was left behind when the mythic oil was extracted from the earth and used to fuel so-called Western religion, as well as the secularist reactions to it.

As we recover this psychic territory, we may be able to release the ways we seek, as a culture, to fill an inner void by taking more and more from the earth around us. Put another way, the extent to which Western culture has been unwilling to look at its own religious roots in terms of indigenous, earth-based spirituality reflects the extent of its denial of the body and the earth.

This collection offers to begin a process of recovery by sharing the words of Native Middle Eastern visionaries, poets, shamans and mystics, linked to the indigenous spiritual practices that make their wisdom an embodied experience. Ultimately, myth arises from a profound, direct experience of the natural world and intimations of its connection with the entire cosmos. Spiritual practice opens the door to such direct experience. Trying to take the myth without the embodied practice is at best a form of voyeurism. At worst it is a form of cultural strip-mining. It raises psychic and mental energy without grounding it—that is, giving it back to the earth through the resonance of our own embodied experience.

For the past twenty years, I have studied the spiritual practice of the Native Middle Eastern tradition with Sufis, dervishes, rabbis, Kabbalists, monks, mystics and shamans. I have researched their sacred writings in Hebrew, Aramaic, Arabic and other languages. I am well aware of the religious and theological differences that divide creed from creed and sect from sect. I leave these to those for whom they have interest. I am also aware of a greater common ground of spirituality that unites not only the "great" religions but all religious experience in this region. What I have experienced and understood, I offer here in translations, commentary and meditations that evoke the wisdom of the Native Middle Eastern tradition.

—Neil Douglas-Klotz, April 1994

Introduction: Weaving a Magic Carpet

The image I carried while completing this book was that of a nomadic, hand-loomed carpet, created from various interwoven strands in which certain patterns emerge depending upon one's distance and angle of viewing. In addition to the main table of contents, two additional indexes allow the reader to hear the voices in different ways: by tradition/textual stand and by the type of meditation offered.

A. The Larger Pattern: Sections and Chapters

The book is divided into three main sections. Each corresponds to one of the three main areas of questioning that have united human beings throughout history:

1. **Diversity:** Why am I here? What is my purpose in life?
2. **Interiority:** Who am I? What is the "self"?
3. **Communion:** How do I relate to other people, nature and my surroundings? How do I love and how do I die?

These three areas also correspond to the three foundational principles of how the life of the universe and on this planet has evolved based on the research of modern physics, paleontology and biology. These three principles were articulated by scientist Brian Swimme and historian Thomas Berry (1992), who gave them the above names.

To the extent that modern culture has lost touch with nature, it exhibits faces of collapse in all three areas. The resources of the Native Middle Eastern tradition, in the form of orthodox religion, have been used to justify this collapse. But its voices of wisdom, prophecy and mysticism speak strongly to all three of these universe—and universal—principles. And they may help us recover parts of our psychic life that have been suffering from collective amnesia.

Within each section, the chapters offer wisdom clustered around particular themes that I feel are unique gifts from this tradition.

To contribute to our experience of **diversity and purpose**, the Native Middle Eastern tradition offers rich understandings of the sacred realities of vibration and form, creativity, light and dark, time, space and voice. Each of these produce questions that arise in our daily life and that I've paired with the chapter titles. As noted in the "Quick Start," this allows the book to be used as an oracle to address a situation in life.

To contribute to our experience of **inner presence and the self**, this tradition offers practical and subtle insights about inner sensation and emotional feeling, the subconscious soul-self, its relation to the universal "I Am," the self's journey of discovery and how it relates to an "other." Similarly, these themes produce personal questions like: "Who is the 'I am' within?" and "Is this a step on my path?"

To contribute to our experience of **communion and relationship**, this tradition offers a clear, rich expression of the interplay between sexual passion, desire, love, devotion, death, healing, and thankfulness. Questions that might arise here include: "What attracts me?" and "What needs to be sacrificed?"

B. Interweaving Your Own Experience: Meditations

The meditation threads are: Sound and Embodiment, Simple Presence, Heart Awareness, Depths of the Self, Celebration and Thankfulness. An index in the back of the book lists all of the meditations in the book by these themes.

I have based these meditations on authentic spiritual practices from the Middle Eastern region. Some derive from Jewish or Sufi mystical practices that are actively used today. I have recreated others based on my understanding of the texts. Some of the ancient practices have not been previously published. This is not because they are dangerous but because what makes them work is the spiritual relationship in which they are usually prescribed. This one-to-one spiritual relationship is like a current that flows from one pole to another in a battery. When the poles are not connected, no current flows.

I encourage readers to (1) use the meditations individually to find their way into the world of experience suggested by the text and (2) use them with others in small, cooperative study groups in which experiences can be shared freely. I feel that the need of the planet at this time calls all of us to the integration of feeling and wisdom that previously was the province of selected people later called mystics, shamans or adepts. I also encourage readers to carefully seek out open-hearted, experienced teachers from these traditions who can serve as touchstones for an ongoing, deeper growth in wisdom. In this sense, my work only introduces a rich territory that requires a lifetime to explore.

Many of the meditations rely on intoning, chanting or breathing with some of the sacred phrases used in the texts. My rendering of Hebrew, Aramaic and Arabic into English characters does not use formal transliteration script and, like my previous work, is not intended to teach a person these languages. The latter requires long, patient study. My transliterations intend only to approximate the sounds involved so that the general reader can understand how the translations arose and participate in the meditations.

The meditations in each thread work with different aspects of one's being. They also develop progressively, building gradually on the ability to sense, feel, concentrate and articulate one's inner awareness. So one might follow the "Depths of the Self" meditations through various chapters and, helped by the texts linked to them, discover a growing inner capacity to hear clearly "the voices at the table of Holy Wisdom" (as the selections from Proverbs or the Nag Hammadi might put it). Some meditations may work for you immediately, some only over time or after practice, some not at all. Please take what you find of value and do not concern yourself with the rest. The Native Middle Eastern tradition is a wild field, not a monoculture. It tells many different stories and shares many different practices to point to something that is, ultimately, inexpressible in words.

C. The Threads of Wisdom: Texts Used

Below I have listed the major threads of text and the reasons why I chose them.

1. Genesis Threads.

This includes the original seven "days" of creation according to the Hebrew text (Genesis 1:1-2:4). This text has had an unparalleled impact on Western culture. The literalistic, and sometimes plainly wrong, translations, of the Genesis story have rendered deep divisions between "heaven" and "earth" as well as between "man" and the rest of "nature." As I point out in chapter ten, key among these texts was Genesis 1:28, which in its most common mistranslation from the Hebrew, charged human beings with "dominating" and "subduing" the earth. In reality, the Hebrew text clearly speaks about ruling "with" or "alongside of" all the other beings created before the human.

My expanded translation and interpretation from the Hebrew could be called a mystical commentary on the scripture (or *midrash*). In these renditions, I have taken full advantage of the vocabulary that the new physics and chaos theory has evolved to describe the origins of the universe. At the same time, I have been as faithful as possible to the sense of the Hebrew words and their roots. Details of this are explained in the textual notes.

Genesis neither explains nor predicts all of the new scientific cosmology. Yet this recent research has created a new vocabulary in English that offers the possibility to go beyond previous literal and mechanistic renditions like those of the King James Version (KJV). At the same time, many of the mystical ideas of the Genesis creation stories (like creation through sound and vibration) correspond well with the more poetically-named theories of modern scientific cosmology, like "super-string" theory. The account of the first seven days in Genesis in fact goes far beyond current scientific and psychological insights in its subtle teachings about how the interiority of a self actually organizes itself. As a number of philosophers and scientists have pointed out, questions about the origins of the cosmos, including time and space themselves, have much to do with the nature of consciousness. The Genesis thread runs throughout this book and in many ways helped organize the location of the primary questions I have chosen to explore.

2. Other Hebrew Threads.

These include translations from the Hebrew of Proverbs (the voice of Holy Wisdom), the Song of Songs (the passage about love and death), Deuteronomy 6:4 (the Shema) and

Isaiah 6 (the vision of the divine "throne/chariot"). Kabbalists have historically connected the Isaiah passage with one of the earliest recorded Jewish mystical practices, which involves re-experiencing the divine *merkabah* (the chariot or throne of the Holy One). According to Jewish scholar Gershom Scholem (1954, p.47), paradoxical references to the experience of this practice mention both "descent" and "ascent" in order to attain the divine vision. In retranslating the Isaiah passages and composing meditations that accompany them, I have offered one way in which the mystical practice might have been performed.

For comparison with my translations of all these Hebrew texts, I have also given the most common (and popularly influential) previous English translation—that of the King James Bible.

I have also included a later "Hebrew thread" from the Dead Sea Scrolls (as noted below) and from the thirteenth century Aramaic mystical treatise called the Zohar, which illustrates the three faces of the soul or self.

3. Ancient Middle Eastern Threads.

These sacred texts, liturgies and poetry from Sumer, Babylonia, Assyria and Egypt sometimes contrast, sometimes harmonize with others around them. I hope that my renderings expand and illuminate this older heritage of native mysticism, which has influenced all of our classical religions.

In this category I have also included brief texts from the Mandaean and Zoroastrian traditions, both of which were once as powerful and influential as Judaism, Christianity or Islam, and both of which still survive today in vitality if not in great numbers.

These older voices reveal wild, stark, intense passion and awe at the processes and mysteries of the universe. The poets and storytellers grope for explanations that can express both the terror and wonder of being alive. As human beings, we need to recover these qualities today as we face different terrors and wonders, with far too many unquestioned assumptions of "the way things are."

For comparison with my translations and versions of these texts, I have given the first few lines of some previous literal translations. Since most people are unaware of these texts, or don't regard them as anything more than curiosities, none of these previous translations has really affected the popular mind in the West. My versions seek to place them clearly within the overall wisdom tradition of the other selections rather than to obscure them with awkward syntax.

4. Aramaic Gospel Threads.

Building on my previous work in *Prayers of the Cosmos* (1990), these are expanded translations of the reported words of Jesus (*Yeshua* in Aramaic) from the Gospels. My source text is the Peshitta version of the scripture in Syriac Aramaic commonly used by Aramaic-speaking Christian churches in the Middle East from the 5th century C.E. up to the present day. Without going into an extensive explanation, which is contained in a number of my subsequent books, particularly *The Hidden Gospel* (1999) and *Blessings of the Cosmos* (2006), these translations and versions illuminate an aspect of Jesus' native language, idiom and culture very distinct from the Greek versions, especially as they were later interpreted through Platonic and neo-Platonic philosophy. Imagine, for example, trying to render the Tao Te Ching exclusively from a Latin version, then suddenly discovering it was composed (or at least originally spoken) in Chinese.

In these selections I have retranslated sayings that have proved problematic to many readers because of later theological interpretations based on inadequate Greek versions of his words. Whatever the textual origins of what we know as Christianity, if or when Jesus said what the Gospels report, he said it in Aramaic. Looking at an Aramaic version of the Gospels opens a window of interpretation into the Semitic mind that no Greek text can do. Again, for comparison with my translations of these texts, I have given the King James Version.

5. Dead Sea and Nag Hammadi Threads.

Here readers will find a new translation of a blessing from the Dead Sea Scrolls (itself a version of Aaron's blessing in Numbers 6) and a new version of the Coptic text usually called *Thunder, Perfect Mind* from the library of scrolls found buried near Nag Hammadi, Egypt in 1945.

Controversy still rages about the communities that buried each set of books. Up until the early 1990s, the Dead Sea Scrolls were dated and analyzed as sufficiently far removed from the early "Jesus Movement" to have no influence on it. The community of ascetics living at Qumran, on a bluff overlooking the Dead Sea, had no direct connection to the origins of Christianity or to Jesus himself, according to the small group of scholars who monopolized the scrolls' translation (and often non-translation) for almost fifty years. In 1992, due to increased pressure, the scrolls were released for the perusal of other scholars. Previously untranslated scrolls revealed versions of a set of "beatitudes" as well as references to phrases like "son of God." Consequently, previous assumptions about the date, purpose and nature of the Qumran community as well as the scrolls themselves have been largely discarded. There are a number of excellent, and usually conflicting, scholarly texts on the subject of the scrolls' interpretation, some of which I have cited in the bibliography.

The Nag Hammadi texts have been in translation much longer, even though they were discovered in the same year. Until the late 1990s, scholars referred to these books as "gnostic" texts from a period before the "Jesus Movement" became an orthodox religion. However, the varieties of belief that the texts represent make it difficult to attribute them to any one group, with any one belief system, including "gnostic." Today most biblical studies scholars consider them a fair reflection of the extreme diversity that existed in the Jesus Movement for at least three centuries after his time. When the Emperor Constantine made Christianity the official religion of the Roman empire in the 4th century C.E., an orthodox version was created, articulated and enforced. Books like those found in the Nag Hammadi collection were banned, which is most likely why this particular library was hidden.

The Coptic language text that I have re-rendered is clearly in the tradition of *Hokhmah* or "Holy Wisdom" as mentioned in Proverbs, even though some scholars were originally at pains to give it a Greek parentage. In addition, the text illustrates a very Middle Eastern view of the subconscious soul-self and its unfoldment, an aspect that previous works have not explored. You will find more on the background of this text in the notes.

No doubt both sets of books deserve better representation than I have given them here. I returned to various of these texts, particularly the Gospel of Thomas, in *The Genesis Meditations* (2003). For comparison to my versions of the Nag Hammadi text and translation of the Qumran text, I have again given the first lines of previous literal translations.

6. Qur'an and Hadith Threads.

No Middle Eastern tradition has been stereotyped as badly as has Islam, especially by the Western popular media. From the

Muslim point of view, there can never be an adequate word-for-word translation of the Qur'an. Muslims view the text as a material symbol pointing to the divine presence in every atom of being. It not only *relates* meaning, its Arabic words *are* Sacred Meaning. For this reason, I hope that my interpretive meditations on the Arabic of the Qur'an will inspire readers to look further for wisdom from this source. The essence of the Qur'an, particularly the early Meccan Surahs, has much to offer toward re-envisioning the entire natural world and cosmos as a sacred sanctuary, a point of view much needed today. I also recommend the book *Heart of the Qur'an* (2003) by Sheikh Nur Lex Hixon, which I was honored to introduce and annotate in the current edition.

The surahs (chapters) and portions of surahs I have rendered include those that are commonly used as part of the ritual prayers of Islam, which were initiated after the example of the Prophet Muhammad. In addition, I have included one of the *hadith* (traditional sayings) of Muhammad. The distinction made by Muslims is that in the Qur'an the voice of the One is said to speak directly; in the *hadith,* Muhammad speaks.

Since there is no common, popularly-influential English translation of the Qur'an, I have cited for comparison that of Yusuf Ali, which is considered a standard in the field of English translation. My recommendations for other Qur'anic translations, including that of Muhammad Asad, can be found in the Bibliography.

7. Sufi Threads.

The roots of Sufism are very ancient, yet as a Middle Eastern mystical movement and path, it attained an outward brilliance during the 9th to 12th centuries as expressed in writers and poets like Mevlana Jelaluddin Rumi, Sa'adi of Shiraz, Hafiz of Shiraz and Mahmud Shabistari.

The origins of Sufism are shrouded in mystery. By some accounts, a circle of mystics formed around Prophet Muhammad while he and his community were in exile in Medina (about 623 C.E.). According to other scholars, some of this circle were already members of or influenced by pre-existing circles of Christian mystical ascetics living in Arabia and Syria. According to still other scholars, there was no prior influence from other traditions, a position frankly difficult to maintain considering that Muhammad himself acknowledged and honored the previous influence of Jesus and all other Semitic prophets.

The origins of the term *sufi* are in doubt. By one reading, it is based on a root meaning "wise," "pure" and "wool" (from the robes of wool that many in some early pre-Islamic desert groups wore). The word also has its origins in early Semitic sacred phrases, particularly in the words of Jesus. According to most accounts, the term "Sufi" was not formally adopted until almost 150 years after the time of Muhammad by the Syrian mystic, Abu Hashim. For more on the practice of Sufism and a new translation of the "99 Beautiful Names of Allah," see my later work, *The Sufi Book of Life* (2005).

While the works of Jelaluddin Rumi are relatively well known through the fine work of Coleman Barks, the other Sufi poets whose work I offer here have not had as good a hearing due to the lack of contemporary English versions. By employing Barks' method of "informants" (that is, comparing previous antiquated English language translations) and keeping in mind the underlying Sufi terminology and psychology used, I have attempted to add my own versions to the growing body of poetry already available. Rather than render the poetry so freely that the original is unrecognizable, I have stayed close to the meaning of various stanzas and lines, if not to the poetic form itself (which fits the original Persian but tends to torture

English). I have not given any comparison to my versions from previous literal translations here, since most of the latter suffer mainly from outdated syntax and word choice. In most cases, the nineteenth and early twentieth century British translators were also clearly unaware of certain key sacred terms in Sufism. However, like many others, I remain in the debt of these early translators for their pioneering work to open the Western mind to classical Sufi poetry.

D. Changes to the Second Edition

In its original composition, *Desert Wisdom* was part scholarly endeavour and part vision quest. Of all my books so far, it is the one organized least by logic and most by intuition. This makes it a puzzle for some readers and a delight for others, primarily those who like to discover meaning for themselves rather than be told why something is important before they read it. I have kept this intuitive feature of the book intact. One very good way to read *Desert Wisdom* remains simply to open it at random, with a question or situation in mind, and begin.

In this edition, I have made many revisions and additions to the translations, meditations and textual notes. Notably, I have re-worked many passages in the Genesis creation story that were not included in my fourth book *The Genesis Meditations* (2003). As part of this *midrash*, I have re-introduced the "storyteller" voice from *Genesis Meditations* to re-create one experience of how the story might have been told and heard orally.

I have also expanded the translations of Jesus' "I Am" sayings from the Gospel of John. These sayings, in their broader context, form part of Jesus' farewell teaching to his disciples and begin approximately a year before he leaves. They illustrate one way that a Native Middle Eastern wisdom teacher can show his students how to benefit from his presence while at the same time learning to follow their own guidance in connection with him.

The reader will also find several new interpretive meditations on passages of the Qur'an, including the "zikr of Jonah" in the belly of the whale and the Qur'an's account of the creation of the soul.

The textual notes have been rewritten and reorganized so that they are now all in the back of the book. If you want to read about word meanings and the origin of a particular text, you will need to become a "two-handed" reader, flipping back and forth. If, on the other hand, you simply want to contemplate a text combined with a meditation, you can do that as well. As a carrot for the "two-handers," most of the textual notes have been rewritten and updated to reflect my subsequent work.

In addition, I have revised all of the transliterations of non-English words and made them more regular than in the first edition. They are still intended only as a guide for lay readers. You can find formal scholarly transliterations of Aramaic, for instance, in the notes of my third book *The Hidden Gospel* (1999).

Hebrew readers will notice one peculiarity in my transliterations of that language. Along with some other scholars, I have been convinced that ancient Hebrew, like other ancient Semitic languages, never had the "v" sound (often used in synagogue Hebrew for some pronunciations of the letter *beth*). The "v" sound seems to be a borrowing from another language, perhaps Persian or German. For most readers this may seem a small point but, as at least one Jewish Kabbalist has pointed out, the "v" sound, emulating "f" expresses the mystical sense of division. The Hebrew letter *beth* (b/w) expresses creation and connection. So, for instance, placing the sound of division in the middle of the word for love (*ahava* vs. *ahaba*) can make a big difference in its "sound-meaning."

In transliterating the Aramaic pronunciation, I have primarily kept to the Assyrian style, although I realize that there are differences between it and what is used by Syrian Orthodox scholars. The best reconstruction of Jesus' first century C.E. Aramaic would likely be a combination of the present Syrian Orthodox and Assyrian pronunciations with a "tablespoon" of late ancient Hebrew mixed in. This is what I use in the published recordings I have made of Jesus' prayer and other sayings (which you can find at www.abwoon.com).

My thanks to all of the friends and supporters of the Abwoon Circles and Abwoon Resource Center, who gently prodded me to revise *Desert Wisdom* for a new edition. It has been a pleasure to do so, as it has offered me a reconnection to the stream of inspiration and blessing out of which the book arose. For the latter, I thank my teachers, including all those mentioned in the first edition. I also thank my critics, who have helped me make the second edition even stronger than the first.

As with all hand-woven carpets, I beg the reader's indulgence for any stray threads that I have left unknotted or hanging out. Most traders will tell you that the lack of machine-fabricated perfection adds to the uniqueness and value of each nomadic *kilim.* The looseness of the weave also leaves some room for you to weave in your own threads of experience. The Middle Eastern storyteller would say that your own personal confidence and magnetism increases the magic of any carpet. If I have succeeded, I hope that this piece of weaving transports you through the power and beauty of the Native Middle Eastern tradition to a new view of your home in the universe.

—Neil Douglas-Klotz, January 2011

Section One: Voices of Diversity: Why Am I Here?

Where do we come from? Why are we here? What is the purpose of our life? Ancient Middle Eastern voices raised these questions and reflected on diversity as a sacred principle of the cosmos. The universe tends to create what is new, unique and complex. No two cells, blades of grass, fingerprints, bodies or events are ever exactly alike. On a personal level, these storytellers and wisdom voices prompt us to find our purpose in life as well as the work that expresses this purpose rather than deadens our soul. On the deepest spiritual level, these voices ask us to hear own unique role in the story of the universe.

1. Vibration and Form: How Do I Begin Again?

The instant of beginning contains the seed of what follows, according to Native Middle Eastern spirituality. Middle Eastern creation stories focus our attention at the beginning, where we find two intertwined cosmic energies—vibration and form—that constantly create new life. These two creative forces help us understand the communal and individual dimensions of our existence.

When life draws you to selections in this chapter, you might consider how you begin projects and relationships, and how you balance inner needs with those that seem to draw you from outside.

1. Vibration and Form:

Particle and Wave (Hebrew)

(a midrashic, or interpretive, translation of Genesis 1:1)

bere'shit bara' 'elohim 'et hashamayim we'et ha'aretz
KJV: In the beginning God created the heaven and the earth.

The Storyteller begins:
In the beginning...
which means:
in archetypal form—
    with the power to be something in principle—
like a point that unfolds itself
in wings and flame,
in all directions,
conceiving the idea of a universe
for better *and* for worse...

In that time before time and space,
the Being of beings,
the I-They-Who-Are,
the One that is Many,
the Ultimate Pronoun,

drew upon unknowable Otherness,
to convert into knowable Existing
two tendencies of our universe-to-be:

the cosmic tendency toward the limitless:
the ocean of light, sound,
name and vibration—
all that shines in glorious space,
and rises in sublime time—

as well as
the cosmic tendency toward the limited:
a formed and fixed energy that moves
straight toward goals and solutions—
the sense of purpose that we see in
earth, water, fire and air.

In Principle,
In Beginning-ness,
Oneness created the wave and the particle.

Meditation—Sound and Embodiment 1: Wave and Particle

For helping balance a healthy sense of both individuality and relationship:

1. When feeling out of contact with your body and with the earth, due to mental distraction, exhaustion or just plain busy-ness:

Sit comfortably on the earth directly, or on a chair. Then sit briefly on your hands, feeling a distinct connection between the solid part in you, the bones of your pelvis, and what is solid underneath you and supporting you, the body of the earth. While feeling this connection (either with hands underneath or removed), intone the Hebrew word *aretz* for four counts (for instance, "A-AH-REH-ETZ"). Feel your bones vibrating with the sound. After a few times, breathe with the sound and feeling.

2. When feeling introverted, locked up within yourself or overly constricted:

Place your hands lightly over your heart and begin to sense all the movement pulsing underneath, for instance, the blood radiating out to all parts of the body. You might feel your own heart's pulsation as a continuation of the mysterious pulse that began the cosmos. While doing so, intone the sound *shamayim* for four counts (for instance, "SHAM-AY-EE-EEM"). As much as possible, feel the sound radiating outward from the center of the heart. Once you feel this, try opening your hands and arms to allow the sound and feeling to radiate outward. To emphasize your own creative fire in unison with the cosmos, you might imagine your heart as the center of a creative fireball, such as might have happened at the beginning of the universe. To feel the freedom of the cosmos in you, you might slowly open your arms like wings spreading while you chant, allowing the heart to fly. After some moments of intoning, simply breathe with the feeling of the sound silently.

3. To balance the two sensations, intone one sound after the other. Feel both the particle and wave realities of your being balance each other and work in harmony together. Then breathe with both sensations while sitting or walking: Try inhaling, feeling the sound *aretz* inside and exhaling feeling the sound *shamayim*. Then reverse these and notice the difference in feeling.

Character Development (Sumerian)

(version of a portion of a creation song, approximately 2nd millennium B.C.E.)

C.J. Gadd version: When in heaven and earth the steadfast twain had been completed, and the goddess-mother Innana, she (too) had been created, when the earth had been laid down in the place made (for it), when the designs of heaven and earth had been decided....

After the beginning,
Vibration and Form, the two elementary principles,
individuated and divided.
(Yet we always find them intertwined.)

After this Inanna, the divine Mother of life, took form:
She begins the countless generations of relationship,
the primordial lineages, clans and families who
caravan together throughout created time,
new emanations linked to prior waves and forms.

Then the earth began to find its place in space and time,
its heights and depths fastened
like a jewel into the cosmic bezel of the prior void.
And wave-atmospheres-sky—earth's partner—
responded harmoniously, embracing it.

From this embrace of partnership,
the denser waves found form on earth
and limited themselves to stream and sea.
Tigris and Euphrates, our two glistening ones,
remind us of that time,

when wave and form
set bounds and banks,
developing their characters more uniquely
to further life's unfolding.

Meditation—Gratitude and Celebration 1: Setting Bounds and Banks

For supporting a deeper sense of flowing, support and spaciousness:

Imagine yourself at a place in nature where earth meets sky and sea in pristine beauty. Or if you have the opportunity, go to such a place. Breathe with the essence of natural, flowing water and feel your own inner essence of flow— emotional feeling, the fluids within you that encourage health, the flow of your life. Imagine water feeling you as you feel it, water tasting you as you taste it.

Do the same for earth. Imagine it as part of your own essence—the sensation of support through your bones, the feeling of healthy "standing," neither pressing down nor holding yourself away from the earth. You are supported for the essence of your being rather than for what you may do or accomplish. Imagine the earth feeling you, touching you, as you touch it.

Finally, do the same for the sky. Its spaciousness and breath is part of your own. Where does this openness and freedom touch you most clearly? Open your ears to the vault of space that resonates with the sounds of the cosmos. Imagine the sky and air touching you, hearing you, as you hear and touch it.

Then, allow yourself to breathe with thankfulness for all the ways in which life has helped you develop your own uniqueness. Feel this unique essence of you as changeable, yet just as natural, as that of earth, sea and sky around you.

Binding and Letting Go (Aramaic)

(a translation of Matthew 18:18-20 from the Peshitta version of the Gospels)

wa'miyn 'amar 'na' lkhuwn dkhul ma' dte'sruwn ba'r'a' nehwe' 'asiyr bashmaya' wmedem dteshruwn ba'r'a' nehwe' shre' bashmaya' (18).

KJV: Verily I say unto you, Whatsoever ye shall bind on earth shall be bound in heaven: and whatsoever ye shall loose on earth shall be loosed in heaven (18).

By the living ground on which we stand, I say:

In whatever you deeply bind your individual self,
whatever passion you harness in earthiness,
whatever foundation you build
on the particle reality,
that same earthy part of you is tied up,
the passion occupied
within the communal reality of the universe,
the wave-penetrated cosmos.

On the other hand:
whatever passion you liberate and release,
whatever circles you open, giving birth,
letting go of the created,
freeing the loved one
in form, substance and earthiness,
that same part of you is unbound,
the passion released
within the vibrating communion of the cosmos—
heaven, within and among you (18).

tuwb 'amarna' lkhuwn de'n treyn menkhuwn neshtwuwn ba'r'a' 'al kul tzbuw dneshe'luwn nehwe' lhuwn men lwat 'aby dshmaya' (19).

KJV: Again I say unto you, That if two of you shall agree on earth as touching any thing that they shall ask, it shall be done for them of my Father which is in heaven (19).

Another way to say this is:
If two of you, in your earthy, individual natures,
agree with each other,
imitating the harmony of the heavens
    (the continuum of wave, sound and name),
then anything that you ask in that mind of communion—
peaceful, straightforward, without deception—
will occur by the power that gave me birth,
the breathing life of All,
the Mother-Father of the cosmos (19).

'ayka' geyr datreyn 'aw tlata' kniyshiyn bshemy taman 'ena' baynathuwn (20).

KJV: For where two or three are gathered together in my name, there am I in the midst of them (20).

This occurs because
wherever two or three
gather and wrap themselves
bshemy—in my sound and name,
in my atmosphere and light,
in my experience of
the wave reality of the cosmos—
wherever this power becomes tangible
and names itself through their devotion,
then "I Am" is really there
among, around and inside them.

My being is present in their own simple presence,
ready for the next instant of reality (20).

Meditation—Simple Presence 1: Boundaries

When feeling not present, unintegrated or without safe boundaries:

Visualize a point at the center of a circle (or perhaps draw an actual circle with a dot at the center). Inhale from and exhale to this point, feeling the unique sense of "I-ness" you experience now. What is the particular essence or atmosphere of the divine expressing itself through you at this moment? From what places in your body do these feelings or sensations arise? After a short period, continue to inhale from the "point" and gradually begin to exhale to the circumference of the imagined circle, sensing your boundaries as whole and complete. After a time, you may also allow the body sensation of boundaries to become porous, yet complete on all sides. Release the image of the circle and continue to breathe and feel for a few moments.

Your "I am" is connected through the heart, by wave, breath and devotion, to the creative "I Am" of the cosmos.

The Next Thing, Part 1 (Arabic)

(a meditation on the Qur'an, Surah *al-Fatiha* 1:1a, "The Opening")

Bismillah

A. Yusuf Ali version: In the name of Allah...

We affirm that
the next thing that happens occurs only
through the waves of the whole universe yearning toward a goal,
By means of the entire unfolding cosmos,
In the light of one single unity of purpose—
    the clear sign and name of the Only Being,
    the ultimate force behind being and nothingness.
We begin
with the Divine Void
calling our name
before we rayed into existence.

Meditation—Heart Awareness 1: Breath and Heartbeat

Beginning a project or relationship, or upon awakening:

With eyes closed, breathe easily and naturally, noticing the rise and fall of the breath and the way in which it forms its own rhythm in combination with the sensation of your heartbeat. To feel this, it may help to place one hand lightly on or near your heart. Now bring into the swing of your breath one of the two words of power in the last two selections: *bismillah* (Arabic) or its earlier Aramaic cousin *bshemy*. Simply feel the sound inside without speaking. Allow a natural four-count rhythm of the phrase to shape the breath (for instance, "bis-mil-la-ah" or "be-sheh-em-ee"). Allow yourself to feel your heartbeat and breathing as though they were forming a clear, conscious, creative space in the middle of your chest. Hold this sacred space free and expectant, ready for the next instant of being.

During the silence, you might also contemplate the face of the universe before its origin. Consider the intelligence, passion, creativity and blessing that has rippled backwards from the beginning of the caravan of creation, from the very beginning of the universe, throughout its entire story and continuing with you, breathing, reconnecting to your place in it.

Gradually release the word you're breathing and follow the feeling that arises. If you try this meditation at the beginning of the day, you might conclude by continuing to breathe in the heart while you focus on what lies ahead. At the same time, allow yourself to continue to feel a breath of the mysterious Unity that was there before all being came into existence. If beginning a project, allow any images or intuitions to arise in this pregnant silence of possibility that precedes all differences. Then open your eyes and go on to "the next thing."

I Am Not (Persian)

(From "The Diwan of Shams-i-Tabriz," by the Sufi poet Mevlana Jelaluddin Rumi, 13th century Anatolia)

Muslims! What can I do? I have lost my identity!
I am not a Christian, Jew, pagan or Muslim.
I am neither an Easterner nor a Westerner,
    neither a land nor a sea person.
Nature can't fully account for me,
    nor can the whirling cosmos.
I don't exclusively belong to earth, water, fire or air.
I am not of the invisible-ineffable, nor of the dust—
    I am not a process or a being.
I am not of this world or the next, and deserve
    neither eternal reward nor eternal punishment.
I am not of Adam or Eve,
    not of the original Garden nor the final one.
My home has no address; my tracks leave no trace.
I am neither body nor soul—What can I say?
I belong to the Self of the Beloved.

I have laid all "two's" aside:
this world and that world are one.
I search for One, I recognize One,
I see One clearly and I call the name of the One.
That unnameable One, the breath of the breath,
is the first and last, the outside and the inside.
I identify no one except by "O Thou...O Thou!"
I am drunk on the cup of Love:
here-now and everywhere-all-the-time have vanished.
I can't handle any business except celebration.
If I spend an instant without you,

that instant makes my whole life seem worthless.
If I can win one moment with you,
I will crush both worlds under my feet
as I dance in joy forever.

My beloved Shams-i-Tabriz,
I am living permanently intoxicated:
I have no more stories to tell
except ones about drunks and parties.

2. The Breath from the Womb: What Wants to Be Created?

There is a breath of warmth, compassion and creativity that comes from inside, from the darkness. Some stories and myths call this the "womb of the world." According to the Native Middle Eastern tradition, the womb reality was present at the beginning, preparing for the primeval fireball. In this process of birth, some part of individuality is sacrificed and cleansed with each new creation. This womb reality is available in our bodies and our collective psyche both as the fear of darkness and the power of rejuvenation.

When life draws you to selections in this chapter, you might consider breathing into and with the hitherto unknown resources of power and creativity that lie within you.

2. The Breath from the Womb:

Before the Fireball (Hebrew)

(a midrashic, or interpretive, translation of Genesis 1:2)

weha'aretz hayeta tohu wabohu (A) wechoshekh 'al-penei tehom (B) weruach 'elohim merachefet 'al-penei hammayim (C)

KJV version: And the earth was without form, and void (A); and darkness was upon the face of the deep (B). And the Spirit of God moved upon the face of the waters (C).

The Storyteller continues:
Now particles—the Power of Limits—
didn't really exist yet in our reality
and were still only "things" in principle.
They were like the germ of a solution
within the shell of a surrounding problem,
the inkling of an answer
to the question of "What next?"
a kernel of purpose embedded in
a dream of the Universe's heart.
This "earthiness" of all the elements was still
unformed and waiting (A).

Meanwhile...
on the surface of the Primordial (yet unawakened) Womb,
that billowing edge of the abyss of existence
where phenomena, time and space had yet to appear,
a struggle raged:

A spark of cosmic desire wanted to
return to the Source immediately,
leaving behind the realm of constriction and contraction.
This self-involved fire forgot its purpose.

It set off the first violence of a being
that wants to be somewhere it's not.
Its barren wanting strangled its own voice until (B)

The breath of Universe Being touched
the face of Beloved Possibility.
Pure expansive power stirred the primordial soup.
The Being of Beings
inspired, animated and reminded Flow,
that same edge of possible phenomena,
of the expansive growth awaiting it.
One could say that Cosmic Breath
moved with pregnant possibility
into the deep and massive nether of Chaotic Dark—
awakening Womb for what?
An intimacy yet unknown (C).

Meditation—Depths of the Self 1: Layers of the Deep

When feeling tense, contracted or overly stressed by life:

Follow the feeling of breathing down inside you. Sense it actually going lower in your body. As much as possible, relax into the bottom of your breathing wave, where the breath is all out and pauses momentarily before it begins to come in naturally.

Don't hold the breath. Simply allow yourself to enter the gentle darkness at the "bottom" of things. Use the awareness of breathing as a way to remain connected to the part of you that observes and witnesses all of the interactions within. Are there any sensations or feelings on the "surface" of your own depths that have been waiting to be heard and recognized?

If so, you might begin by asking their names and needs. This process can begin a long, gradual journey to establish a relationship with the subconscious self, called *nephesh* in Hebrew (*naphsha* or *nafs* in Aramaic and Arabic respectively). You can return to the process layer by layer as a regular "check-in" and subsequent meditations entitled "Depths of the Self" may help.

To conclude the journey, breathe toward this deeper self (or selves) with as much love and thanks as you are capable of. Ask for help by aligning your breath to the breath that began the cosmos, the "Holy Breath." Feel your own potential for creation arising from what waits to be born in the darkness.

The Mother Womb Creates the Human (Babylonian-Assyrian)

(a version from portions of Old Babylonian and Assyrian incantation texts, approximately 2nd millennium B.C.E.)

First lines of E.A. Speiser translation: That which is slight he shall raise to abundance; the word of god man shall bear! The goddess they called to enquire, The midwife of the gods, the wise Mami....

"From what is small and fragile
let abundance and power come:
let humanity take on the consciousness
of the whole creation
and be absorbed by this task."

So spoke the Great Ones,
    shining centers of awareness,
    the original archetypes of existence,
in the primordial beginning.
From the energizing dark waves
they summoned the Great One (Inanna)
in the form of
the Mother, Wise Mami—
    she whose name means
    the one who responds to cries:

"You are the Mother-Womb,
radiant source of warmth and life,
the one from whose depths
humanity may arise.
Create this unique form

as a spiral of life into matter—
one force of its being always leaving,
the other always returning home,
the tension balanced
by the awareness of the void.

"Create humanity as a thin veil
that shrouds the Universal Reality.
Let its purpose spread open and fertile
like a fresh field to be plowed.
Let it embrace the empty core of Being
covered in layers of activity
like an onion's skin."

Then the Great One in the form of Nintu—
    she who bears all new generations,
    preserver of the chain of being—
told the other shining archetypes:

"From my essence comes everything
that helps the cosmos unfold.
So let *lullu*—this new spiral being—appear!
Let the universe develop through its efforts!
Let this new human being be
formed from the earth
and enlivened with blood!"

Then Enki,
    the "I Am" compressed into form,
    the archetype of being made manifest,
suggested to the others:

"In the month when the land is cleansed,
when it returns to healing emptiness,
when the earth's beings
see the fruits of their labor
and feel the mother's support underneath,
let them kill one of us holy ones,
    shining centers of awareness,
    mythic shells of life energy,
and let us all be cleansed thereby.

"With the flesh and blood of the divine
let the Great One, also called Ninhursag—
    she who expands the circle of illuminated being—
mix and mingle the clay of the earth.
Let both the worlds—
shining-waved and particle-formed—
be forever changed by
this new mixture—
the human being.
And we shall hear its tale unfold
from ages to ages."

From Their Inner Wombs (Aramaic)

(alternate, expanded translations of Matthew 5:7 from the Peshitta version)

tubwayhuwn lamrachmane' da'layhuwn nehwuwn rachme'
KJV version: Blessed are the merciful; for they shall obtain mercy.

Ripe are those who from their inner wombs birth mercy;
 they shall sense the relief of all prayers answered.

Ripe are those who from their inner wombs birth compassion;
 they shall feel the delivery of unconditional love.

Ripe are those who from their inner wombs birth radiance;
 upon them shall be the rays of divine warmth and heat.

Ripe are those who from their inner wombs birth ardor;
 they shall feel a breath from the heart of the Universe.

Ripe are those who from their inner wombs birth light;
 upon, around and within them will the Cosmic Body shine.

Meditation—Sound and Embodiment 2: Blessings of the Womb of Life

When feeling in need of a renewed sense of creativity and warmth:

Lie or sit comfortably and place your hands lightly over the belly, sensing all the movement and fluidity that is there. Breathe into this center, gently feeling the word meaning "womb-reality" and "compassion," from Yeshua's Beatitude: *rachme* (pronounced "RACH-MAY"). You might imagine the power of creativity that can come from the unknown, for instance, the layers of "dark matter" throughout the universe from which new stars and galaxies are born.

Then, with one hand lightly over your heart, slowly begin to intone the sound on one note, sensing the movement it evokes in your body. Try it in three parts: RA-CHM-AY. "RA" is the raying forth energy; "CHM" is the breath from the inside, the sound of Holy Wisdom (who returns later in our journey), "AY" (as in "day") opens outward to further new life. To conclude, allow yourself time to simply breathe again with the sound while you integrate the feeling of this creative "going out" with its connection to a grounded, embodied yet mysterious knowing within.

The Womb is a Great World (Aramaic)

(version based on a Mandaean text from Iran from around the first century C.E.)

First lines of E.S. Drower translation: In the name of the Great Life.... each of them that existeth in the Body is a world; when separated (taken separately) each of them is a world.... The head is one world; one world the neck, one world the breast...

In the name and light of the most powerful Life!

Worlds combined to form the first human flesh.
Each head, neck, breast, leg, liver, spleen, stomach,
each male and female organ, skin, hair, nails
was originally its own world.
They all carry on a friendly conversation.
When they don't—or one does not join in—
then the whole human flesh is in trouble.

Next came the soul, a renewing, gracious self that
links us to the sphere of luminous vibration.

After soul took shape,
the flesh formed the breath of its own radiant life.
This vital spirit animates and connects it to all other selves.
And after flesh, soul and breath took shape,
then the womb was formed:
an enclosing darkness from which new life radiates.

The womb is a great world,
there is none greater or more powerful.

The blood within the womb radiates pure purpose.
The blood within the heart radiates precious refinement.
The blood within the liver radiates plentiful beauty.
The blood within the veins radiates pure surrender.

These four radiant vibrations control the whole human.
If there were only three, there would be no human.

Meditation—Gratitude and Celebration 2: The Blood of the Womb

To cultivate a deeper sense of thankfulness and gratitude:

Lie comfortably, perhaps before going to sleep, and sense the blood renewing your creative depths, the womb, with a sense of purpose. According to this tradition, all human beings, female and male, can have a connection to this "womb reality," even though in women it is more embodied. Next you might feel this renewing power refining the many feelings the heart experiences each day. Third, allow yourself to feel the blood circulating through the liver to distinguish between the beauty which we can use and that which we can't. In our physiology, the liver is an "organ of elimination," but ancient Middle Eastern people also saw it as a center of passion. Finally, feel the blood return to the heart through the veins as the blood surrenders what we need to release with each breath.

Each "world" is a vastness for which we can be thankful, pulse by pulse, heartbeat by heartbeat. They all provide doorways for the renewal and rebirth of our connection to a sacred cosmos.

A Conversation About Rebirth (Aramaic)

(an expanded translation of John 3:2-8 from the Peshitta version of the Gospels)

hana' 'eta' lwat Yeshua' blilya' we'mar leh rabiy yod'iynan dmen 'alaha' 'eshtadart malpana' la' geyr 'nash meshkach haleyn 'atwata' lme'bad da'nt 'abed 'ant 'ela' man da'laha' 'ameh (2)
KJV: The same came to Jesus by night, and said unto him, Rabbi, we know that thou art a teacher come from God: for no man can do these miracles that thou doest, except God be with him (2).

He [Niyqadimaws] came to Yeshua at night and said to him:
Teacher, we know that you are sent from Alaha, the Source,
because no one can do what you are doing
unless the One is with him.

'no' yeshuw' we'mar leh 'ameyn 'ameyn 'amar 'na' lakh
de'n 'nash la' metiyled men driysh la' meshkach dnechze' malkuwteh da'laha'(3)
KJV: Jesus answered and said unto him, Verily, verily I say unto thee, Except a man be born again, he cannot see the kingdom of God (3).

Yeshua answered and said:
By the earth on which we stand
what I am going to say is
the ground of truth and
the source from which my actions grow.

Unless a human being is completely regenerated,
propagated and reborn
from the Center of existence,
from the primal origin of light and fire,
that person will not see the sudden vision,

or be illuminated by the flash
of the 'I Can' of the cosmos,
the creative arm of the soul's Source.

'amar leh niyqadimaws 'aykana' meshkach dnetiyled gabra' sobo' dalma' meshkach tuwb lkharsa' de'meh dtarteyn zabniyn lme'al wnetiyled (4)
KJV version: Nicodemus saith unto him, How can a man be born when he is old? Can he enter the second time into his mother's womb, and be born (4)?

Niyqadimaws then said to Yeshua:
How can an old man be reborn?
Can he physically pass through his mother's vagina
and enter the space inside a second time?
Can he be born again?

'na' yeshuw' we'mar leh 'ameyn 'ameyn 'amar 'na' lakh de'n 'nash la' metiyled men maya' wruwcha' la' meshkach dne'uwl lmalkuwta' da'laha' (5)
KJV: Verily, verily, I say unto thee, Except a man be born of water and of the Spirit, he cannot enter into the kingdom of God (5).

Yeshua answered:
As surely as I stand on this earth,
unless a human being returns
to that sameness with the cosmos
that feels like death—
the dark, moist place of birthing,
the place where only flow and animating spirit,
only water and breathing,
only giving way and stirring exist—
that person cannot enter
the reign of Unity,

2. The Breath from the Womb:

the "I Can" of the cosmos,
the queen- and kingdom of the One.
That person cannot stretch
to touch and feel at home in
the power and beauty of the Source.

medem diyliyd men besra' besra' huw wmedem diyliyd men ruwcha' ruwcha' huw (6)
la' tetdamar de'mret lakh dwale' lkhuwn lmetiyladuw men driysh (7)
KJV: That which is born of the flesh is flesh; and that which is born of the Spirit is spirit (6). Marvel not that I said unto thee, Ye must be born again (7).

That which arises from a base sense of things,
crushed down and tread upon with heavy feet,
will show the impression of that density.
That which arises from inspiration,
breathed from and with the spirit of the cosmos,
will show the force that
moves the universal winds (6).

Is it surprising that I have told you
you must be born from the First Becoming,
leaving everything else behind (7)?

ruwcha' 'atar dtzabya' nashba' wqalah shama' 'ant 'ela' la' yada' 'ant 'aymeka' 'atya' wla'yka' 'azal' hakhana' 'iytawhy kulnash diyliyd men ruwcha' (8)
KJV: The wind bloweth where it listeth, and thou hearest the sound thereof, but canst not tell whence it cometh, and whither it goeth; so is every one that is born of the Spirit (8).

The breath, the wind, the spirit—
all move by becoming small and large,

by heating and cooling.
They obey their own impulses and
their own harmonious laws.
You are touched by their signature,
you know they exist without a doubt
when you hear their gentle, rapid voices.
But you do not notice or understand
how they attract each other and come together
or how they rise and fall as they
seek their own relationship to the earth.

Just as mysteriously moves every human being
who has returned to the Source
and been reborn from the Great Dark
through the power of breathing and of spirit.

Meditation—Sound and Embodiment 3: Celebration of the First Winds

For cultivating an embodied sense of freedom and "spirit":

About 4.45 billion years ago, the earth began to develop an atmosphere of methane, ammonia, hydrogen and carbon dioxide. This highly ionized, violent atmosphere seethed with gigantic lightning storms for about a half billion years, charging and changing the primeval earth and seas. From this one-time (as far as we know) spectacular manifestation of the universal winds, the first living cell arose.

As you feel the wind passing over your skin, open to its sound and texture as well as its resonance with the first life on the planet.

This ancient wind still lives as a memory within you. Feel your own being as breath and wind inside and outside, with only a thin layer of skin in between. The skin itself evolved from the same embryonic layer in you as your brain. It is, so to speak, the part of your intelligence most in contact with the cosmos.

Intone gently on one note the Aramaic word for breath and wind that Yeshua uses above, *ruha* (pronounced "ROO-CHA" with "ch" as an aspirated "h" sound). Allow yourself to feel your voice uniting with that of the air around you and the wind in nature. Follow the feeling of the wind back to its source, through the atmosphere of the planet back to the cosmic winds that helped form the earth. Celebrate those earlier winds that began life here, and thank the intelligence behind them. What wants to be revealed now through this breath in your life?

The Next Thing, part 2 (Arabic)

(a meditation on the Qur'an, Surah *al-Fatiha* 1:1ab, "The Opening")

Bismillah (A) ar-rahman ar-rahim (B)

A. Yusuf Ali version: In the name of Allah (A), Most Gracious, Most Merciful (B).

We affirm that
the next thing that happens occurs only
with the Divine Void calling our name
before we rayed into existence (A).

From this Original Womb comes both grace and mercy.
The first, a supreme unconditioned love:
    before any need arose, a vital power enveloped itself,
    creating warmth and heat, radiating from a center
    without regard to what was lost or gained,
a natural gift of the cosmic Self.
This always continues.
The second, a tender response to all cries,
all unfulfilled potentials:
    the primordial pull of cosmic kinship bears
    acts of compassion, responding to all needs
    as though heard for the first time,
the breath of love in response to a sighing universe,
the quality of mercy (B).

We begin
by means of the unfolding Unity of Being,
from whose Womb is born the Sun and Moon of Love.

3. The Gift of Light and Dark: What Do I Know?

Light and dark arrive together as a package in one of the original gifts of the universe's diversity. In developing the fullness of our humanity, we develop an awareness of both. Neither can exist without the other and both lead us back to the Source of all Being.

When life draws you to selections in this chapter, you might consider how what you know about yourself, and your place in life, contrasts with what you don't yet know. Can you shine a light on the situation before you, and find there a resonance with a part of yourself?

3. The Gift of Light and Dark:

Light Shall Be (Hebrew)

(a midrashic, or interpretive, translation of Genesis 1:3-4)

wayyo'mer 'elohim yehi 'aor wa yehi 'aor (3)
KJV: And God said, Let there be light: and there was light (3).

The Storyteller continues:
And then the Universe declared—
that is, its own intelligence,
reflected from the depth of Being,
surfaced and focused a straight
storyline of light and power
toward a path ahead.

It called potential wave and form to action:
"Light Shall Be!"
and because in its "beginningness"
this massive radiance and
flaring forth of light, heat
and all elements already was,
so "Light Shall Be!" meant "Light It Was!"
The push of the future from "behind" and
the pull of the past from "ahead"
ignited the presence of the present
as the caravan moved further (3).

wayyar' 'elohim 'et-ha'or ki-tob wayyabdel 'elohim ben ha'or uben hachoshekh (4)
KJV: And God saw the light, that it was good: and God divided the light from the darkness (4).

Next, that Universe Being that brought
elementary life into existence

from nonbeing to being
sent a pure, straight ray of its intelligence toward
the flaring forth of pre-elementary
wave and particle—the Light.
The cosmos drenched itself in lucidity
and recognized the Light as ripe, that is,
capable of advancing the cosmic story for now.
It was an appropriate balance to the older Dark.
This new character development led to the instant
that would begin what we call time.

Within the tendency of the Universe Being
to foster peculiarity for the sake of abundance,
a natural differentiation then occurred:
The Being of Beings divided
Light,
the flaring forth, expanding energy—
straightforward, direct, intelligible,
the mystery of all illumination,
teaching and knowing—
from
Dark,
the gyrating, concentrated ardor—
self-involved, curved, unknowable, dense,
the mystery of all chaotic
and violent creation.

Meditation—Gratitude and Celebration 3: Moving Toward the Light.

For encouraging a sense that your life's purpose is unfolding naturally:

At dawn, find a quiet place to observe the changing of darkness into light as the earth rolls to face the sun. Instead of seeing the sun as rising, imagine that you (and the rest of the earth in your region) are moving forward to meet the sun. This is the actual condition. With your eyes half open, take the feeling and sensation of the sun into your inner being by breathing gently and inhaling the feeling of its warmth and light. You may also find it helpful to gently intone the word for light or knowing, *aor* ("AH-OR") on one note. Feel the outer sensation of moving toward the light awaken the inner sensation of clarity and purpose. These sensations are linked, according to this tradition. Our purpose is part of that "light shall be" moment in the early childhood of our universe.

If you are willing, ask the Being behind the universe to shape your life in accordance with its own best unfolding. Follow whatever light you feel, inner or outer, back to its source. You might begin a relationship with your personal source of guidance, a greater Self or Soul that awakens the potentials created by your past in the opportunities of the present with the inklings of your future purpose.

Your Radiance Suckles Every Blade of Grass (Egyptian)

(from a Hymn to Aton as the Sun from the time of Akh-en-Aton, Pharaoh Amen-hotep IV, 1380-1362 B.C.E.)

First lines of John Wilson translation: Praise of Re Har-akhti, Rejoicing on the Horizon, in His Name as Shu Who Is in the Aton-disc, living forever and ever....

Praise to the Three-in-One of the Sun:
Praise to *Re*, the streak of light we see.
Praise to *Har-akhti*, who appears pregnant at dawn.
Praise to *Shu*, who balances heat and power.
All live eternally in the disk of *Aton*—
the ultimate Thou-and-I in all beings,
our Mutual Soul.

You appear with beauty on heaven's horizon,
beginning life anew each day.
When you approach in the east, glistening and gracious,
your rays embrace all you have made.
Though you are far away, we feel your radiance.
Though you touch our faces,
no one knows your coming and going.

When you leave us in the west,
the whole earth lies in death's darkness.
We sleep in our rooms, heads wrapped in night:
One eye does not see the other and
everything we think we own
can disappear without our knowing.

3. The Gift of Light and Dark:

Lions roam around, things creep and sting.
Darkness covers us like a shroud.
The earth becomes still like a tomb,
as the one who made us rests,
beyond our horizon.

At dawn you approach us again,
appearing from beyond the border of being.
The symbol of our Mutual Soul,
you drive away all darkness and give
the Two Lands cause for daily joy.
Awake, standing on our feet—
for you have raised us—
we wash and pull our clothes on over our heads,
our arms raising in praise as we see you.
The whole earth takes up your work again!

You create women's seed, men's semen.
You comfort and nurse the child in its mother's womb,
you soothe even its inner weeping.
When the time comes for it to descend,
to breathe and face the outer world,
you open the infant's mouth wide to
receive what it needs from you.
When the chick rouses and
speaks within the egg,
you give it enough breath
and the fullness of time,
to break the shell
and come forth into the day.

Your radiance suckles every blade of grass.
When you approach, each sprout lives and grows for you.
You created seasons to teach us maturity:
The winter cools us, the heat reminds us of your taste.

You appear, shining,
you approach and withdraw:
By this alone, millions of forms have come from you.

Every being that glances up sees you,
radiant one of the earth's day,
symbol of our Mutual Soul.

The "I Am" Illuminates (Aramaic)

(translations of John 8:12 from the Peshitta version of the Gospels)

tuwb deyn malel 'amhuwn yeshuw' we'mar 'ena' 'na' nuwhreh d'alma' man dbotary 'ate' la' nhalekh bcheshuwkha' 'ela' neshkach leh nuwhra' dchaye'

KJV: Then spake Jesus again unto them, saying, I am the light of the world: he that followeth me shall not walk in darkness, but shall have the light of life.

Then Yeshua spoke again to them, saying:
The "I Am" in you, in me,
illuminates all the worlds of form.

It clarifies and reveals the force
behind creation's shining joy.
When you follow this inner light of the self,
conscious of the Only Self, the One Being,
you do not stumble blindly
but find your way through the darkness,
guided by the light of inner life energy.

The ego fully aware of its impermanence
guides the infant selves of the world
toward their purpose in life.

The eye of the whirlwind of self-interest
instructs each leaf growing
on the tree of life.

Simple Presence is the radiant force
guiding us all along the path of
nature's expansive power.

Meditation—Simple Presence 2: The "I Am" and Radiance

For cultivating a clearer, conscious sense of being in the moment:

Sit comfortably, eyes closed, and with one hand lightly over your heart, allow yourself to feel the rise and fall of your breath. With each breath, reach out to whatever feelings or sensations appear. Feel the breath illuminating each with love and respect. Each sensation is also an "I"—a momentary individual awareness. Where does it find its source? You might breathe and feel inside the sound of the Aramaic word for light that Yeshua uses above—*nuwhra'* ("NUH-RA"). Allow the inner sound to help you build a bridge of awareness between the individual feelings and sensations that are arising in you and their source. Try opening your eyes very slowly and, breathing in the heart, maintain the same awareness of presence for a few moments.

Metaphors of Light (Arabic)

(A meditation on the Verse of Light, Qur'an Surah *an-Nur* 24:35)

Bismillahir-rahmanir-rahim (A)
'Allahu nurus-samawati wal- 'arz (B)
masalu nurihi ka-mishkatin-fiha misbah (C)
'al-misbahu fi zujajah (D)
'az-zujajatu ka-'annaba kawkabun durriyyuny (E)
yuqadu min shajaratim mubarakakin (F)
zaytunatil-la sharqiyyatinw-wa la garbiyyatiny-yakadu
zaytuha yuzi-'u wa law lam tansas-hu nar (G)
nurun 'ala nur (H)
yahdillahu li-nurihi many-yasha' (I)
wa yazribullahul-amsala linnas (J)
wallahu bi-kulli shay-'im 'alim (K)

A. Yusuf Ali version: In the name of Allah Most Gracious Most Merciful (A). Allah is the Light of the heavens and the earth (B). The parable of His Light is as if there were a Niche and within it a lamp (C): the Lamp enclosed in Glass (D): the glass as it were a brilliant star (E): lit from a blessed Tree (F) an Olive neither of the East nor of the West whose Oil is well-nigh luminous though fire scarce touched it (G): Light upon Light! (H) Allah doth guide whom He will to His Light (I). Allah doth set forth Parables for men (J): and Allah doth know all things (K).

We begin with the Light of Unity,
radiating and reflecting the Source
of all creative loving, and being loved.

One Being illuminates all waves, all particles—
    both communal and individual existence (B).
Models and symbols surround us:
Our consciousness sculpts space like
a shade designed to hold and focus light (C).

Within the shade, glass surrounds the fire element,
protecting, magnifying it, or—if dusty—
obscuring the light.
This glass is the way our embodied life develops—
    the contours of our personal history,
    its twists and turns (D).
Finally, within the glass is light itself—
    pure fire, heat, illumination,
    soul-force, produced from
burning earth, burning matter.
This fire, light, illumination is
the same as the stars we see (E).
All stars are lit from another growing force,
a tree of light and life
we cannot find in space or time (F),
neither of East nor of West.
Our soul is of the same stuff,
transmitting light like
the oil from an olive tree.
At moments we can see this light
break the bounds of self
and shine, producing brilliance
before fire touches it (G).
Light upon light upon light—
    back and back we trace it to its Source (H).
From this One comes the ultimate ray of
light and sound—
a voice, an echo—
guiding those who hear the desire behind
the unfolding universe's story,
who come to its call
like flocks of thirsty birds to water (I).

3. The Gift of Light and Dark:

The Universal One is the
meeting place of all meaning.
It creates models, signs, symbols and parables
everywhere we look to remind us
of our Source (J).
And the One behind all
understands and embraces all—
the past and future journey of primal matter,
all particles, from seed to star (K).

Meditation—Sound and Embodiment 4: Light Upon Light

For cultivating an inner, embodied sensation of light and knowing:

Breathe the words *Allah Nur* ("AHL-LAH NOOR") in and out, with one hand gently over the heart, asking for a renewed sense of guidance in your life. Then slowly intone the sound on one note several times, feeling the sounds resonate through your body as much as possible. Return to breathing the sound inside. Finally release it while you hold only the feeling of the sound, and your connection with the Source of all Knowing, the consciousness behind the universe, for a few more breaths.

To this meditation you might also add a brief contemplation on the clear light transmitted by a substance like olive oil, along the lines suggested by the surah itself. Place the oil in a clear glass before you, and, placing one hand gently over your heart, breathe with your feeling there, slowly connecting your heart-feeling with the light being reflected through the oil. Soften your gaze and allow your mind to take in the feeling of the oil more than its exact details.

After a few minutes, close your eyes, and still breathing in the heart, hold the feeling of the light and the oil that remains in your awareness. It's best to start with the eyes opened for about a minute and then closed for a minute, gradually lengthening the time each session. At some point, you will find that, after holding the feeling, you can allow the feeling to hold and lead you. Follow the feeling to its source. End by opening the eyes again slowly and breathing the phrase *Allah Nur* a few more moments, finding the presence of the light everywhere you look.

Unity's Disguises (Arabic)

(Meditation on a recorded saying (*hadith*) of the Prophet Muhammad)

Inna lillahi la-sa`bina alfa hijabin min nurin wa zulmati
A. Yusuf Ali version: God has seventy thousand veils of light and darkness.

Cosmic Unity has 70,000 ways to hide.

The One Being wraps itself in countless disguises:
It veils itself in light and darkness,
in appearance and disappearance,
in sage guidance,
    a torch to understanding,
and in foolish advice,
    the extinction of wisdom.

Sacred Unity reveals itself
in the rising and setting of enlightenment.

It hides in the straight, clear line,
drawn between knower and known,
as well as in
the spiraling, confused reflection,
the opaque mystery of the cosmos.

We understand or misunderstand the "self"
in the projection and shadow of the divine image.
One moment we shield our eyes from the glare,
the next we shudder in the shade.

Eclipse and brilliance both obscure the mind's limited view
of the Universe's single-hearted purpose.

The Back of the Mirror (Persian)

(From "The Diwan of Shams-i-Tabriz," by the Sufi poet Mevlana Jelaluddin Rumi, 13th century Anatolia)

David asked God: "We know you don't need
either this world or the one beyond,
so what was the wisdom in creating them?"
God replied: "Since humanity is enmeshed in time,
how shall I answer so you can understand?

"I was a hidden treasure,
abundant, radiating love.
To reveal this treasure
I created a mirror—
its face the heart of being,
its back the worlds of phenomena.
The back seems better than the face—
if that's the only side you know."

When dust clouds the glass,
how can the mirror be clear?
When you remove the dust,
the rays return without a detour.
Grape juice does not ferment overnight—
wine ages a while in a bottle.
If you want your heart to brighten,
expect to exert yourself a bit.

Listen to this story:
When the soul left the body,
it was stopped by God
at heaven's gates:
"You have returned just as you left!

3. The Gift of Light and Dark:

Life is a blessing of opportunity:
Where are the bumps and scratches
left by the journey?"

Everyone knows the legend about
the alchemist who turns copper into gold.
A rarer alchemy has transmuted our copper,
my beloved Shams and I:
Shams, the sun, needs no hat or robe
to block the intense, uncompromising
rays of Grace.
His being alone covers a hundred bald heads
and clothes ten naked bodies.

My child-self!
For humility alone, Jesus rode an ass.
Why else should the divine breath mount a donkey?
My intuitive self!
On this path, better move your head
to match the river's flow to the sea.
My logical self!
If you want a life worth living,
walk the path holding death's hand.

Remember Unity until you forget separation.
Then you may lose your way in the Named,
without the side-trip
of namer and name.

Meditation—Heart Awareness 2: The Mirror

For developing a healthy sense of receptivity:

This meditation comes from an ancient Sufi practice. With one hand placed lightly over the heart, imagine or feel the heart as a mirror. With each gentle breath in and out, feel the mirror becoming clearer and clearer. After a few minutes, imagine the heart as a sacred space, an altar, a place of possibility. What images or sensations appear there as a gift from the One Being? What healing or inspiration is needed to feel the blessing of opportunity life presents, *now*?

4. Time and Timing: Is it Ripe?

In addition to the alternation of light and dark, the Universe creates vibration, pulse and rhythm. This further gift of diversity allows us to create various ideas of what we call *time*. The pulse from the heart of the Universe also calls us to tune our own pulse to the unfoldment of its purpose.

When life draws you to selections in this chapter, you might consider the *ripeness* of the situations before you. How does your own heartbeat, the inner heart-time, respond to what is arising, inside and outside?

The First Day (Hebrew)

(a midrashic, or interpretive, translation of Genesis 1:5)

wayyiqra'(A) 'elohim la'oryom (B) welachoshekh qara' layela (C) wayehi-'ereb wayehi-boqer (D) yom 'echad (E)

KJV: And God called the light Day, and the darkness he called Night. And the evening and the morning were the first day.

The Storyteller continues:
To further engrave their character
and move creation along,
the Universe Being compressed
the fate of Light and Dark
into two gatherings (A):
The first, a mass of definite,
luminous manifestation and intelligence—
a fireball of straight rays of all spectra
moving with purpose,
formed the quality of Primordial Day (B)
The second, a mass of indefinite,
endarkened manifestation and unknowing—
swirling energies moving out and back from a center,
formed the quality of Primordial Night (C).

These forces alternated once:
All events and forms condensed through the Grace of Primal Night,
all events and forms expanded through the Grace of Primal Day,
the Dark brought the possible to a close through density,
the Light opened up again the expansive course of destiny (D).

Once over and back again,
forever after entwined,
this first round of closing and opening,
condensing and expanding,
off and on,
also marked the beginning of a
different sense of universe time.
There were no seconds, minutes or years,
but this we know:
It was the first period of
manifest luminous phenomena
in our cosmos—
the First Universal Day (E).

Meditation—Gratitude and Celebration 4: Density and Destiny

For improving the ability to relax without collapsing:

At twilight, take some moments to face the horizon and breathe with the fading light. Visualize yourself, and the other beings in your region, rolling away from the light, backwards into the darkness (rather than the sun "setting"). As you breathe with the darkness gathering around you, begin to feel the effects of the day consolidating, congealing and coming to a close. This is easier to feel in nature, as each plant prepares to use the energy and natural elements gathered during the day. For a moment at least, allow yourself to relax, to stop pushing and consciously to enter the darkness.

Before going to sleep at night, complete this process by consciously releasing the impressions attached to any events, circumstances and encounters during the day that do not carry you toward ripeness. This can easily be done by placing your forehead on the earth or floor and breathing a few times with gentle emphasis on the exhalation.

At dawn or the next morning, as you roll again toward the sun, take a few moments to breathe with the light and feel your destiny opening up before you. Gently emphasize the inhalation as you breathe a few breaths feeling the sun in your heart.

The Right Time and Place (Avestan)

(a version of the Zoroastrian prayer from the Avestan language recorded in Yasna 27:14, from ancient Persia, approximately 1700-1500 B.C.E.)

ashem vohu vahishtem asti (1) ushta asti. (2) ushta ahmai hyat ashai vahishtai ashem. (3)

Dastur M. N. Dhalla translation: Righteousness is man's best acquisition (1). It is happiness (2). It is his happiness when he is righteous for the sake of Best Righteousness (3).

To do rightly by the cosmos depends on timing:
right doing, right being at
the right time and place.
This right guidance, found in every heart,
finds its source in the universal Heart (1).
This rightness is ultimate good,
ultimate happiness and joy (2).
The joy comes naturally to and through a life
lived in moment-by-moment contact
with the truth behind all nature,
for its own sake and not for anything else (3).

Meditation—Heart Awareness 3: A Breath from the Heart of the Universe

For aiding a sense of being in the right place at the right time:

Breathe easily and gently in the center of the chest, and again feel your heart as a mirror. After a period of "clearing the mirror" (as suggested in Heart Awareness 2 in the previous chapter), visualize your heart reflecting the purpose at the heart of the Universe, as though connected to it by a ray of light. Slowly intone the Old Avestan word *ashem* ("AH-SHEM"), meaning timeliness and the ripeness found in nature, into your own heart. Direct the sound into your chest, keeping the neck relaxed. Then, slowly raising your head from your heart upwards, intone *vohu*, ("VO-HU"), the source of that ripeness, found in every being, in the heart of the cosmos. Allow yourself to feel a renewed connection between your own heart and that of the universe. Begin with your own best note as felt in the heart. Feel the sound more than you hear it, and allow the vibration of your own voice to bring you back into right timing and rhythm with the cosmos.

Tomorrow Means Things Depart (Aramaic)

(a translation of Matthew 6: 33-34 from the Peshitta version of the Gospels)

b'aw deyn luwqdam malkuwteh da'laha wzadiyquwteh wkhulheyn haleyn mettawspan lkhuwn (33)

KJV: But seek ye first the kingdom of God, and his righteousness; and all these things shall be added unto you (33).

If you're going to be anxious and rush around about anything,
do it first about finding the "I can" of the universe
and how it straightens out your life.
Line up your starting place with that of the cosmos:
Search and ask and boil with impatience
until you find the vision of the One Being
that empowers all your ideas and ideals,
that restores your faith and justifies your love.

All the rest—the universal and endless "things" of life—
will then attach themselves to you as you need them.
You will stand at the threshold where
completeness arrives naturally
and prostration leads to perfection.
Pouring yourself out makes the universe do the same (33).

la' hakhiyl ti'tzpuwn damchar huw geyr mchar yatzep diyleh sapeq leh lyawma' biyshteh (34)

KJV: Take therefore no thought for the morrow: for the morrow shall take thought for the things of itself. Sufficient unto the day is the evil thereof (34).

4. Time and Timing:

Don't torture yourself standing watch over things,
accomplishments or states of mind
you still want to possess tomorrow.
It doesn't work that way.
Tomorrow means things depart.
Time and the elements wash them away
just as they came, with abundance,
as the future stands by watching.

Each day completes itself with
its own share of unripeness.
Every illumination carries enough
inappropriate action
without carrying any forward.

The Day is Nearly Over (Arabic)

(A meditation on the Qur'an Surah 103, *Al 'Asr,* "Time Through the Ages")

bismillahir rahmanir rahim (1) wal 'asr (2)'innal insana lafi khusr (3) 'illallazina 'amanu wa 'amilus sallihati (4) wa tawasaw bil haqqi wa tawasaw bis sabr (5)

A. Yusuf Ali version: In the Name of Allah, the Compassionate, the Merciful. By (the Token of) time (through the Ages) (1), Verily Man is in loss (2), Except such as have Faith and do righteous deeds and (join together) in the mutual teaching of Truth and of Patience and Constancy (3).

We begin with the light of Unity,
the womb that bears compassion and mercy (1).

Unity also includes the root of everything solid,
the origin of everything compressed;
the feeling of being pushed from outside in—
the steepness of a mountain, the hardness of a rock,
the bits and pieces we sense as matter,
the bits and pieces we experience as time.
"Time and again...Day after day..."
The awareness we have
when late afternoon light
reminds us that the day is nearly over,
again (2).

Because of this, if you count material gain,
human existence always comes up a loss.
Energy contracts to form a being,
a vortex of "I-ness" envelopes the Self.
This creates a temporary shelter, a hostel for the night.
But we miss the journey

if we hold on to the shelter:
Its nature is to fall away behind us
as we travel farther,
just as do the moments of time (3).

Time's loss doesn't affect those whose
lives arise from the mother-principle, the giveaway:
who radiate beneficence without counting the cost,
whose actions are fully formed, a work of art,
because they are always opening softly
to the divine One (4).

Time's loss also doesn't affect those who
come together simply and with feeling,
to point out and celebrate
the presence of holy wisdom all around,
who recognize the sacred ground of being,
the home of truth within embodiment;
who share the glory of patience and of limits
as they function like channels
for the sacred fire to flow (5).

Meditation—Sound and Embodiment 5: Ground and Patience

For working with practical wisdom within limits:

Both *haqq* and *sabur*, mentioned in the final line above, are numbered among the "99 Beautiful Names of Allah"—qualities of feeling that express the essence of Being. Most if not all of these sacred words of power have predecessors in Aramaic, Hebrew and other ancient Semitic languages. Rather than imaging these qualities as clothes that we try on, it is more helpful to use the sounds to connect the feeling and knowing already within our cells and selves to their source in the cosmos. In the most profound sense, there is nothing "outside" the One Being, a point that the Qur'an makes again and again.

1. For sensing what is practical and possible for this moment:

Intone the phrase *Ya Haqq* ("YAH HAHQQ"), the truth in this moment, several times (the traditional number is thirty-three). The word "ya" is a form of address: we call to the quality as something living in ourselves, seeded there as part of the divine image at the first Beginning. Feel the sound going down through the body, and release the muscles of the pelvic floor as you feel the double "q" sound. This practice may also be done walking in a rhythm of four, either speaking or simply breathing the phrase. After a few minutes, continue to breathe the phrase, then release the sound and breathe only with the feeling, making a gradual transition to "normal" consciousness. Gradually, this sacred phrase will transform what is "normal."

2. *For developing gratitude for limits*, or for slowing down to maintain energy in a project or relationship over a longer period of time:

Slowly intone on one note the phrase *Ya Sabur* ("YAH SAH-BOOR"), calling to the part of the self that knows how limits can help the self grow. Feel each part of the sound vibrate through your body. Imagine a light that is able to maintain itself within, releasing radiance and energy over a long period of time. Our consumer society encourages the opposite tendency: throwaway goods, throwaway relationships, throwaway lives. There is enough "ripe" loss in the universe without adding what is unripe. Again, after several minutes, simply breathe with the phrase, and then with the feeling of the phrase. Reach deeply into yourself to connect with the places that need "staying power."

The Past Flies Away (Persian)

(from "The Secret Rose Garden" by the Sufi poet Mahmud Shabistari, 13th century Persia)

The past flies away,
coming months and years do not exist:
Only the pinprick of this moment
belongs to us.

We decorate this speck of a moment—time—
by calling it a flowing river or a stream.

But often I find myself alone
in a desert wilderness,
straining to catch the faint echo of
unfamiliar sounds.

Time, Patience and Love (Persian)

(from the "Diwan" of the Sufi poet Hafiz of Shiraz, 14th century Persia)

At dawn,
the nightingale spoke to the rose:
"Don't look down on my passion for you,
for while hovering around this garden, I have seen
many like you blossom and die."

The rose, smiling, replied:
"The truth doesn't bring me any tears,
but what a way for a lover to speak!"

From now until time's end,
you will never know the perfume of love
until you have swept dust from the
doorstep of the tavern of ecstasy
with your forehead.

If you want to taste red wine from
a cup encrusted with jewels,
expect to pierce many pearls
with the hair of your eyebrows
before you have a sip.

Yesterday at dawn
I entered the garden of Identity.
The morning breeze wafted a blessing
across the hair of a hyacinth.
"Where," I cried in ecstasy, "is the cup that
satisfies all the thirst in the world?"

4. Time and Timing:

A voice replied,
"Poor man, you'd have better stayed in bed
than tempt fate with such questions."

Love's talk doesn't touch the tongue—
O cupbearer—
stop interrogating me!

With his own tears, Hafiz has poured
both wisdom and patience into the sea.
Love's pain made any cover-up
or delay impossible.

5. Sacred Spaciousness: What is Opening and Resonating?

The Universe creates newness and diversity by creating possibility itself. The power of sacred space and spaciousness created our planetary atmosphere. Because atmosphere makes resonance and sound a possibility, our ears and vocal cords wrap themselves around this reality just as our eyes wrap themselves around the reality of light and dark. In this tradition, the power of hearing and the power of the word are creative—they engrave space with a possibility for further sacred diversity.

When life draws you to selections in this chapter, you might consider what resonates with you in the situation before you. How does your own voice sound when you speak of it—wholehearted or half-hearted?

The Earth's Personal Space - Day 2 (Hebrew)

(a midrashic, or interpretive, translation of Genesis 1:6-8)

wayyo'mer 'Elohim yehi raqia' betokh hammayim wihi mabdil ben mayim lamayim (6)
KJV: And God said, Let there be a firmament in the midst of the waters, and let it divide the waters from the waters (6).

The Storyteller continues:
Again the Universe's intelligence
tapped a more complex future for inspiration.
It invoked a new process,
one more rarifying, spacious and possibility-enlivening,
right in the middle of the primordial, compressed
Dark Wave-Matter.
By imagining more opening and expansion,
the cosmos called forth Spacious Choice—
the mother of all the universe's listening, receptive habits—
from the center of the primal cosmic Flow.

wayya'as 'Elohim 'et-haraqia' wayyabdel ben hammayim 'asher mittachat laraqia' uben hammayim 'asher me'al laraqia' wayehi-khen (7)
KJV: And God made the firmament and divided the waters which were under the firmament from the waters which were above the firmament: and it was so (7).

By calling forth the future possibility,
the Universe began to assemble
the waves and particles needed to embody
this Spacious Choice as the firmament or atmosphere
that receives sound in our vicinity.

This plotline caused more change in the whole universe.
The contracted Dense Flow—Dark Matter—
remained a mystery locked inside itself,
compressed on the far side of Spacious Choice.
Expansive Flow remained on this side—
the "Great Beyond" of the sky that embodies
the living metaphor of extension and exaltation.

wayyiqra' 'Elohim laraqia' shamayim wayehi-'ereb wayehi-boqer yom sheni (8)
KJV: And God called the firmament Heaven. And the evening and the morning were the second day (8).

To further engrave this distinction,
the Universe gave Spacious Choice in our locale
the embodied form of one of its first archetypes:
the character of infinite vibration or *shem*—
the wave reality of name, sound and light,
the atmosphere that creates, surrounds and
unites all beings here in a mutual communion of breath.

Once over and back again,
this second round of opening and closing
marked the second large manifestation
of luminous, intelligent happenings
in our vicinity since the Great Beginning:
the creation of the earth's "personal" Space.

Meditation—Gratitude and Celebration 5: Sky and Space

When feeling overly burdened or constricted:

Sit or lie comfortably in nature with as much expanse of sky in view as possible. Breathe for a moment as though from the whole sky, and allow yourself to gaze at and take in the amount of space that surrounds you. Then gently close your eyes and sense the air passing over the pores of your skin. Imagine that you are only air and space, inside and out, with only a thin layer of skin in between. Imagine the same amount of space inside you as you sensed outside. Breathe a regular breath and feel the rhythm of heartbeat and breathing resonating in the inner space.

Allow yourself to focus on creating spaciousness for new possibilities and choices to appear. These new choices may not appear immediately. Often we need practice to overcome the neurotic modern habit of filling our entire lives, inner and outer, with things and busyness.

The Depths of Shamash (Babylonian)

(A version of a Hymn to the Sun, approximately 7th century B.C.E.)

(First lines of Ferris J. Stephens translation: Those who traverse the wide earth, Those who tread upon the high mountains, The monsters of the sea which are full of terror....)

We humans travel the breadth of the earth.
We place our footsteps on the highest peaks.
The sea contains terrible monsters
as well as unknowable creatures in its depths.
The rivers spawn their own life cycles.
All these, O Shamash,
live in your unfolding harmony of song.
They occupy a sphere of name,
a glorious place of vibration
that has no "outside"—
your border continues to expand.
You dress the mountains with your brilliance.
Every region warms itself by you.
You even illuminate light's absence and
cause darkness itself to shine.
You open the depths and unfurl space.
From the bright days, torrid with midday heat,
to the long nights of cold and frost,
you open the ears of the whole world.
On the twentieth day of the month, you rejoice.
You eat and drink in ecstasy.
Taverns open their pure beer and aged wine.

5. Sacred Spaciousness:

Everything is poured out in your remembrance.
The flood goes over some of our heads,
but you drink with all pure toasts
of desire, love and gratitude.
Everything asked in this spirit
will surely come to pass.

Hear the Sound (Hebrew)

(A meditation on the Hebrew words of Deuteronomy 6:4)

shema' yisra'el (A)
YHWH 'elohenu (B)
YHWH 'echad (C)
KJV: Hear, O Israel: the Lord our God is one Lord.

Hear the sound,
Hear the tone,
Hear the name
of the unnameable.
Be thunderstruck by its flash.

Listen all beings—
all you who make an effort
to manifest the rays of the One,
who persevere to express Unity's radiance,
who struggle with the inheritance
of the image of the One (A):

Ever-living Life Energy, before, now and later,
as intimate as the sigh of our own breath,
is the essence of Sacred Diversity:
the Nameless one expresses itself
in the complex tangle of our lives
where being and absence exist together (B).

Ever-living Life Energy, before, now and later,
as immediate as the pause within the breath,
is the essence of Sacred Unity:

the Nameless one is the center
where all lines meet,
where there is only one Being (C).

Meditation—Sound and Embodiment 6: The Harmony of the Universe

For developing a greater awareness of choice:

Begin by breathing in the heart. Then intone slowly the word *shema* ("SHEM-AH")—hearing, listening, awakening—feeling the sound in the area of the heart. Allow it to resonate through the entire inner space of your body. Focus your feeling and intention on allowing the Universe Being to wake up the awareness of choice in your life. You might also try cupping your hands behind the ears, a traditional gesture for a meditation using *shema*.

Here a little struggle is necessary, as the passage presents. Our job description as human beings involves expressing life energy as unity but also as our own unique diversity. As you intone *shema,* maintain a sense of the boundaries of the skin: do not dissolve completely into the sound. To aid this, feel your bones and their connection to the earth. To conclude the meditation, feel the entire body receiving sound from all around, as though being bathed in a universe of sound. Somewhere in this universe is a note that will bring out the melody of your unique purpose in life.

By the Heart and By the Tongue (Egyptian)

(a expanded version of a ritual chant to Ptah, 3rd millenium B.C.E.)

First lines of J.H. Wilson translation: There came into being as the heart and there came into being as the tongue (something) in the form of Atum. The mighty Great One is Ptah, who transmitted [life to all gods], as well as (to) their *ka's*, through this heart, by which Horus becomes Ptah, and through this tongue, by which Thoth becomes Ptah....

By the heart and by the tongue
all things came into being.
By the heart and by the tongue of
the Opening Mouth, the Space-maker,
who is called *Ptah*,
arose the creating principle,
the universal Mind
called *Atum*.

The great one is *Ptah*, cosmic Space,
who gave life to all *ka*-spirits,
the limited soul reality—
of the gods, those shining archetypes.

By the heart of Space,
the Mind's creative conception
extends throughout the universe:
Then *Horus*, this conception,
also becomes *Ptah*.

5. Sacred Spaciousness:

By the tongue of Space,
Mind completes itself through Speech
extending throughout the universe:
Then, *Thoth,* this completion, becomes *Ptah.*

So it came to pass that
the heart and tongue of *Ptah*
gained power over all bodies.
Ptah's sacred Opening dwells in every atom—
of archetypes, humans, animals,
creepers, plants and dust.
The manifested cosmos relies
on the commands of Space.

The eyes see, the ears hear, the nose smells:
They all report to the heart.
When the tongue announces
what the heart conceives, only then
does anything take a step
from non-being into being.

All work and crafts,
all movements of arms and legs,
every stirring tendril of life
follows the process of Ptah:
space unfurls,
heart reveals,
voice clarifies,
life creates.

Meditation—Heart Awareness 4: How Space Creates

For help in taking a new direction:

Begin with breathing and feeling the heart area. Allow yourself to re-create the clear, spacious boundaries set by the feeling of your breathing and heartbeat (for instance, cultivated in Heart Awareness 1 in chapter one). If necessary, proceed to "clear the mirror" (described in Heart Awareness 2 in chapter three). Nothing new can arise if one's entire life and awareness has no space for it. As much as possible breathe with a sense of fullness, remembering the sense of blessing that has infused the journey of the universe from the very beginning.

Breathe the sound *ptah* ("PTAAH")—opening—in and out, using the "ah" sound to support a feeling of opening from the heart. If you are looking for a new direction, allow the space to evoke the various possibilities that your life presents at this moment.

If you are considering several possibilities, bring each of them into your awareness and notice how they affect your heartbeat and breathing. Take a moment between each alternative to "clear the mirror" again. Notice the changes, if any, and do not immediately attempt to interpret them. Often this practice must be done several times in order to begin to understand the wisdom coming through one's own body sensations. They are a bit like dreams in that regard—there is no one, stereotypical interpretation of what these sensations mean. This deeper wisdom connects to the sacred guidance that is throughout the universe at all times, which can come through our own nature as well as through the nature that surrounds us in its wilder state. In this sense, our bodies can become our own oracle.

Ethphatah – Be Opened! (Aramaic)

(A version of Mark 7: 32-35 from the Peshitta version of the Gospels)

wa'ytiyw leh charsha' chad pi'qa' wbo'e' hwaw meneh dansiym 'lawhy 'iyda' (32) wnagdeh men kensha' balchuwdawhy wa'rmiy tzeb'oteh be'dnawhy wraq waqreb lleshoneh (33) wchor bashmaya' we'ttanach we'mar leh 'etpatach (34) wboh bsho'ta' 'etpatach 'ednawhy we'shtariy 'esora' dleshoneh wmalel pshiyqa'yit (35)

KJV: And they brought unto him one that was deaf, and had an impediment in his speech; and they beseech him to put his hand upon him (32). And he took him aside from the multitude, and put his fingers into his ears, and he spit, and touched his tongue (33); And looking up to heaven, he sighed, and saith unto him, Eph-pha-tha, that is, Be opened (34). And straightway his ears were opened, and the string of his tongue was loosed, and he spake plain (35).

They brought Yeshua a man who could not speak or hear,
asking that he lay a healing hand upon him (32).

Yeshua took the man aside, so the crowd could not see,
and placed his fingers gently into the man's ears.

As they breathed together,
Yeshua united his sensing self with the man
then spat on the ground and
touched the man's tongue (33).

As Yeshua focused on the Source
of all sensation and knowing,
he raised his glance and awareness upward,
and breathed one long, powerful breath
with *shemaya*—the universe of vibration.

Releasing his hands from the man's ears,
he said forcefully "*Eth-phatah!*"
"Be opened, expand, clear the way—
allow yourself to be penetrated by the waves of space
that give and receive all sound,
hearing and speech (34)."

At that instant, the man's ears were opened,
the belt binding his tongue loosened
and he spoke clearly (35).

Meditation—Sound and Embodiment 7: Be Opened

For opening a way, or strengthening a new choice:

Following from the previous meditation, this new choice will have come from a contemplation of sacred space and from allowing the often still, small voice of the Only Being to enter one's heart. There is a place where the desire from the Heart of the cosmos intersects with one's own desire. This need not always involve a goal that is "spiritual" or profound. As the Sufi Mevlana Rumi once said, "Whether you love the One or love a human being, if you love enough in the end you will come into the presence of Love itself."

Place the fingertips of both hands lightly on the heart. Breathe the sound "ETH-PHA-TAH" as the hands and arms open (inhale on "eth" and exhale on "pha-tah"). Allow your eyes to remain open. Then begin to speak the word gently, feeling the sound in the heart and focusing on opening a way for the Universe Being to work through your life.

If you are focusing on a particular goal, the feeling of it may get either stronger or weaker after doing this meditation. Perhaps another alternative arises. If you are willing to receive any answer, you are in a good position to benefit from the practice. If an inspiration comes, remember to thank the Source.

As a focus on sound, this meditation is also good for "letting the voice out." Feel the resonance that develops as the power of the universe breaks through any old messages you may have internalized that say that your voice should not be heard or should not be creative.

The Opening (Arabic)

(a meditation on the Qur'an, Surah *al-Fatiha* 1:1-7, "The Opening")

Bismillahir rahmanir rahim (1) alhamdulillahi (2a) rabbi-l'alamin (2b) arrahman irrahim (3)

A. Yusuf Ali version: In the name of Allah, Most Gracious, Most Merciful (1). Praise be to Allah (2a), the Cherisher and Sustainer of the Worlds (2b). Most Gracious, Most Merciful (3).

Upon hearing the Irresistible Voice
of Love's Wellspring and Goal,
we affirm with this breath that (1):

The One is acting to fulfill its purpose,
through individual beings,
through communities of beings,
through large acts and small,
and that every act is celebrating
the Source of our unfolding story.

The essence of all praiseworthy qualities
everywhere in the cosmos
is constantly returning to Unity
as we celebrate our service
and dedicate our gifts
toward the One (2a).

This Being of beings is mysteriously
nurturing and sustaining,

growing and bringing to maturity
all worlds, universes and pluriverses,
all aspects of consciousness and knowledge,
all storylines and lesson plans (2b).
This Source is the Original Womb of Love in all its aspects (3).

maliki yaumadin (4)
A. Yusuf Ali version: Master of the Day of Judgment (4)

It says "I Can" on the day when
the elements part company and return home,
when the threads of interweaving destiny unravel
and the invoices come due.
This Universe Being resolves the irresolvable
at the time when time ends
just as it says "yes" to the birth movements
that are beginning it (4).

iyyaka n'abudu wa iyyaka nasta'ain (5)
A. Yusuf Ali version: Thee do we worship and thine aid we seek (5).

Cutting through all distractions, addictions and diversions,
all conflicting taboos, theologies, offenses and misunder-
standings,
we will act only from this Universe Purpose,
we will develop abilities only in service to the Real,
we will bow to and venerate only the deepest Source of all Life
and we will expect help only from this direction,
the ration of what we need,
freely given by the One (5).

Ihdina sirat almustaqim (6) sirat alladhina an'amta 'alayhim ghayril maghdubi 'alayhim wa laddalin. (7)

A. Yusuf Ali version: Show us the straight way (6), the way of those on whom Thou has bestowed thy Grace, those whose portion is not wrath, and who go not astray (7).

We ask you to reveal our next harmonious steps.
Show us the path that says, "Stand up, get going, do it!"
That resurrects us from the slumber of the drugged
and leads to the consummation of Heart's desire,
like all the stars and galaxies in tune, in time, straight on. (6)

The orbit of every being in the universe is filled with delight.
When each travels consciously,
a sigh of wonder arises at the expanse, the abundance.
This is not the path of frustration, anger or annoyance,
which happens only when we temporarily
lose the way and become drained, roaming too far
from the Wellspring of Love. (7)

Section Two: Voices of Interiority and Presence: Who Am I?

Who are we? How do we know ourselves? How do we understand the feelings, thoughts and sensations that arise within us? Ancient Middle Eastern voices also raised these questions and reflected on interiority, or inner presence, as a sacred principle of the cosmos. Everything in the universe seems to have organized a self that shows evidence of moving spontaneously, toward its own goals and purposes. From the primeval fireball to the early galactic clouds to the planets in their infancy, each revealed an ability to act as unique "selves" moving toward their own destiny, according to modern scientists. Our universe, it seems, is a collection of subjects not objects. Nothing is inert or dead. On a personal level, these storytellers and voices of wisdom prompt us to be more aware of how and why we sense, feel, imagine and experience. On the deepest spiritual level, these voices question how our personal "I" is connected with the "I" behind the universe's existence.

6. Holy Wisdom: What is the Breath from Within Saying?

In the Native Middle Eastern tradition, we begin to develop a sense of depth or interiority by recognizing that something greater than ourselves is moving with intention through our life. When we confront the "knower" within us, the one that experiences, we enter the presence of what these storytellers call *Hokhmah,* Holy Wisdom or the "sacred sense." From the meaning of her name, she is "the breath of awareness from underneath and within." The developed sense of an inner "I am" has gifts to give, including the fulfillment of needs we often try to satisfy by looking outside.

When life draws you to selections in this chapter, you might consider what inner impulses, impressions and voices you have been ignoring. What is the wisdom that wants to be heard from within?

The Essence of Seed - Day 3 (Hebrew)

(a midrashic, or interpretive, translation of Genesis 1:9-13)

wayyo'mer 'elohim yiqqawu hammayim mittachat hashamayim 'el-maqom 'echad wetera'eh hayyabbasha wayehi-khen (9)

KJV: And God said, Let the waters under the heaven be gathered together unto one place, and let the dry land appear: and it was so (9).

The Storyteller continues:
Opening and closing once again
the luminous intelligence of the Universe
vibrated radiance toward Flow,
allowing part of it to settle, in density and destiny,
toward a lower vibration than the Atmosphere—
all this driven by the unfolding purpose
of the whole cosmos.

This denser face of Flow became more stable.
Its previous, exalted state of wild ecstasy,
which made for a very unpredictable personality,
gave way to an embodied, slightly more sober character
that you could rely upon.

With Dense Flow as a model,
the Universe Being then created a more
individualized form of Primordial Fire,
a burning, pulsing presence from within
that warmed and magnetized the whole planet (9).

wayyiqra' 'elohim layyabbasha 'aretz ulemiqwe hammayim qara' yammim wayyar' 'elohim ki-tob (10)

KJV: And God called the dry land Earth; and the gathering together of the waters called he Seas; and God saw that it was good (10).

Carving, engraving destiny further,
the Holy One created more diversity:
Our land and sea
reflect particle and wave
throughout the cosmos.
Sea arose from the cosmic Waves,
"squared," compressed into themselves.
Our great waters on earth reflected
the Great Flow of the cosmos and
its greater question:
"What happens next?"

All this was still evolving, but the
pebble of character had been thrown
into the sea of possibility.
So far, the Holy One saw it all as ripe—
in tune, in rhythm—a "timely" way
for the purpose of the cosmos
to unfold (10).

wayyo'mer 'elohim tadshe' ha'aretz deshe' 'eseb mazria' zera' 'etz peri 'oseh peri lemino 'asher zar'o-bo 'al-ha'aretz wayehi-khen (11)

wattotze' ha'aretz deshe' 'eseb mazria' zera' leminehu we'etz 'oseh-peri 'asher zar'o-bo leminehu wayyar' 'elohim ki-tob (12)

wayehi-'ereb wayehi-boqer yom shelishi (13)

KJV: And God said, Let the earth bring forth grass, the herb yielding seed, and the fruit tree yielding fruit after his kind, whose seed is in itself upon the earth: and it was so (11). And the earth brought forth grass, and herb yielding seed after his kind, and the tree yielding fruit, whose seed was in itself, after his kind: and God saw that it was good (12). And the evening and the morning were the third day (13).

Next the Universe called forth
a more embodied interiority—
that inside-outside tension also
present in the beginning:
The essence of *seed-cell* appeared—
a being or body unfolding and evolving
from a center at its core.

Seed came with sprouts,
like a center comes with a circumference.
Most of each seed's "children"
followed in the path of their ancestors—
they behaved within the boundaries of
what had gone before.

But a few veered off from the limits of
previous expectations.
They tried out new scenarios based on
the needs of the moment (the outside)
and their own self-organization (the inside).
Moving to model the consciousness that created them,
they learned by "trial and error."

Some seed-cells offered food to the
various senses of other beings by
gathering and mixing elements around them,

creating the meal we now call *fruit.*
Yet all the primordial seeds and cells
bore children within their own family.
They didn't mingle their inner
essence with other types of seeds (11).

By creating the habit of *seed-ness*
the Universe moved growth into high gear.
Everywhere that this experiment of
unfolding from a center could happen,
it did happen, and more beings
with their own interior seed of "self"
began to take shape.

In a mysterious way, these new seed-selves
had already taken shape previously.
They just hadn't recognized that they
belonged to a pattern that led *somewhere.*
Now they began to act in harmony with the whole cosmos
as it shaped the next part of the story.
Once again, the future called to and awakened the past
in the possibility of the present.

And once again, the Universe Being
saw it all as ripe—
in tune, in rhythm—a "timely" way
for the purpose of existence
to unfold (12).

Once over and back again,
this third round of opening and closing

marked the third large manifestation
of luminous, intelligent happenings
in our vicinity since the Great Beginning:
the creation of selfhood's Seed (13).

Meditation—Depths of the Self 2: The Seed of the Self

For developing an ability to feel what you really feel:

Our modern world does not encourage depth. It encourages feeling compulsively swept away by our perceived needs, which are often programmed into us based on someone else's priorities. Without apportioning blame to education, religion, business, government or unhealthy family dynamics, we can simply say that, in the modern era, we are not encouraged to contact our own inner, unrehearsed nature any more than we are encouraged to contact the wildness of nature around us. As the integrity of nature outside rapidly deteriorates, there is a certain urgency for us to contact the depths of our self, in order that both might be nurtured and preserved.

As mentioned previously, the seed of the self in the Native Middle Eastern tradition is called *nephesh* in Hebrew (*naphsha* in Aramaic, *nafs* in Arabic). Most of the selections in this chapter center on cultivating a relationship to our own inner, self-organizing depths. Of course, there are many psychological models for working in this way. The Native Middle Eastern tradition contributes its own model and practices, and the meditations offered provide possible doorways to begin a lifelong journey of understanding.

While in nature, consider the entire unfolding story of the cosmos that led to your being alive at this place and time. Breathe with the force and power of the cosmos, and consider the sense of purpose that empowered it. This takes a certain amount of surrender, of opening yourself to a feeling of guidance, at the "ripe" time and place. Breathe with and call with love and respect to this sense of deep intuition within you. It was there in the first human beings, otherwise we wouldn't be here. So it is also there in you.

From this place, ask about the timing of working with your inner depths, the *nephesh* or subconscious self, now. If you feel a sense of spaciousness or openness, breathe further into your depths, into the darkness of the original womb of feeling. Notice all sensations of the body and breathe with the intention that all growth will support your fulfilling the purpose of your life.

To help focus this intention, you might place a word from our story on the breath: *desha* ("DESH-AH," to grow from a center). As you continue to follow the breath, feel into what *feels* in you: Who is the experiencer? There may be voices waiting to be heard, parts of your self, your inner family, your inner nature, that have not been heard. Ask them with respect to identify themselves. Sometimes the responses come in words, sometimes images, sometimes body sensations. Some patience is required. When they come, thank them and thank the Source. The process unfolds from here.

Sacred Power and Sacred Sense (Hebrew)

(an expanded translation of Proverbs 1:7)

yir'at YHWH re'shit da'at Chokhema umusar 'ewilim bazu

KJV: The fear of the Lord is the beginning of knowledge: but fools despise wisdom and instruction.

When we feel awe for the Life behind all life;
when we feel fear before the mystery of the Universe's energy,
    past without beginning, future without edge;
when we feel terror at the source of nature's power—
    turning forms to nothingness and back again,
then we begin to touch the Knower behind all knowing.

Reverence for the unknowable strength and mystery
behind the cosmos begins to create our inner lives,
opening our senses, tuning our understanding
to Holy Wisdom (*Hokhmah*):
The breath of life from underneath,
the Sense behind all senses,
the one within that grasps meaning
out of the bewildering swirl of existence.

In other words,
the reverence of Sacred Power naturally unfolds
the understanding of Sacred Sense.

Only the foolish—
those who allow their limited desires to control them,
who close their senses to the natural world,
who are addicted to their own small power and

think they can extend it everywhere—
only these despise self control—
the power of limits that creates, fashions and teaches
everything embodied,
that opens our eyes to
the sacred architecture of Holy Wisdom.

For All Time Wisdom Rules (Assyrian)

(a version from the Sayings of Ahiqar in Aramaic, fifth-seventh centuries B.C.E.)

First lines of H.L. Ginsberg translation: Two things [which] are meet, and the third pleasing to Shamash: one who drinks wine and gives it to drink, one who guards wisdom, and one who hears a word and does not tell....

Shamash approves of two things and blesses a third:
First, the one who drinks wine and shares it.
Second, the one who guards Wisdom.
Third, the one who hears a word but does not speak it.

Wisdom is precious to the gods, the shining ones.
She rules the psychic world of vision and ideal for all time.
She was established in the shining realm,
wave reality, by the order of the holy one.

More than anything, watch your mouth.
A word is a bird. Once released, it's gone.
First number the secrets of your mouth,
then unpack your words in solitary bundles.

Meditation—Gratitude and Celebration 6: Silence

For developing a relationship to silence:

It is virtually impossible to develop interiority without developing a relationship to silence and to being with one's self without distractions. One of the best ways to do this is to spend a day or two in nature, walking, breathing and taking in the presence that imbues every living being. Take some minutes to gaze at and breathe intimately with several beings you encounter: perhaps a mountain, a flower or a stream. Begin by breathing and gazing with eyes open, then after several minutes allow the eyes to close and continue to breathe with a feeling of connection to that being. Can you feel this being inside you as well as outside?

By not talking you are doing two things: First, you open other senses to communicate with what is around you—you are developing, in fact, greater "social" skills. Second, you conserve the enormous amount of energy that talking requires and that "small talk" consumes in much greater proportion than meaningful, heartfelt conversation does. The energy saved can be directed toward our relationship with our inner self. This is not an invitation to become a hermit, which few of us are called to, but to moderate the outwardly directed, addictive pace of modern life, which distracts us from the voice of nature, whether inside or outside.

Thunder Speaks: Mind Embraces All Opposites, Part 1 (Coptic)

(from the Nag Hammadi Library text "Thunder, Perfect Mind")

First lines of George W. MacRae translation: I was sent forth from [the] power, and I have come to those who reflect upon me, and I have been found among those who seek after me....

The Voice

The Power sent me.
I appear in the minds I make restless.
I am found within by those who look for me.
If I disturb your mind with images, why not look at them?
If you can hear me in a sound, why not listen?
Whoever waits for me—here I am, embrace me!
Don't deny you've seen me,
Don't shut my sound out of your ears—or your voice.
You cannot fail to "know" me, anywhere or anytime.
I am both what knows and what denies knowledge.
Be aware, this moment—
don't claim ignorance of this mind.

For I am first and last,
honored and dishonored
prostitute and saint,
experienced and virginal.
...
I am the silence not grasped by the mind,
    the image you can't forget.
I am the voice of every natural sound,
    the word that always reappears.

I am the intonation of my name—*huu-khm-aah*—
the breath returning from form to its source.

The Bodies Who Come After

I am knowledge and ignorance,
I am timid and bold,
shamed and shameless.
I am strength.
I am fear.
I am war and peace.
Listen to me:
I am infamous and renowned.

Listen to my poor voices,
Listen to my rich ones.

Don't look down on me in the earth under your feet:
I compose the bodies of those who come after you.
Don't look away from me in the shit-pile:
I am the remnants of great civilizations.
Don't laugh inwardly at me when I am
disgraced, homeless or uneducated.
Don't isolate my voice as "another" victim of violence.
I am compassionate, but also cruel.

Be aware, this moment!
Do not indulge in obedience or self-control
because you love one or hate the other.

Do not turn your back on my weakness
or fear my power.

6. Holy Wisdom:

Why despise me when I am afraid
or curse me when I am inflated?

I am she who shudders in all your fears and
who shakes in your moments of power.
I am the one in you who becomes sick and
I am the one who is completely healthy.
I am no sensation and I am the Sense,
the Wisdom of all.

Meditation—Sound and Embodiment 8: The Intonation of My Name

To strengthen a connection to your inner wisdom:

Begin by breathing the name *Hokhmah* with the sound "hukh" on the inhalation and "mah" on the exhalation.

Then begin to elongate and emphasize the sounds even more as you intone them on a note that feels as though it vibrates within. Try this slowly in three parts.

Begin with the sound "HOO" with one hand lightly over your heart. The open "oo" sound is preceded by a gentle "h," slightly aspirated, like the "ch" sound in the word *loch*. With this sound feel the source of the breath and life behind all beings.

Then proceed to "CHM"; be gentle with the initial "ch" sound so that that the throat doesn't constrict. Feel a humming resonance deep in the body, the embodiment of the life-breath-knowing within you.

Finally intone "MAH," feeling the breath returning to the Source and to all beings, carrying wisdom from this experience of embodiment.

Try intoning all three parts of the name on one breath. This may take a bit of practice to do easily in a balanced way. Allow yourself to release any clinging to the beginning, middle or end of the process. After some minutes, simply breathe each part of the sound: "hu" as you inhale, the middle "chm" where the breath turns over and "mah" as you exhale. Then after some moments release the word itself and breathe naturally with the feeling that remains. Follow the feeling where it wants to lead, perhaps to a better relation to the "I Am" within you, the source of what feeds and empowers you.

Wisdom's Gift (Aramaic)

(An expanded translation of Matthew 26:26 from the Peshitta version of the Gospels)

kad deyn lo'siyn shqal yeshuw' lachma' wbarekh waqtza' wyahb ltalmiydawhy we'mar (A) sabw 'akhuwlw hanaw pagry (B)

KJV: And as they were eating, Jesus took bread, and blessed it, and brake it, and gave it to the disciples, and said (A), Take, eat; this is my body (B).

Then, while they ate, Yeshua embraced and picked up the bread, sign and symbol of the earth's support and understanding.
He did this as though becoming one with the loaf, absorbing himself into it.
He breathed into this *lachma*—daughter of Holy Wisdom—with blessing.
He divided it, just as a seer might divide something in order to prophesy from the shapes that the will of the Holy One causes to form.
He gave these pieces to his students and said (A):

Take and eat,
Surround and enjoy,
Convert and consume,
Envelop and devour:

This is my dead body.
This is my corpse.
This body (*pagry*) extends itself and wanders this world.
It eventually loses strength and heat.
Read the signs yourself:
My future, your future
is to be food—*lachma*, Wisdom's gift—
for those who come after us (B).

Wisdom's Bread (Aramaic)

(a translation of John 6:35 from the Peshitta version of the Gospels)

'amar lhuwn yeshuw' 'ena' 'na' lachma' dchaye' (A) man da'te' lwaty la' nekhpan wman damhaymen biy la' netzhe' l'alam (B)

KJV: And Jesus said unto them, I am the bread of life (A): he that cometh to me shall never hunger; and he that believeth on me shall never thirst (B).

Yeshua said to them:
The "I Am" is the bread of renewable life energy.

When you reconnect your small self—
the elemental "I"—
to the only "I,"
Depth and Source of all identity,
you energize the animal life in you.

The freshness of food—its palpable "I am"—
feeds the life of all beings receiving it.
This Simple Presence is Holy Wisdom's daughter,
the fruit of natural vigor created in the beginning.

So the "I" fully aware of its ephemeral nature,
the germ of individuality's seed,
fuels a passion for what's fresh and verdant.
The self that is conscious of its Self,
resting in the eye of desire's hurricane,
touches the energy-filled, energy-less center—
the Living One that was, is and will be,
present in every breath.

6. Holy Wisdom:

Whoever travels with and through
the Simple Presence coming through me,
joined with the I-I of Holy Wisdom,
uniting one to many at the table of the One,
will find themselves fulfilled on all levels of life,
from age to age, from gathering to gathering.

Their inner voices will gather at Wisdom's table
without the gnawing that remains after
consuming food that doesn't nourish or
drink that leaves us weakened and dried out inside—
all that separates us from our own Simple Presence.

Meditation—Simple Presence 3: Food from Within

For working with unhealthy hunger or thirst:

Return again to a place of simple presence. Sit comfortably, eyes closed and feel the rise and fall of the breath in the heart. With each breath, reach out to whatever feelings or sensations arise, and feel your breath illuminating each sensation with awareness. Follow the feelings and body sensations associated with the object of your need. To help center, you might also breathe with the word *inana* ("INA-NA"), the connection of small "I" to the Only "I." Notice the effect of the sound on what seems to be needed, or wanted, at the moment. What is the deeper origin of your feeling of hunger or thirst? Is there another way to fulfill these feelings, one that brings you more into health and able to fulfill the purpose of your life?

Like Seed and Fruit (Persian)

(from "The Secret Rose Garden" by the Sufi poet Mahmud Shabistari, 13th century Persia)

Look around you!
This world is tremendously mingled:
Angels, devils, Satan, Michael—
all mixed up like seed and fruit!
Atheist with fundamentalist,
materialist with mystic.

All cycles and seasons,
years, months and days
converge at the dot of now:
"In the beginning" *is* "world without end."

Every point in this circle becomes
the first stroke for a million new forms.
Every point follows its own orbit,
but sooner or later
revolution meets itself,
coming and going.

7. The Seed of a Soul: Who is the "I Am" Within?

The inner life of all nature, as well as of each individual being, organizes itself around simple things that we often take for granted: the sensuous pleasure of sunlight or moonlight; the flow within our bodies; the voices of need, desire and struggle within. If we follow the experience back to the Experiencer, the sensation back to Sacred Sense, a door opens toward a more integrated self, the seed of a soul that can contain the whole universe.

When life draws you to selections in this chapter, you might breathe with a breath of "simple presence," clearing the heart's mirror so that a more real sense of self can arise from within. Who is the deeper "I Am" in you?

How to Organize a Self – Day 4 (Hebrew)

(a midrashic, or interpretive, translation of Genesis 1:14-19)

wayyo'mer 'elohim yehi me'orot birqia' hashamayim lehabdil ben hayyom uben hallayela wehau le'otot ulemo'adim uleyamim weshanim (14)
wehau lim'orot birqia' hashamayim leha'ir 'al-ha'aretz wayehi-khen (15)
KJV: And God said, let there be lights in the firmament of the heaven to divide the day from the night; and let them be for signs, and for seasons, and for days, and years (14). And let them be for lights in the firmament of the heaven to give light upon the earth: and it was so (15).

The Storyteller continues:
During the next Big Day,
Seeds and cells developed a
more private sense of Light.
Looking, sensing outwards from a center,
they felt light collect in bundles
right in the middle of Great Spaciousness.

Their illumination led to more choice
(just as it does in us),
and so light helped living beings
organize their ability to know—
their intelligence—in new ways.

Feeling light localized in space
allowed a being to turn toward
or away from it, further clarifying an
early sense of "I" and "Thou."
We could have a relationship

with something far away
that we didn't understand.

Being "in tune" and "on time"
also became a possibility as
seeds and cells could now
pulse towards or away from what
pleased or repelled them in their
meetings with the remarkable lights,
which sometimes appeared
and sometimes disappeared.

Of course, the lights' own
seed-selves acted and reacted
to other beings,
so they changed, too.

And so the Universe Being itself
became more and more conscious through
this new way to organize a self.
As a result, reality itself began to shift (14-15).

7. The Seed of a Soul:

wayya'as 'elohim 'et-shenei hamme'orot haggedolim 'et-hamma'or haggadol lememshelet hayyom we'et-hamma'or haqqaton lememshelet hallayla we'et hak-kokhabim (16)
wayyitten 'otam 'elohim birqia' hashamayim leha'ir 'al-ha'aretz (17)
welimshol bayyom uballayla ulahabdil ben ha'or uben hachoshekh wayyar' 'elohim ki-tob (18)
wayehi-'ereb wayehi-boqer yom rebi'i (19)
KJV: And God made two great lights; the greater light to rule the day, and the lesser light to rule the night: he made the stars also (16). And God set them in the firmament of the heaven to give light upon the earth (17), and to rule over the day and over the night, and to divide the light from the darkness: and God saw that it was good (18). And the evening and the morning were the fourth day (19).

Lights above, lights around—
no longer light only
everywhere and all-the-time.

But this wasn't like turning on a light
in a room already arranged.
As selves and cells whirled
toward unknown ends and purposes,
light bundles touched them with
heat, color, magnetism and waves
for which we still don't have names.

The closest radiant bodies—
sun, moon and stars—created
the deepest relationships.
Like symbols in a poem,
they came to represent the local reality
of day and night, reminding us
of the Universe Being's larger cycle

of opening and closing—
the expansion of intelligent creative cause,
the contraction of mysterious creative effect.

So day and night allowed seed-cells
to alternate times to grow
with times to rest and absorb.

And once again, the Universe Being
saw it all as ripe—
in tune, in rhythm—a "timely" way
for the purpose of existence
to unfold (16-18).

Once over and back again,
this fourth round of opening and closing
marked the fourth large manifestation
of luminous, intelligent happenings
in our vicinity since the Great Beginning:
the creation of personal
enlightenment and endarkenment,
the rhythm of growth and rest (19).

Meditation—Heart Awareness 5: Gathering Bundles of Light

For deepening a relationship with your inner nature:

Find a quiet place, perhaps in nature, where you can contemplate a plant or a flower and its relationship to light. Closing your eyes, return to breathing in the heart, and clear the mirror that can take impressions. Then open your eyes with a soft focus and allow your being to absorb the impressions of the plant before you. Notice not only its visual details but also its capacity and desire to turn toward the light. Particularly powerful times to do this are dawn and dusk.

Feel yourself absorbing and remembering the qualities of the plant that are still part of your being. Then with eyes closed, internalize even more the feeling rather than the visual image of the plant. Become the plant for a few moments and find the place within you that resonates with it in all its unfoldment: seed, sprout, fullness and fading. Follow your feeling where it leads you in your developing relationship to the soul-self (*nephesh*) within you. As you complete the meditation, breathe gratefulness toward the plant and the Source of its creation.

The "I" Joins the Journey (Hebrew)

(a midrashic, or interpretive, translation Proverbs 8:22-24)

yhwh qanani re'shit darko qedem mif'alaw me'az (22)

KJV: The Lord possessed me in the beginning of this way, before his works of old.

(Wisdom speaks:)
The Life behind Life, eternally now in past and present,
possessed me at the beginning of beginnings:

As the first principle of setting up an ordered existence,
this Universe Life Force absorbed me,
Hokhmah, Holy Wisdom—
Breath from Within and Underneath—
into itself.

Cosmic appetite combined with the power of density,
the desire to compress and condense,
and I—the first Interior Experience—
joined the journey from the very start.

This was the first and most ancient mystery:
how the power of growth can be contained
and fixed around a center,
the identity of the self.
This is the axis on which the universe turns (22).

me'olam nissakhti mero'sh miqqadmei-'aretz (23):

be'en-tehomot cholaleti be'en ma'yanot nikhbaddei-mayim (24)

KJV: I was set up from everlasting, from the beginning, or ever the earth was. When there were no depths, I was brought forth; when there were no fountains abounding with water.

7. The Seed of a Soul:

From the first gathering of sensing and feeling,
I was poured out like a libation,
a consecration of the cosmos.
At that ancient pivotal moment,
before particles or form were even imagined,
I flowed out, baptizing all in sacredness (23).

This was even before the primordial abyss—
that dark kernel of purpose—formed in the Universe's heart.
Even before this I danced into existence.
When everything we call reality was still a "Not!"
when even the abundant springs of chaos
    had not yet begun to flow,
I hoped, I waited,
I twisted and turned, I struggled
my way through the birth canal of the Holy One (24).

Meditation – Gratitude and Celebration 7: Flow, Struggle and Dance

To support a better relationship to your physical health:

Begin again with natural, relaxed breath, and gently sense your way into the "involuntary" pulsations of the body: heartbeat, lymphatic flow, peristalsis in digestion and the pulse of the spinal fluid. Anywhere a body sensation arises, thank it for the blessing it pours out. Feel the flow, even when the body struggles or seeks better health, as part of the dance of life. Allow each pulsation to lead you to *that which senses*, which one might call the "wisdom of the body," part of the *nephesh*, seed-self within you. At the end, thank each sensation as a gift of the Sacred Sense.

Thunder Speaks: Mind Embraces All Opposites, Part 2 (Coptic)

(from the Nag Hammadi Library text "Thunder, Perfect Mind")

(First lines of George W. MacRae translation: [I am...] within. [I am...] of the natures. I am [...] of the creation of the [spirits]. [...] request of the souls. [I am] control and the uncontrollable....)

The Within

I am the "within."
I am the "within" of all natures.
In the beginning, all spirits claim my creation.
In the end, all souls request my presence.
I am control—and uncontrollable.
I bring things together, I scatter them.
I persist, I fall apart.
I am the one felt as "below,"
but all rise in my presence.

I am the verdict: guilty and innocent.
I make no mistakes,
but all errors have their root in me.
I look like lust, but within I am restraint.
I am easy to hear, difficult to grasp.
I am mute and verbose together.
Hear my gentle voice or
learn the hard way, from experience.
I am the one who cries out
and gets a bad reputation.
I prepare the bread, the understanding,
earth's food for all needs.

I am the *Hokhmah* of my name:
earth-wisdom,
breath of the mother,
source of all livingness in form.
My voice is all around.
My ears listen everywhere.

Meditation—Depths of the Self 3: Selves Speaking for Themselves

For calling a circle of inner wisdom:

The process of establishing a relationship with the inner self or selves, begun in previous chapters, may continue by allowing each aspect of the self to have its own "I"—its own name, atmosphere, voice and expression.

Begin again by breathing in the heart, and connecting with your source of guidance, the guidance behind the entire universe. Then breathe gently into the depths of the body and ask with respect that any voices of the *nephesh* that have something to say present themselves and offer their names. Often this will feel like coaxing a frightened or angry child into the light. Orders and threats have no place here, only love and acceptance. After a name is exchanged, you could ask each self to express its needs. Listen without judgment, but also without any compulsion to act on everything you hear. Contacting an "inner family of selves," all aspects of the *nephesh* in this tradition, can help clarify your inner life. Keep the boundaries of each session definite, determined by your ability to maintain a concentration with both breathing and body awareness. Begin with a shorter period of time and then lengthen it as your ability to focus increases. Consciously end each session with thanks for what has been experienced and a willingness to continue the relationship. Then take some moments to integrate the feelings and sensations in your body and bring your awareness into the present moment before proceeding onto anything else.

The Door Between the Worlds (Aramaic)

(a translation of John 10:9 from the Peshitta version of the Gospels)

'ena' 'na' tar'a' wbiy 'en 'nash ne'uwl niche' wne'uwl wnepuwq wre'ya' neshkach

KJV: I am the door: by me if any man enter in, he shall be saved, and shall go in and out, and find pasture.

The connection of one to One,
I-I, is the door between the worlds.
The self conscious of its Self
opens a passage between times and spaces.
The ego, aware of its moment-by-moment existence,
conveys us between realities.
Simple Presence in Unity
shuttles us back and forth,
from limitation to freedom.
The eye at the center of diversity's hurricane
turns us from one face of life to another.

Those who enter into form
with awareness, each moment,
the way I have done,
will find the Source of all life energy.
They come into embodiment
and leave again freely
with every breath,
all the while finding relief
from the cares and sorrows
of human life.
They return to themselves
in conscious peacefulness
finding rest and pasture for their souls.

Meditation—Simple Presence 4: The Door of "I"

For balancing responsibilities and needs in life:

Return again to a place of simple presence: sit comfortably, eyes closed, and feel the rise and fall of the breath in the heart. It can help to place one hand very lightly over the heart to help center your awareness there. With each breath, reach out to whatever feelings or sensations arise and feel the breath illuminating each with awareness. Explore the different arenas of your life, including the various ways you are known by others, as well as the images you hold of yourself. Where in you is the door that allows you to move between these various "you's" and to keep all the aspects of yourself integrated and whole? Who sits in the door between them? Consider each image and sensation as a gift, with gratitude for an increasing sense of the sacred "I Am" within.

In the Doorway (Persian)

(From "The Diwan of Shams-i-Tabriz," by the Sufi poet Mevlana Jelaluddin Rumi, 13th century Anatolia)

My eyes gleam because there is Another inside.
If water scalds you, there was fire behind it—understand?
But I have no stone in my hand,
you won't find an argument here.
We know a rose garden for its sweetness, not its thorns.
So what you see in my eyes comes from another place.
Here's a world, there's a world—
I'm seated in the doorway.
Only those who sit between can deliver wordless lectures.
It's enough to give this hint:
Say no more—
stop talking and
follow your tongue inside, not out!

Drops and Specks (Persian)

(from "The Secret Rose Garden" by the Sufi poet Mahmud Shabistari, 13th century Persia)

Penetrate the heart of one drop of water—
you'll be flooded by a hundred pure oceans.
If you examine carefully a speck of dust,
you'll see a million unnameable beings.
Look closely: the limbs of a fly are like an elephant.
A hundred harvests reside in a germ of barley seed.
A millet seed holds a whole world.
The reflection in an insect's wing unfolds an ocean.
Cosmic rays lie hidden in the pupil of my eye,
and somehow the center of my heart
accommodates the pulse of the cosmos.

The Soul's Three Faces (Hebrew)

(a version of selected portions of the Zohar, Book of Radiant Life, a collection of mystical Jewish commentaries, assembled in the 15th century)

(First lines of Gershom Scholem translation: The names and grades of the soul of man are three: *nefesh* [vital soul], *ruah* [spirit], *neshamah* [innermost soul, supersoul]. The three are comprehended one within the other, but each has its separate abode....)

The human soul has three faces: *nephesh, ruach* and *neshemah.*

Nephesh is the animating and animal self,
that which scatters and gathers.
Ruach is the breathing self,
conscious in the present moment,
a portion of the Breathing Life of All.
Neshemah is the illuminating self,
light of the light of guidance from the One.
The three are contained,
one inside the other,
though each has its own sphere of activity.

Nephesh is intimate with the body:
It nourishes and supports it.
It is the "below"—the first instant of
the arising of all sensation.
Having fulfilled its purpose, conscious of itself,
it becomes a throne, a resting place for
the breathing, conscious self—

a place for *ruach* to rest—
as Isaiah writes (32:15):
"when the breath pours upon us
from the first Source."

When these two selves fulfill their purpose
and prepare themselves, they can welcome
the illuminating self (*neshemah*),
which then rests in the home
created by the breath.
Neshemah goes through and beyond
the normal ways of sensing:
It fulfills all sensation.
Throne upon throne, vehicle within vehicle:
One place to rest, one accommodation,
rests upon another and again upon another.

Study and experience these faces of the soul.
It can lead you to *Hokhmah*, Sacred Wisdom.
Then the Source of Sacred Breath and Soul
brings together mysteries
that otherwise seem separate and divisive.

Nephesh is the dark light
at the bottom of a candle's flame,
the part close to the wick you can't see through
but without which there would be no flame at all.
When fully lit, the "bottom" of the flame
creates a seat for the visible light above it (*ruach*),
the only one we usually see.
When these two burn fully, they

build a foundation for another light,
one sensed as a shimmering essence—
the illuminating aura of *neshemah*.
All three lights only complete themselves
in partnership with the others.
This one light then embraces the All.

8. The Soul's Journey: Is This a Step on My Path?

The journey into the depths of self begins with the question from the previous chapter: "Who is doing the traveling?" First we might differentiate various parts of the self, then hear their voices and call them together. Often these voices are as disturbing and surprising as the sound of thunder. We each journey on our own from here. There is no one right way to proceed.

As resources, we can draw on what Middle Eastern wisdom calls, by various names, Sacred Sense and Holy Wisdom. This inner, "gathering self" helps guide our soul's journey toward fulfillment, integrating a deeper purpose with the challenges of everyday life. In our inner world, who leads and who follows? Perhaps we do not so much follow the soul-self as lead it to follow us, all the while asking who the real "I" might be.

When life draws you to selections in this chapter, you might consider how the situation before you is part of a longer, larger journey that helps you understand yourself, and your place in life, with more depth and passion. Is the choice before you a step on your authentic path?

The Preferential Option for a Soul - Day 5 (Hebrew)

(a midrashic, or interpretive, translation of Genesis 1:20-23)

wayyo'mer 'elohim yishretzu hammayim sheretz nephesh chayya we'of ye'ofef 'al-ha'aretz 'al-penei reqia' hashamayim (20)

KJV: And God said, Let the waters bring forth abundantly the moving creature that hath life, and fowl that may fly above the earth in the open firmament of heaven (20).

The Storyteller continues:
The Being behind the Universe
shined again, radiating, pulsing,
it "said" something more (but not in our words).
It sang for a new possibility,
drawing forth a new character in the
unfolding reality as it tried to express
its own freedom of choice in form.
It stirred more life energy into Primal Flow
adding a dash of liberation as well.

Like a centrifuge, or a whirlpool,
this swirling caused the interiority of living beings
to "precipitate" out new forms, inside and out.
So what we call inner psyche and outer form
evolved together, feeling their way toward completion
even as they became more different from one another.

As life proceeded, it dawned on these new beings,
"Hey! I'm not part of one large smudge!
I'm an individual with
life to use as I choose!"

Here's how it happened:
Outer and inner arose together as usual.
First came the *nephesh* way—
we call it the subconscious, or soul-self,
but it was really another way for the Holy One
to experience reality as it changed and evolved.
The *nephesh* could inhale (NPh) and exhale (PhH),
be inspired and effusive,
be affected by what was outside
as well as initiate action from within.
As an additional, sometimes hidden, feature:
Within *nephesh* you find
an inner, impassioned, rising fire
causing it to grow, trying to fulfill its own purpose (ASh).
These beings began to swim around
under "their own" power.

Then came the '*hoph* way,
we might call it our "instincts,"
an even more obscure feature of
the new, developing "I-ness."
Its movements came swiftly and easily,
as though soaring on wings.
This way of experiencing life
reacts quickly to changes in
atmosphere, space and vibration.
With the addition of instinct,
a being could respond to danger
instantly to keep itself alive and
maintain the integrity of its own evolving life.
Outwardly the forms took wings and flew (20).

wayyivra' 'elohim 'et-hattanninim haggedolim we'et kol-nephesh hachayya haromeset 'asher shartzu hammayim leminehem we'et kol-'of kanaf leminehu wayyar' 'elohim ki-tob (21)

KJV: And God created great whales, and every living creature that moveth, which the waters brought forth abundantly, after their kind, and every winged fowl after his kind: and God saw that it was good (21).

At this point the Holy One unleashed even more diversity,
wondering whether "scale"—largeness and smallness—
would have any effect.
Some interior soul-selves developed very large bodies,
swimming along together
in the primal psychic flow.
Some instinctual selves began to
travel together in large flocks.
These inner "animals" and "birds"—
the consciousness they evolved—
guided the outer development
of material forms, types and communities.

But they didn't exist in isolation.
These new types of beings began to
generate their own offspring,
leaving behind the forms and ways
of their parents, springing and flying off
toward their own destiny.
So each self pursued its own inspiration
and then expressed it in action.
In this way, by its in-breath and out-breath,
it showed it was part of the Universal soul.

As the experiment proceeded,
the Holy One articulated what we might call
"the preferential option for a soul."
Yes, it already existed as one among many options
in the original heart of the Cosmos, but now
the call of the Holy One from the Beginning
activated it everywhere.

Once again, the Universe Being
saw it all as ripe—
in tune, in rhythm—a "timely" way
for the purpose of existence
to unfold (21).

wayebarekh 'otam 'elohim le'mor pheru urebu umil'u 'et-hammayim bayyammim weha'of yireb ba'aretz (22):
wayehi-'ereb wayehi-boqer yom chamishi (23)
KJV: And God blessed them, saying, Be fruitful, and multiply, and fill the waters in the seas, and let fowl multiply in the earth (22). And the evening and the morning were the fifth day (23).

After this new breakthrough,
the Universe Being breathed radiantly—
with magnetism and love—
(what we call blessing)
toward the new beings
of subconsciousness and instinct,
of *nephesh* and *hoph.*
Translating the Holy One's energy
into words, it said:
"Bear more fruit!

Become more frequent and diverse!
Swimmingly fill the flow
of inner and outer life!
And because they can,
let the flying, instinctual ones also
spread over and through earthiness
(the particle reality, too!)
where those who swim can't go (22)."

Once over and back again,
this fifth round of opening and closing
marked the fifth large manifestation
of luminous, intelligent happenings
in our vicinity since the Great Beginning:
Souls joined the caravan of life (23).

Meditation—Depths of the Self 4: The Soul of Life

For improving healthy instincts:

After beginning with a remembrance of the Source, consciously breathe in the heart, feeling each aspect of your subconscious self that you have been able to feel or identify. Try using the elongated sounds and roots of the word *nephesh* slowly as a meditation. With the inhalation, feel the sound "NEPH" and focus on the infusion of new energy. With the exhalation, feel the sound "PHAH" and focus on passing along life energy. In the brief natural pause after the exhalation, and without extending the pause, feel the sound "ASH" and honor the fire and passion that each aspect of the *nephesh* carries to fulfill its purpose for existence.

At the end of the session, breathe with the self of your bodily instinct. See if there is anything that you are neglecting in the health of your body. Thank the instinctual self for all that it does to keep you together, body and soul. After a few minutes, breathe thanksgiving to all parts and to the Source.

Wisdom's Dinner Party (Hebrew)

(a translation of Proverbs 9:1-6 from the Hebrew)

chakhemot baneta betah chatzeba 'ammudeha shib'ah (1):
KJV: Wisdom hath builded her house, she hath hewn out her seven pillars (1):

From the primordial, chaotic "within,"
Hokhmah—the breath of nourishing insight—
has created a separate place to live:
By enclosing her unknowable, inner mystery,
Holy Wisdom has created an address for her temple.

She has done this by dividing the Dark,
pushing from outside until the
foundations of her dwelling—the necessary basic "selves"—
join together by their own mutual attraction:
This natural union creates the first conscious "I am."

tabecha tibchah masekha yenah 'af 'arekha shulchanah (2)
KJV: She hath killed her beasts; she hath mingled her wine; she hath also furnished her table (2).

She has resisted her inner resistance to having limits,
ripened her ripeness for inner and outer diversity,
killed the beast, sacrificed and cooked it for nourishment.
From her own intoxication of the "All,"
she has mixed spiced wine of spirit-soaked Mind
which can be drunk and digested by the "small."
She has spread out a table to nourish the selves
by ordering matter and light, form and vibration
in a reliable and harmonious way.

shalecha na'aroteha tiqra' 'al-gappei meromei qaret: (3)
KJV: She hath sent forth her maidens: she crieth upon the high places of the city (3).

From the first bursts of desire
coming from this new union of her soul-selves,
Wisdom sends out messengers, children of her own being.
From the new center of her unfurling reality—
the enclosure of dynamic relationship we call *soul*—
diversity engraves itself on the life of the universe,
expanding, spreading, rising further.
Wisdom proclaims and pleads, she calls together more selves,
she calls for ever more integrity and inter-being
from her inner and outer creation.

mi-feti yasur henna chasar-leb 'amera lo (4)
lekhu lachamu belachami ushetu beyayin masakheti (5)
'izbu feta'yim wichu we'ishru bederekh binah (6)
KJV: Whoso is simple, let him turn in hither: as for him that wanteth understanding, she saith to him (4), Come, eat of my bread and drink of the wine which I have mingled (5). Forsake the foolish, and live; and go in the way of understanding (6).

"You who are open, susceptible, ready to learn,
You who are simple enough to take a new direction—
right this way, change here, this moment!"
To those who lack heart,
whose vital passion is diminished,
whose center of courage is blocked,
she radiates certainty, command and praise,
she promises (4):

8. The Soul's Journey:

"Absorb my understanding of radical wetness—
of greening, growing, vital force.
Eat my bread of freshness and beauty:
In the form offered here, it's all digestible.
Drink wine distilled from my experience, my embodied breath,
arising through the power that
stands under and supports you.
This liquor offers the intoxication of your soul (5).

"Free your open-heartedness and feel the energy of life!
Release the power of your simplicity,
stop getting ready and start actually living!
Find the direct way,
follow a path which goes somewhere.
Begin a journey which leads to the education
and understanding of your soul (6)."

Thunder Speaks: Mind Embraces All Opposites, Part 3 (Coptic)

(from the Nag Hammadi Library text "Thunder, Perfect Mind")

(First lines of George W. MacRae translation: Why have you hated me in your counsels? For I shall be silent among those who are silent, and I shall appear and speak....)

Appearing, Disappearing

Why am I hated wherever the powerful meet?
I am silent with those who are silent,
I stand up with those who speak out....
I am the one who has caused hate and love everywhere.
Some call me Life, some Death.
Some Law, some Anarchy.
You have pursued me and
you are my captive.
I have been scattered and gathered.
Shamed, shameless you appear before me.
I honor no holy days and
they all belong to me.
I have no god and my god is great.

You would like to forget me,
but I am everywhere in your mind.
I am uneducated, but everyone learns from me.
You despise me,
but you cannot remove me from your mind.
You try to hide from me,
but my gaze sees you everywhere.
For whenever you hide, I appear.
Whenever you are truly present, I hide from you.

8. The Soul's Journey:

Embrace Me

Embrace me from the place in you
that understands and which grieves,
from the place which seems ugly and in ruin,
from the self which steals from its neighbors
though they are really no better off.

From the self which feels shame,
embrace me shamelessly.
From the middle of shame and shamelessness,
the place where grandiosity and depression merge,
find a center that brings sense and order
to all my dismembered members in you.

Advance together to me:
you who know my unity and disunity,
the One Self or my separate selves.
Bring the "great," the spiritual Self
to live among the small, the animal selves.
Advance together to childhood:
the small, the simple, the poor
living with
the great, the complex, the rich.
Don't isolate "great" from "small,"
"rich" from "poor" within you.
By one you know the other
and none can live in health divided.

Why, then, do you curse me in one form
and honor me in another?

You have wounded some of mine, had mercy on others.
Do not separate me from the First Ones
who were here before you.
Do not cast anyone or anything away
because you think them primitive.
I know the First Ones and
those who followed in their ways know me.

Meditation—Depths of the Self 5: Calling the Selves Together

For help when feeling contradictory or conflicted feelings:

After remembering the Source, breathe gently in the heart, as you have done previously. Begin to breath with the name of Holy Wisdom ("HU-KHM-AH") as in the meditation under "Sound and Embodiment" in chapter six. Through the sound, call to a feeling of life-giving support from your own connection to guidance. Then call the various aspects of your subconscious to a round table at which they can share. Call together even those aspects that do not get along. Allow the "rich" and the "poor" to come to the same table together. Allow each aspect to express its own needs and desires. Again, listen without judgment but also without any compulsion to fulfill anything. Listen with the ears of *Hokhmah*. Find the place of simplicity, openness, susceptibility in each aspect of the self. Open to the possibility that in this simplicity is the power to fulfill the true purpose of your whole being.

In concluding the practice, breathe thankfulness toward each aspect of the self and to the Source. With all such work—which separates, articulates and, hopefully, clarifies the inner territory—take some time afterward to breathe, stretch and re-integrate all parts of the self into a unified whole. Sometimes, we encounter voices of our *nephesh* that can be surprising and disturbing. Viewed as an ancient archetype of inner wisdom, *Hokhmah* can be both severe and nurturing but she can embrace them all.

The Creator of Ripeness (Aramaic)

(a translation of John 10:14-15 from the Peshitta version of the Gospels)

'ena''na' ra'ya' taba' wyoda' 'na' ldiyly wmetiyda' 'na' men diyly (14)

'aykana' dyoda' liy 'aby we'na' yoda' 'na' la'by wnapshy so'em 'na' chlap 'ono' (15)

KJV: I am the good shepherd, and know my sheep, and am known of mine (14).
As the Father knoweth me, even so know I the Father: and I lay down my life for the sheep (15).

The "I Am"—
linking I-I, one-to-One
leads our flock of needs to fulfillment,
at the right time and place.
The peaceful center at the middle of
'Who am I?' leads our desires and anxieties to
the pasture ripe for us.
Simple Presence understands, grasps and gathers
the wandering selves in us,
the attractive, distractive swirl and whirl "outside"
that covers and blinds us to the
light from the Beginning within.
Those 'inner sheep,' just like the outer ones,
recognize immediately their own shepherd,
the guiding Self within,
the one connecting us to the One (14).

The Parent of all,
continues creation each instant,
understanding, grasping, gathering
every living process in Its hand.

8. The Soul's Journey:

This Father-Mother
expresses It(self) through the
one connected to One in unity,
the "I Am."
(That's what's happening in the freely-
given teaching and example here.
It's not like someone who "leads" and "teaches"
you for hire, for reward or compensation.)

The person fully aware of the limited self,
tuned to the Creation's giveaway,
clears a mirror to reveal
"in the Beginning," now.
S/he lays down the small self to reveal
the light of the First and Only (15).

Find a Self, Lose a Self (Aramaic)

(a translation of Matthew 10:39 from the Peshitta version of the Gospels)

man de'shkach naphsheh nawbdiyh (A) wman dnawbed naphsheh metulaty neshkchiyh (B)

KJV: He that findeth his life shall lose it (A): and he that loseth his life for my sake shall find it (B).

Whoever blindly chases the small self
    as mirrored in things outside, in the surrounding world,
    will be isolated from it:
Whoever tries to fulfill all its demands will end up divided.
Whoever unconsciously and constantly
peels the onion of animal desire
    will find only separate, clamoring voices.
Whoever gains only the instinctive soul's diversity,
which scatters all it gathers,
will find that this variety perishes (A).

However, whoever realizes the
perishing nature of self-hood with awareness,
    will find the self's real purpose.
Whoever uproots its limited demands,
will find them entangled in a desire for Unity.
Whoever separates the small self's voices clearly
    will find profound repose
at the Center of the conversation.
Whoever punctures the small self's inflation—
and connects self to Source—
will discover in surrender
its true nature pouring in (B).

Meditation—Depths of the Self 6: Who Follows Whom?

For working with compulsive needs and desires:

Begin again with whatever invocation of the Source you have chosen. Then breathe rhythmically in heart with the word *Alaha* or *Hokhmah* until your breath and heart both settle. Breathe into the parts of your *nephesh* (or in Jesus' Aramaic language *naphsha*) that have demands and desires you have not heard before, or that overwhelm you blindly in moments when you are not conscious of their source. Sometimes these messages from the *naphsha* are very powerful, washing over in waves of compulsive behavior, which can seem inevitable or undeniable. Sometimes they can even masquerade as the voice of genuine guidance. See this all as some part of the self trying to get your attention. There is always a deeper need underneath, perhaps one that you cannot fulfill immediately, or ever. When you come to the bottom of the need, there may be anger, sadness or fear concerning a past event, but ultimately a need for love, acceptance and inclusion.

Cultivate the quality of inner, attentive and understanding listening. Affirm the reality of the need as it is felt. Notice where its sensations are felt in your body, and follow them, affirming the wisdom that is there at the bottom of the feeling. If you have clearly distinguished which voice of the self needs attention, make a list of its likes and dislikes, then consciously seek to fulfill some of the ones that are not harmful to your being or that of others.

Gradually, you will establish a relationship with your inner self in which you feel more cooperation in everyday life. The inner territory becomes less polarized, less a matter of a massive conflagration between good and evil and more one of what is ripe and unripe for this moment. At some point you may begin to ask whether the aspect of your *naphsha* that was previously problematic would like to experience a more direct relationship to the Source—an invitation to Wisdom's party, as we saw in Proverbs. When the time is ripe, the pathway will open. To conclude this meditation, thank all aspects of the self and thank the Source.

The Self of Nature and the Nature of Self (Arabic)

a meditation on the Qur'an, Surah *Ash-Shams*, 91:1-10)

wa ash-shamsi wa zuhaahaa (1)

wa al-qamari 'izaa talaahaa (2)

wa an-nahaari 'izaa jallaahaa (3)

wa al-layli 'izaa yaghshaahaa (4)

wa as-samaa'i wa maa banaahaa (5)

wa al-'arzi wa maa tahaahaa (6)

wa nafsi wa maa sawwaahaa (7)

fa 'alhamahaa fujuurahaa wa taqwaahaa (8)

qad aflaha man zakkaahaa (9)

wa qad khaaba man dassaahaa (10)

A. Yusuf Ali version: By the Sun and his (glorious) splendor (1) By the Moon as she follow him (2) By the Day as it shows up (the Sun's) glory (3); By the Night as it conceals it (4); By the Firmament and its (wonderful) structure (5); By the Earth and its (wide) expanse (6); By the Soul and the proportion and order Given to it (7); And its enlightenment as to its wrong and its right (8); Truly he succeeds that purifies it (9) And he fails that corrupts it (10)!

By the sun—shining, exposing, revealing (1),
By the moon—reflecting, following, shadowing (2),
By the flow of day—expanding, imposing, unveiling (3),
By the ebb of night—covering, concealing, contracting (4),
By the chord of the heavens, birthing and radiating harmony (5),
By the notes of the earth, spreading and extending melody (6),

By the soul-self, being fashioned in harmony and health,
designed to incline toward a purpose,
balancing stability and wildness (7),

able to go off the path as well as stay on,
to break things apart and preserve them,
to dig up and cultivate (8).

Truly, the one who unfolds the seed of self,
revealing the mystery the One has planted there,
continues to prosper more and more in joy,
always purging branches of old fruit (9).
The one who buries the self,
concealing what the One has planted there,
remains rolled up inside,
feeling disappointed at every turn,
the fruit rotting on the tree (10).

Gambling the Self (Persian)

(from "The Secret Rose Garden" by the Sufi poet Mahmud Shabistari, 13th century Persia)

The stakes are high for real prayer.
You must gamble your self
and be willing to lose.
When you have done this,
and your self shakes off
what you believed your self to be,
then no prayer remains,
only a sparkle of the eyes.
Knower and known are one.

If you penetrate the center of time and space,
you can bypass the addictions of the world:
You can become the world yourself.

The Moon and the Sea (Persian)

(From "The Diwan of Shams-i-Tabriz," by the Sufi poet Mevlana Jelaluddin Rumi, 13th century Anatolia)

At dawn, the moon appeared
swooping down from the sky to look at me.
Like a falcon hunting up a meal,
the moon grabbed me, and away we went!
I looked for my self, but my self was gone:
In the moon, by grace, my body became soul.
Luminous, I journeyed on as soul,
but all I saw was that moon—
then the mystery of Self and self dissolved.
Nine heavens mingled in that moon,
as my being disappeared in the sea.

Waves broke. Awareness rose again
and sent out a voice.
It always happens like this.
Sea turns on itself and foams:
With every foaming bit
another body, another being takes form.
And when the sea sends word,
each foaming body
melts immediately back to ocean-breath.

Thanks to my beloved friend,
Shams `l Haqq, Sun of Truth!
Without his strength,
I couldn't see the moon,
I couldn't become the sea.

Meditation—Heart Awareness 6: The Moon

For establishing a better connection between the small self and the Self:

With very profound subtlety, Mevlana Jelaluddin Rumi alludes her to an experience in which the subconscious self (*nafs* in this tradition) becomes totally luminous and glimpses its reality as part of the Soul of the whole universe. The "moon" here symbolizes the experience of a heart-mind or awareness that has become clear of disturbances and can reflect the divine light.

Breathe easily and naturally with awareness in the heart. Calm and clear the mirror of the heart (as in previous "heart awareness" meditations) as much as you can in this moment. Then open your heart to feel a reflection of light, purpose and love from the Only Being—whatever you most need right now. After some moments, direct the mirror downwards toward the soul-selves and let them share this experience. Allow some time for any feelings, sensations, inspirations or images to arise. Allow for a thinning of the boundaries between self and Self that may outshine any of these. This meditation ends with thanks for anything received.

9. The Veil of Separation: Is This a Mirror for Me?

As our interior life becomes richer and more complex, it lives on a knife's edge between creative independence and destructive isolation. The "I" has the choice to remember or to forget its Source. Judgment—of oneself or another—increases with the distance felt between "you" and "I." Here the search for ways to bridge this gap, to remove the veil, begins in earnest.

When life draws you to selections in this chapter, you might consider how the situation or person you find before you mirrors back to you a part of your inner self.

An Experiment in Independence - Day 6, Part 1 (Hebrew)

(a midrashic, or interpretive, translation of Genesis 1:24-26)

wayyo'mer 'elohim totze' ha'aretz nepesh chayya leminah behema waremes wechayto-'eretz leminah wayehi-khen (24):
wayya'as 'elohim 'et-chayyat ha'aretz leminah we'et-habbehema leminah we'et kol-remes ha'adamah leminehu wayyar' 'elohim ki-tob (25)
KJV: And God said, Let the earth bring forth the living creature after his kind, cattle, and creeping thing, and beast of the earth after his kind: and it was so (24). And God made the beast of the earth after his kind, and cattle after their kind, and every thing that creepeth upon the earth after his kind: and God saw that it was good (25).

The Storyteller continues:
Proceeding further toward the call of purpose,
toward the horizon of destiny
that seemed to recede with each step....

The Holy One drew from particle reality (*aretz)*
the basic character of brand new selves
that could exist and thrive as individuals on earth
(not just above it).
As a parallel inner evolution,
these new "souls" could travel and move
in the unseen realm (at least by most of us)
in new ways.
Now there were options for more than
swimming, wiggling, creeping, paddling, floating or winging:
Legs and limbs were invented.
So consciousness could also "walk," step by step.

Two more things happened as a result:
Soul-selves developed more "speed" in relation to "particle" reality:
they could move faster and make more noise
without reconnecting to the shared "wave" reality.
Second, they could now also
gather and pile up more material "stuff,"
again without touching base
with the community of "wave."
Serious consequences unfolded from
this development of consciousness.

Each new way to move and gather
as an "individual"
meant beings could seek to fulfill
their own ends in new ways,
often at the expense of others (24).
Just to be clear:
all the beings we're talking about
came from the assimilated, whole substance of the Holy One
as it had expressed itself through the whole known universe.
That is, it was all divine blood, essence and sap (*adamah*).
No one came from the "outside."
There was no "outside" to the
universal ground of Being.

Once again, the Universe Being
saw it all as ripe—
in tune, in rhythm—a "timely" way
for the purpose of existence
to unfold (25).

9. The Veil of Separation:

wayyo'mer 'elohim na'aseh 'adam betzalmenu kidmutenu weyirdu bidgat hayyam ube'of hashamayim ubabbehema ubekhal-ha'aretz ubekhal-haremes haromes 'al-ha'aretz (26)

KJV: And God said, Let us make man in our image, after our likeness: and let them have dominion over the fish of the sea, and over the fowl of the air, and over the cattle, and over all the earth, and over every creeping thing that creepeth upon the earth (26).

And then it happened:
The Universe Being declared its radiant, burning passion—
its love and desire to know itself more deeply—
in yet another way.
It "spoke," and by speaking also asked the question:
Could all the incredible number of previous experiments
in being and consciousness be experienced by and within
a single individual, a particle-and-wave being?

"By taking into account everything going on,
every tendency, process, destiny and question,
let us draw out the assimilation of all this activity,
as well as the distillation of the essence of Unity,
in a form that will endure, develop and affect our destiny
in an even more powerful way.

"Let this universal assimilation
of the whole ground of Being (*adam*)
take on the veil of the Holy One itself,
the shadow of the totality as projected from the Source,
as it has lived, moved and breathed
through the whole experiment of earthiness so far.

"Let this *adam*, universal collective humanity,
have the complete powers of
differentiation, subjectivity and communion
we have developed so far.

"Let it unfold its course like a wheel covering ground
and have the power to persevere,
for better or worse, in its own destiny,
ruling with, along with and within
the other beings created before it,
the other embodiments of instinctive soul.

"By uniting from within with prior creation,
by identifying with the universe as whole,
let this *adam,* in its own nature, hold the key
to the challenge of being "individual":
It can conceive, imagine and think
as We-I-the Universe does (26)."

Meditation—Heart Awareness 7: The Challenge of Humanity

For balancing outer challenges and inner growth:

At each turning in life, or each opportunity, we have the choice to isolate ourselves or to connect. How do we balance the needs of various voices in our interior reality with our feeling for the purpose of the whole Universe, leading us onward?

9. The Veil of Separation:

Breathing easily and naturally, with awareness in the area of the heart, return to the image of the heart as a sacred mirror. Open your awareness to your sense of guidance, including the support of those whom you feel as teachers or prophetic examples in life. Then breathe into the "back of the mirror" and the door it opens to the depths of the *nephesh* or subconscious self as you have experienced it so far. Finally open your awareness again to the front of the mirror, as it reflects the situations in your outer life. Can you hold a gentle, expansive awareness of all dimensions of existence—sense of guidance, inner self, outer situations? If so, allow yourself to "be breathed," and clear the mirror of impressions that do not lead to the fulfillment of your purpose, inner or outer. Conclude this meditation with thanks for the challenge of being human at this time.

The Old Order: Every Mouth is Crammed With "Love Me!" (Egyptian)

(a version of selections of the "Prophecies of Nefer-Rohu," written down in the Middle Kingdom about 2000 B.C.E. and describing the period at the end of the Old Kingdom, about a 100-200 years earlier.)

(First lines of Adolf Erman translation: "Up, mine heart, that thou mayest bewail the land whence thou art sprung.... Rest not! Behold, it lieth before thy face. Rise up against that which is in thy presence... That which was made is as if it were never made, and Re might begin to found (anew)....)

Try to stay together, my heart,
while you mourn the land
where you first began to beat.
To keep silent is impossible—stifling!
Ra, The Radiant One must build the foundations again.
The land is so devastated that not enough black earth
survives to fit under a fingernail.
The land is so devastated, and no one cares,
no one speaks out, no eyes are even wet.
The sun is covered,
    the rivers are empty,
        the fish ponds are polluted.
Land is fought over, seized and returned,
    seized and returned,
and no one can see or hear the end of it.
Nothing seems important, and everything seems sick.
People make arrows of metal,
    beg to be fed with blood and
    laugh in a sick tone of voice.
Death doesn't cause anyone to weep

or fast or turn toward anything but themselves.
Every mouth is crammed with "Love Me!"
and ripeness has disappeared.
The earth is diminished
but bureaucrats abound.
The earth is bare
but taxes increase.
The less grain we raise,
the more they take from us.
The Radiant One turns away from humanity
and shines only an hour a day.
People can't tell midday,
because they don't see their shadow.
No one's face brightens when they see
the Radiant One, no eyes water with feeling.
Radiance is still there, as before,
but we don't face the right direction.

Thunder Speaks: Mind Embraces All Opposites, Part 4 (Coptic)

(from the Nag Hammadi Library text "Thunder, Perfect Mind")

(First lines of George W. MacRae translation: You honor me [...] and you whisper against [me]. You [who] are vanquished, judge them (who vanquish you) before they give judgment against you, because the judge and partiality exist in you....)

The Judgment

You praise me and plot against me
out of different sides of your mouth.
You cannot win. You are beaten.
Wisdom cries out as judgment.
If you cannot embrace the opposites within you,
you will be judged by your own environment.
Instead, first judge the one who judges within you—
the discriminating power
that calls this worthy and that worthless,
within and among you.
If your inner judge condemns you,
who can set you free?
If your inner judge acquits you,
who can lock you up?
What is inside of you is outside of you.
Your outer appearance is created
by the same one who dresses you inside.
What you judge outside,
what you value, what you call living,
the voices you hear or ignore,
you also judge inside.
You create your inner life in
visible form all around you.

Meditation—Depths of the Self 7: The Inner Judge

For cultivating a healthy sense of judgment and discrimination:

After beginning with a remembrance of the Source, allow your breath and awareness to connect with aspects of the *nephesh* with which you have developed a relationship. Using their support, request the presence of that aspect of the self that feels as though it is judging you and ask for its name. This "inner judge" offers both discrimination and self-criticism, both practical wisdom and cynicism, as well as other two-edged swords that we may feel as both a blessing and a curse. Begin to develop a relationship to this aspect of your soul-self. It will also have its likes and dislikes, its needs and goals. As before, become a good listener and don't react, even if you hear some things you don't like. As support for the healthy growth of this part of yourself, you can breathe with names of Holy Wisdom: *Hokhmah* (Hebrew), *Hakima* (Aramaic) or *al-Hakim* (Arabic, another of the "99 Beautiful Names"). As you bring each session to a close, thank all aspects of self for their cooperation and thank the Source.

Like Vine and Branches (Aramaic)

(a translation of John 15:1-5 from the Peshitta version of the Gospels)

'ena' 'na gpeta' dashrara' wa'by huw palocha'(1)

KJV: I am the true vine, and my Father is the husbandman (1).

I am the vine—rooted, giving, opening to life—
a life leading you in the right direction, at the right time and place.
The Breathing Life of All—Father-Mother of the Cosmos—
is the only source, the germ of all seeds, the Mystery.

kul shbishta' dbiy pi're' lo' yohba' shoqel lah wa'yda' dyahba' pi're' mdake' lah dpi're' sagiye" tayte'(2)

KJV: Every branch in me that beareth not fruit he taketh away: and every branch that beareth fruit, he purgeth it, that it may bring forth more fruit (2).

The vine extends branches—
connected, receiving, passing on life.
A branch connected to me, not sprouting,
not creating life that mirrors the Source,
gets taken up into itself and is embraced by emptiness.
Every branch that bears abundantly
gets purified and pruned so that more fruit appears.

'antuwn men kaduw dkheyn 'ntuwn metul melta' dmallet 'amkhuwn (3)

KJV: Now ye are clean through the word which I have spoken unto you (3).

9. The Veil of Separation:

Through this last talk with you, the whole
ongoing teaching and example I have given,
you have been purified and pruned of all
that stands in the way of bearing fruit,
the holdings and restrictions of your self
that stop the flow of Creation's life.

qawaw biy we'na' bkhuwn 'aykana' dashbishta' la' meshkcha' dtetel pi're' men nap-shah 'ela' mqawya' bagpeta' hakhana' 'ap la' 'antuwn 'ela' tqawuwn biy (4)
KJV: Abide in me, and I in you. As the branch cannot bear fruit of itself, except it abide in the vine; no more can ye, except ye abide in me (4).

Abide in me: Don't think about yourself.
Feel yourself as living earth in the hands of the Creator
who does with it as S/he wishes.
That means: rest in me—be the breath of the Breather.
I also rest in you, rooted in the Holy One.
A branch doesn't fruit separated from its Source.
So also you don't heal, teach, create or do anything
from your own individual sense of self,
your isolated "I,"
without being connected to me.

'ena' 'na' gpeta' wa'ntuwn shbishte' man damqawe' biy we'na' beh hana' mayte' pi're' sagiye" metul dadla' 'ena' la' meshkchiyn 'ntuwn lme'bad medem (5)
KJV: I am the vine, ye are the branches: He that abideth in me, and I in him, the same bringeth forth much fruit: for without me ye can do nothing (5).

I am the vine—rooted, giving, opening to life,
  the out-flow of sacred creation.
You are the branches—connected, receiving, absorbing life,
  the natural receivers and channels for that flow.

The depth of selfhood—connecting I to the Only I—gives life,
the depth of relationship—connecting "I" to "you"—passes it on.
Realizing "I Am" is the vine of interiority;
Realizing "You Are" creates the branches of communion.
The ego hollowed by its own sense of mortality flows with breath;
Sympathy with another receives that flow in harmony.

It is all connected:
You in me, I in you—
bearing fruit, acting, teaching, loving,
doing the "greater Works"—
We all travel together.
With no connection,
you simply do not find anything
to do that exudes the wonder of
the Universe Being,
the Breathing Life of All.

Communion's Gift (Aramaic)

(An expanded version of Matthew 26:27-28 from the Peshitta version of the Gospels)

washqal kasa' wa'wdiy wyahb lhuwn we'mar sabw 'eshtaw meneh kulkhuwn (27). hanaw demy ddiyatiqi' chadta' dachlap sagiye mete'shed lshuwbqana' dachtahe' (28).
KJV: And he took the cup, and gave thanks, and gave it to them, saying, Drink ye all of it (27); for this is my blood of the new testament, which is shed for many for the remission of sins (28).

Then he took up the cup,
symbol of the physical shelter,
the accommodation of the body.
He praised the One, making outward
profession of his inner desire,
he embraced and absorbed himself into
the substance of the cup,
then gave it to them, saying:

Everyone, take and drink,
Surround and enjoy,
Convert and consume,
Envelop and undergo
the depths of Sacred Foundation (27):

This is my wine (*dami*)—
the juice of the Universe that satisfies
all thirsts for communion.
This is my blood, sap of the *adamah*,
the assimilated essence of the cosmos—

part of your name at Beginning—
the bond between all souls and bodies,
all you's and I's.

This renewable prescription fills every need.
It flows out from its Source
in ever greater amounts.
It unties all the knots and
embraces all mistakes with emptiness.

Just like blood
this universal effusion,
in whose likeness we appear,
releases us from the past,
heartbeat by heartbeat (28).

Meditation—Simple Presence 5: Presence and Forgiveness

For releasing past experiences and impressions:

Sit comfortably, eyes closed, and feel again the rise and fall of the breath in or near the heart. With each breath, reach out to whatever feelings or sensations arise and feel the breath illuminating each with awareness. Place one hand lightly on your heart and allow the sensation of your heartbeat to come into it. Allow the touch of your hand to neither press down nor hold itself away, neither reach nor withdraw, but simply be present. Allow this sense of simple contact to lead you to deeper layers of sensing the blood's pulsation, releasing the body, heartbeat by heartbeat, from the past impressions of any kind. What comes to the mirror of the heart to be released now, at the ripe time? This process of releasing and renewal flows continually through the whole universe, according to Yeshua. We should not be surprised that we are also part of this, given that according to the larger story, individual human consciousness is a big experiment by the Holy One. Mistakes, clingings and impressions we need to release are part of the journey.

From the Depths of Divine Shadow (Arabic)

(a meditation on the Qur'an, Surah *al-Anbiya*, 21:87)

wa- Zan-Nuuni 'iz-zahaba mughaadzib(an) fa-zanna 'allan-naqdira alayhi fanaadaa fiz- zulumaati 'al "Laa 'ilaaha 'illaa 'anta subhaanaka 'innii kuntu minaz-zaalimiin"
A. Yusuf Ali version: And remember Zun-nun when he departed in wrath: he imagined that We had no power over him! But he cried through the depths of darkness "There is no god but Thou: Glory to Thee: I was indeed wrong!"

[Just like the other prophets,
through whom we offered compassion,
remember Jonah]
the man of the big fish when
he abandoned his mission, holding a fixed belief
in a state of confusion and biting anger.
He assumed for his own convenience
that We could not focus our power
on his little point in space and time
and return him to Unity.
But he only imagined this.
He was divided within himself,
in exile from the Source, and cried
from the depths of divine shadow—
all humanity's forgetful attempts
to fulfill the divine image:
"There is no Being but You,
the One who is the untouched,
original purity in all things (even me!)
Indeed, I became too separated,
too material-minded, acting
from a confused image of myself,
a crooked shadow of the One Being."

Meditation: Sound and Embodiment 9: Soul at the Beginning

For touching a place of clarity and wonder within:

As in the other meditations, begin by breathing a gentle breath in the heart. Then gradually add into the mirror of the heart the inner sound of the words *Subhan Allah* ("SOOB-HAHN AHL-LAH," based on the word *subhaanaka* in the passage above). This sound can help you contact the place inside your self that is just as it was at the beginning, untouched or unpolluted by any impressions of your life. Even deeper, this place in you remembers before your birth, before any human beings were born.

According to the Sufis, this state of pure, unpolluted wonder is the way we were when all humanity was in the heart of the Beloved at the beginning. We have always carried within us this inner knowing. We need only to breathe with it in order to reawaken it. As your breath deepens, allow yourself to begin to gently intone the sounds of the words on one tone, with your hand gently over your heart in order to feel the vibration there. Allow the vibration and feeling to deepen, then after some time return to simply breathing with the phrase. Rest in this place of wonder and purity, feeling yourself older than the stars and galaxies, before any "I" and "you" appeared.

"I and You" (Persian)

(from "The Secret Rose Garden" by the Sufi poet Mahmud Shabistari, 13th century Persia)

"I" and "you" focus light
like decorative holes cut
in a lamp shade.
But there is only One Light.

"I" and "you" throws a
thin veil between
heaven and earth.
Lift the veil and all
creeds and theologies disappear.

When "I" and "you" vanish,
how can I tell whether I am
in a mosque, a synagogue,
a church or an observatory?

Section Three: Voices of Communion: How Do I Connect?

In a universe of individuals, how do we relate to "others"? What is desire? What is love? When we leave our individual forms, what remains or continues? Ancient Middle Eastern voices also raised these questions and reflected on communion as a sacred principle of the cosmos. Every wave and particle in the universe seems to be connected to every other. Every person and action is related to every other. The tendency of atoms to bond, of animals to herd and of human beings to form communities reflects this principle. On a personal level, these storytellers and wisdom voices prompt us to be aware of our relationships with each other, with nature and with the source and end of Being. On the deepest spiritual level, these voices ask us to consider how we love as well as how we die.

10. Desire and Love: Whom Do I Love?

Increased outer diversity as well as increasingly complex inner lives led the cosmic evolution to some very fundamental differences—like those between male and female. These differences are balanced by the desire of living beings to return to more intimately bonded relationships. Compulsive desire can override other, more objective voices in one's nature. But desire can also develop into love, a more mysterious force that grows slowly from the inside, rather than through the more immediate—and often blinding—force of attraction. According to Middle Eastern storytellers, following desire and love to their source, without holding on to their object, can lead us to communion with the Being behind the universe.

When life draws you to selections in this chapter, you might consider how the situation or person attracting (or repelling) you, is asking you to open to a new part of your inner self. What doors would real love open for you now?

Two Habits of Being Human - Day 6, Part 2 (Hebrew)

(a midrashic, or interpretive, translation of Genesis 1:27-28)

wayyivra' 'elohim 'et-ha'adam betzalmo betzelem 'elohim bara' 'oto zakhar uneqeba bara' 'otam (27)

KJV: So God created man in his own image, in the image of God created he him; male and female created he them.

The Storyteller continues:
Later in that sixth illuminating period
(the "day," you understand),
The Holy One drew from its
own essence of total Presence
(and is still drawing it forth)
a new experiment in consciousness:
Individuated Collective Unity,
sometimes called the "human."
Humans could distill the juice of the
wine of the cosmos, but still
go off on their own tangent
if they forgot their origin and source.

Even within a human unity,
diversity also expressed itself.
Two basic tones or modes
of experiencing human consciousness
presented themselves in
various ways in different "bodies."

One was innocent, obvious and apparent,
growing and rising,
engraving what has been established and
embodying the memory of the origin of things.

The other was innocent, subtle and deep,
hollowed and cavernous,
nurturing the new and
embodying knowledge of space
and the primeval void.

These two ways of knowing and experiencing
evoked the first stirrings of
male and female consciousness
as found in various ways
within each human being.
One music, two modes—
First Human destined to deal
with the harmonics,
in ever-evolving changes.

wayebarekh 'otam 'elohim wayyo'mer lahem 'elohim peru urebu umil'u 'et-ha'aretz wekhibshuha uredu bidgat hayyam ube'of hashamayim ubekhal-chayya haromeset 'al-ha'aretz (28)
KJV: And God blessed them, and God said unto them, Be fruitful, and multiply, and replenish the earth, and subdue it: and have dominion over the fish of the sea, and over the fowl of the air, and over every living thing that moveth upon the earth.

Again the Holy One breathed
with magnetism,
radiating with sound
toward the First Human.
Universe Being "blessed"
this living experiment
with a wordless job description
that, in translation, might
sound like this:

"Bear more fruit!
Become more frequent and diverse!
Fill the particles of
of inner and outer life
as you spread over and through
earth and earthiness.
Help creation to
redeem its purpose (*khibshuha*)
and rule together with,
within, alongside of (*b'*)
the older inner and outer ways
of swimming, flying and creeping,
whether through wave or particle.
This "human" way, able to
reflect on all that has gone before—
self-reflective and reflexive—
can overrule what has gone before,
but needs to learn to rule *together*."

(Yes, listeners,
the "human project,"
being a very centralized fire
of the entire cosmos,
could override and overrule
its older interior structures—
subconscious, instinctual self,
reptilian intelligence and all the other
previous, precious developments
that it received as a heritage.
And yet the blessing clearly given tells us
that we need to learn how to
redeem and fulfill

our own and nature's purpose,
how to manage creation alongside
and within the other beings present in
the sacred story being told
by the Holy One right now
from the first Beginning.)

Meditation—Depths of the Self 8: Partnership

For help harmonizing the male and female sides within:

After beginning with a remembrance of the Source, continue breathing in the heart. Ask within whether it is the right time to make a connection between the original species-level impressions of "female" and "male" within you, ones that come before our cultural conditioning. Then begin with whichever one draws you most. The intention is to harmonize the memory of both within, for a greater unity.

For the "male": Allow your breathing awareness from the heart to contact the side of your body that you associate with maleness. Feel a breath from the beginning of time, a creative breath of humanness that rises, extends itself and engraves something. Breathe and feel.

For the "female": Allow your awareness to shift to the other side of your body. Feel a creative breath from the Beginning that forms a matrix or net of spaciousness, drawing out of the pregnant void what is new.

After a few minutes, breathe in both sides of the body and feel the partnership of the two modes of being. This partnership may not occur immediately. One side of being or the other may feel that it has, in the past, been ignored or slighted. Begin to build some bridges of understanding, as you did in previous "Depths of the Self" meditations.

At the end of the meditation, include the awareness of the other aspects of your subconscious self—inheritances from older species. Consider that the energy of our human interactions may become so dominant that these other needs and voices may fade into the background. Resolve to keep nature's other voices alive inside you. As with the others, this meditation ends with thanks for each voice heard and thanks for the Source behind the universe.

Birds, Crocodiles, Ecstasy, Longing (Egyptian)

(Egyptian love songs from approximately 1300-1100 B.C.E.)

(First lines of Adolf Erman translation: The beautiful songs of thy sister, whom thine heart loveth, who cometh from the meadow. My beloved brother, my heart aspireth to thy love.... I say to thee: "See what I do. I have come and catch with my trap in mine hand...")

The sister, who is the beloved of all hearts,
begins these songs as she returns from the forest:
"O my beloved, my brother,
My heart runs after your love,
You have brought everything to life!
Come along and see what I am doing!
I have just returned from setting a trap:
The bait and snare are in my own hand.
Birds of outrageous beauty and plumage
are traveling from perfumed lands far away,
anointed with myrrh and scents.
One has come and taken my worm,
its fragrance from Arabia, its talons full of raw amber:
Come, let us release him together.
When I am alone with you,
I want you to hear the cry of
that poor bird anointed with spices.
How much better it will be if
you are with me when I prepare the trap.
There's nothing better than going to the fields
with the beloved!"

The brother says:
"My sister's love waits for me

on the other side of a stream.
A crocodile waits in the shallows.
But when I go down into the water,
when I wade through the current,
my heartbeat will master
the rhythm of the tide,
my feet will turn the waves to land.
My love for her steadies me—
it's my water-magic!
As I see my sister coming toward me,
my heart dances
and my arms open to embrace her.
My sister comes to me!"

The sister says:
"The swallow is trying to distract me:
'It's dawn, aren't you coming to the forest?'
Bird—you will not disturb me today!
I have found my brother in his bed.
My heart is light today, for he told me:
'I will not go far—my hand is in yours—
and we will stroll together
through every beautiful place.'
He honors me,
he does not hurt my heart."

The brother says:
"I have not seen her for seven days
and now I am sick.
My body is heavy, I pass out easily.
If the chief doctor visits,
my heart isn't satisfied.

If the priests chant for me,
it's useless, their diagnosis is flawed.
Just tell me, 'Here she is!' and I'll revive—
her name picks me right up.
Letters from her restore my heart.
My sister is a better tonic than any prescription.
She means more to me than all the holy books.
If I see her, I start to recover.
If she throws me a glance, I get younger.
If she speaks to me, my strength returns.
When we embrace, all evil flees.
But I have not seen her for seven days!"

A Song About Love and Desire - Part 1 (Hebrew)

(an expanded translation of the Song of Songs 8:4-5 from the Hebrew)

hishba'ti 'etkhem benot yerushalaim ma-ta'iru uma-te'oreru 'et-ha'ahaba 'ad shet-techpatz (4)

KJV: I charge you, O daughters of Jerusalem, that ye stir not up, nor awake my love until he please (4).

Swear to me, daughters of Jerusalem!
Future sisters who revere peace,
let me captivate you with this insight:
The love that expands and spreads out
gradually, mysteriously, from a secret place,
that seeks to give rather than possess,
should not be excited all at once, without awareness.
Don't ignite it without light,
arouse it without clear sight or
strip it naked, firing it on to
a complete loss of intelligence.
Lay the depths of its foundation
securely: it then finds pleasure in
bowing to the wishes of the beloved.

mi zo't 'ola min-hammidbar mitrappeqet 'al-dodah tachat hattappuach 'orartikha shamma chibbelatkha 'immekha shamma chibbela yeladatkha: (5)

KJV: Who is this that cometh up from the wilderness, leaning upon her beloved? I raised thee up under the apple tree: there thy mother brought thee forth: there she brought thee forth that bare thee (5).

Who is this, rising like a primal plant,
growing with primordial energy

mounting the open spaces
and grasslands that spread freely?
Who is this restoring herself
upon her beloved—
leaning, resting, moving in a
regenerating wave?
Who is this mending
the vessel of love she has chosen,
healing the flower of her desire
like a medicine,
like a redemption of the moment?

I first aroused you below the apple tree,
I blinded you down in the chamber of dark fruit—
the depth of your living, individual breath.
Inside there I astonished and desolated you—
within the light of that dark, fecund place.
Inside there, you were linked to the ancestress.
Inside there, you were brought forth in struggle
by all the women who have carried on life.

Meditation—Heart Awareness 8: Fire and Light

When making love with your partner:

Breathe and allow the sense of simple contact mentioned in the last chapter ("Presence and Forgiveness") to sensitize your connection to your partner. Let go of the past. Allow your awareness of the heart, the depths of love, to keep the light in the fire, the vision of a deeper love in the passion. Allow the feeling of heart to spread throughout the whole body. When the foundations are laid, and there is strength at the bottom, love bends to the wishes of the beloved. Then the blinding fire of desire will find its own right moment. You will be linked to the ancient, sacred healing power of love and passion, mentioned in the Song. These moments should not be assumed as a right, but valued as an astonishing grace. They can be prepared for, but not expected.

A Prayer for Seed, Bread and Water (Sumerian)

(a version of a Sumerian hymn of Inanna and Damuzi, 3rd millennium B.C.E.)

(First lines of S.N. Kramer translation: Oh, wild bull, 'eye' of the land, I would fulfill all its needs, Would make its lord carry out justice in the princely house....)

Inanna says:
Wild bull—pulsing, single-eye of the whole land!
I want to fulfill all your needs:
I want to force your master to wage justice
    in the royal place inside.
Leave no voice unheard,
leave nothing undone!
I want to make your seed grow
    to fullness in my mansion.

Damuzi says:
Inanna, your breast is an open field,
your wide open spaces gush with greenery
like a freely spreading meadow flowing with grain.
Your deep waters pour down on me
like bread from the source.
Water flowing and flowing,
bread and understanding from on high.
Release the flood for its desired goal,
I will drink it all from you.

Meditation—Sound and Embodiment 10: Call and Response

For helping to free a heartfelt voice:

Some of the oldest chants of humanity involve call and response between two attracting yet different energies. As each "pole" of the battery, so to speak, feels more and more clearly the differences in the other's voice, tone and atmosphere, the "corrosion" on the senses falls away and the current flows even more strongly between the two. This process can take place within a person, in the *nephesh* or subconscious soul-self, as well as between people. Such old responsive chants can lead us beyond stereotypes of male and female since they work underneath our mental conceptions. They can also open a doorway of feeling to earlier, simpler human responsiveness, when sexuality and eroticism were not commercialized and exploited as a way to sell, manipulate and control.

Try chanting the names *Inanna* ("IN-AN-NAH") and *Damuzi* ("DAH-MU-ZEE") on one note, placing one hand lightly near your heart to allow the sound to be felt there. Feel the sound as a call and response between the female and male aspects of yourself. Begin softly and slowly, feeling each open sound, directing it inside. After some practice, your voice may begin to clear and open. Follow the feeling of resonance that you find in the heart, and allow this to bring more "heart" into your voice. It can then become a touchstone for you to notice, in your own voice, when your heart is "in" something or not. This is another part of recovering our real human heritage. As before, for any changes noticed or insights received, offer some thanks and gratitude toward the Source.

As the Cosmos Opens and Closes (Aramaic)

(an expanded translation of Matthew 7:7 from the Peshitta version of the Gospels)

sha'lu wnetiyheb lkhuwn (A) b'aw wteshkchuwn (B) quwshw wnetptach lkhuwn (C)
KJV: Ask, and it shall be given you; seek and ye shall find; knock, and it shall be opened unto you.

Ask intensely—
    like a straight line engraved toward
    the object you want;
pray with desire—
    as though you interrogated your own soul about
    its deepest, most hidden longings;
and you will
receive expansively—
    not only what your desire asked,
    but where the elemental breath led you—
    love's doorstep, the place where you
bear fruit
    and become part of the universe's
    power of generation and sympathy (A).

Search anxiously—
    from the interior of your desire
    to its outer embodiment—
    let the inner gnawing and boiling lead you to
act passionately—
    no matter how material or gross
    your goal seems at first;
and you will
find fulfillment

of the body's drive to accomplish its purpose
and see its destiny.
Like a spring unbound, you will
gain the force
of profound stillness after an effort—
the earth's power to grow new each season (B).

Knock innocently—
as if you were driving a tent stake or
striking one clear note, never heard before.
Create enough space within
to receive the force you release;
hollow yourself—
purified of hidden hopes and fears,
and it shall be
opened easily—
a natural response to space created,
part of the contraction and expansion
of the universe;
and penetrated smoothly—
as the cosmos opens and closes
around your words of satisfied desire (C).

Meditation—Simple Presence 6: Love's Doorstep

For actively pursuing a goal with heart:

Find a place, perhaps in nature, where you can walk freely and not be disturbed. Breathing in the heart, with eyes open, begin to walk and feel as though the impulse to move were coming from the heart. You can again use Yeshua's word of power *Ina-na*, connecting one to One in simple presence, as rhythmic support while you walk. Then bring the image or feeling of your goal into the heart. Feel the desire, passionately engaged, yet leave space inside for the response of the Universe. Allow what is real and from the heart to separate from what is compulsive and habitual. Follow the real.

Her Eyebrows Have Kidnapped My Heart (Persian)

(from the "Odes" of the Sufi poet Sa'adi of Shiraz, 13th century Persia)

The first breath of spring!
But do I smell a garden or
the aroma of two friends meeting?
Like calligraphy, which transports
our eyes from thought to beauty,
her eyebrows have kidnapped my heart.
Bird! My heart snared you once.
Why not return to nest voluntarily?

Nightly, the candle and I both melt,
but my fire burns within.
All my focus is on road noises,
my eye lingers on the doorstep.
When the call to prayer resounds,
I hear only the caravan's bell.
Even if you hate me, return—
that would be some kind of relationship!

Love has strong-armed my patience—
my writing hand trembles!
When lovers separate,
soul and body do, too.
Sa'adi, moaning, is your security
for this proposed contract of love:
Fire consumes my reed pen,
the ink you see here is smoke.

Cups and Wine (Persian)

(from the "Diwan" of the Sufi poet Hafiz of Shiraz, 14th century Persia)

You there, carrying that cup!
Fill it with the joy of youth—
bring me another cup of the wine of ecstasy.
Bring me medicine for the disease of love—
bring pure, passionate intoxication,
the remedy of young and old.
Musician! Don't whine to me about the wheel of time—
how it turned this way and not that for you.
Quiet! Just touch the strings in peace.
Too much wisdom is boring:
Let's bring the noose of wine for its neck.
When the rose starts to fade, say "Let it go!"
and drink the present moment, as the rose does.
If the dove's coo has vanished, who cares—
we can make the same "hoo" with the wine jug!
The sun is the wine, the moon is the cup:
Pour the sun into the moon if you want to be filled.
Drinking such wine can be good or bad—
drink anyway!
If you can't see the beloved's face except in dreams,
then what's wrong with a little sleep?
More cups of wine! Keep them coming for Hafiz:
Whether it's sin or salvation—keep pouring!

11. Love and Death: What Must be Sacrificed?

The desire of the Universe to pursue communion leads to various types of sacrifice—willing and unwilling—including the acts of eating and being eaten. Ultimately, love and death prove to be forces than are more interwoven than our culture wishes to acknowledge. The denial of death splits the modern psyche. We tend to act as though we will live forever, and that the earth's resources are also endless. Yet part of us knows that this isn't true. Returning to a sense of "simple presence" heals the split and provides a refuge of creative peace, according to the wisdom voices here. In addition, deep bonding with another invokes the death of who we thought we were and the birth of something new.

When life draws you to selections in this chapter, you might consider how love is asking you to sacrifice a known part of your inner being in order to uncover more of the unknown treasure within. Is there a more real sense of yourself waiting to be resurrected if, as the Sufis say, you "die before you die"?

Eating and Being Eaten - Day 6, Part 3 (Hebrew)

(a midrashic, or interpretive, translation of Genesis 1:29-31)

wayyo'mer 'elohim hinne natatti lakhem 'et-kol-'eseb zorea' zera' 'asher 'al-penei khol-ha'aretz we'et-kol-ha'etz 'asher-bo feri-'etz zorea' zara' lakhem yihyeh le'okhlah (29) ulekhal-chayyat ha'aretz ulekhal-'of hashamayim ulekhol romes 'al-ha'aretz 'asher-bo nefesh chayya 'et-kol-yereq 'eseb le'okhla wayehi-khen (30):
wayyar' 'elohim 'et-kol-'asher 'asa wehinne-tob me'od wayehi-'ereb wayehi-voqer yom hashishi (31)
KJV: And God said, Behold, I have given you every herb bearing seed, which is upon the face of all the earth, and every tree, in the which is the fruit of a tree yielding seed; to you it shall be for meat (29). And to every beast of the earth, and to every fowl of the air, and to every thing that creepeth upon the earth, wherein there is life, I have given every green herb for meat, and it was so (30). And God saw every thing that he had made, and, behold, it was very good. And the evening and the morning were the sixth day (31).

The Storyteller continues:
As a completion to the
sixth illuminating period,
the Holy One next instituted
eating and being eaten.
Perhaps up to this point,
inner beings and outer creatures
had not mingled their essence in
such an intimate way as this.
Or perhaps sustenance came
through wind and wave and contact
rather than through consuming one another.

Introducing "bread" (*lakhem*),
which could be outer food or

inner understanding,
meant that now one being could
assimilate another's interior wisdom.
It could, as it were, receive bundles of
energy and understanding,
the living "freshness" of another,
so that the desire for a deeper communion
with the whole universe (and the Holy One)
would also evolve.

As a menu for the "human," the Holy One offered
a complete, yet radical diet:
First, the essence of "personality," that is,
all new fragile desires
producing strange, lavish experiments in diversity.
This part of the menu was like the ever-changing
"melody" produced by the music
of those beings created earlier.
Second, the essence of "character," that is,
a more sturdy and predictable ability
to sense, organize and remember.
This "food" offered, through memory,
more bonded offspring, children or "fruit."
This part of the menu was like the
"rhythm" produced by the music
of those beings created earlier.
While more "regular," the food of character
also contained the fire of life and
could, through spontaneity, unfold
new seeds of diversity to pass on to
the next generation. (29)

To the other soul-selves created
before the human (at least those
associated with earth and "particle")
the Holy One
offered a reduced menu:
new desires, "personality,"
and those spontaneous, improvised
riffs on life's *leit motif*
sometimes called "mutations."
Somehow, they could not "eat,"
or assimilate to their benefit,
the character of another being. (30)

Maybe not "fair," maybe not balanced,
yet the Universe Being saw that
to follow a new course, learning as it grew,
the creation could not be completely "ripe,"
all the time, in all places.
A fire had been lit,
smoke was rising.
Choices made in freedom
must run their course.
So this development in creation was as
close to Unity as relative unity could get,
ripe for the moment,
good "enough."

Once over and back again,
this sixth round of opening and closing
marked the sixth large manifestation
of luminous, intelligent happenings
in our vicinity since the Great Beginning:

The melody of Humanity
joined the music of Life. (31)

Meditation—Gratitude and Celebration 8: Conscious Eating

For developing a more fulfilling relationship to eating:

When we eat, we bond with the interiority, diversity and communion of other beings. The personality of the universe, lavish in diversity, presents itself to us as the subtle differences in each herb, vegetable or grain. Wildness and freshness, not uniformity, are nature's gifts. Fruit results from a longer, more bonded relationship. So, of course does any food from animals, birds or fish. All willingly or unwillingly give their life to us in a very literal sense.

For one meal, consider the gifts of diversity, interiority and communion that you receive by eating. Sense or imagine the personality and character of each being that feeds you and how this adds to your own sense of being totally human—that is, aware of the consciousness of the entire universe. This may take a little preparation. For one thing, you may need to discover what you actually *are* eating. For another, you may have to slow down to actually sense the beings that are feeding you. This may initiate more changes in your normal pattern. Eating simpler and less for a period of retreat can reawaken this sensitivity.

The only other question to consider is the one raised by Jesus earlier: For which future beings will our bodies be bread?

Create Again the Rising Waters (Babylonian)

(a liturgy of a lament of Inanna for her lost lover, Damuzi, approximately 1800-1200 B.C.E.)

(First lines of Stephen Langdon translation: The heavenly queen who brings the verdure in abundance, Innina [sic] who brings the verdure in abundance. The sprouting things abundance where....)

Inanna, who is always bringing us
green life in plenty, asks her consort,
who has departed to the underworld
and sleeps in the buried grain:
"Where did it go—all the abundance,
all the springing fruit of nature?
Brother, who has taken it?
Where has it gone?"

Damuzi replies:
"My queen, this springing plant,
vigorous and rising like a bull,
I will restore for you,
I will raise it for you.
All that was taken away
will return again."

Inanna still wants to know:
"But whom shall I embrace?
It is you, husband, that I *must* embrace!
With whom shall I join?
With the one who has risen
from the great flood,
from the whirlpool after death!

I want to join with you!
With the one who created life
in my holy chamber.
I want to embrace you!
Return, my plentiful one,
return and create again
the rising waters,
create again the rising waters.

A Song About Love - Part 2 (Hebrew)

(an expanded translation of Song of Songs 8:6-7 from the Hebrew)

shimeni khachotam 'al-libbekha kachotam 'al-zero'ekha (6A)

ki-'azza khammawet 'ahaba (B)

qasha khish'ol qin'a (C)

reshafeha rishpei 'esh shalhebetyah (D)

KJV: Set me as a seal upon thine heart, as a seal upon thine arm (6A): for love is strong as death (B); jealousy is cruel as the grave (C): the coals thereof are coals of fire, which hath a most vehement flame (D).

Engrave my essence
like a seal on your heart.
Let my memory resound
through the core of your being.
Let me shine and rise
through the center of your passion,
through the fringes of your action,
through every part of you that
becomes a traveler and leaves home.
Engrave me like a monogram
that alerts everyone:
"This is the sign of integrity:
The strength of the cosmos
hides underneath." (A)

For this love that expands us
boldly faces death's contraction.
This mysterious self-effacing power—
a double-strong, fully physical force—
is as audacious and potent as
anything with juice and sap,

as fierce and violent as
the withering, the decay
that returns us all to sameness
with the universal Self (B).

This blinding passion,
this jealous, envious desire that
possesses and redeems us,
this tense, compressed ardor
is as confusing and mixed up
as the world after physical death.
It binds us as closely as
the whirlpool of sensation and calm,
the abyss of delirium and peace,
the netherworld of questions and answers
that we find on the other side (C).

It sparks like lightning.
It spreads like the plague.
It burns like the fire
inside the fire inside the fire.
It radiates like the inside
of the first moment of the cosmos (D).

mayim rabbim lo' yukhelu lekhabbot 'et-ha'ahaba uneharot lo' yishtefuha (7A)
'im-yitten 'aish 'et-kol-hon beto ba'ahaba boz yabuzu lo (B)
KJV: Many waters cannot quench love, neither can the floods drown it (7A): if a man would give all the substance of his house for love, it would utterly be condemned (B).

Not the many waters of the Great Dark,
the collected possibilities of chaos...
Not the rivers of Directed Light,

the vibrating stream of purpose…
Neither can contain or put out,
neither can overwhelm or drown
the secret power of expansive love.
Not the great passive flow,
womb of all chance...
Not the great active flow,
storyline of the Universe...
Neither can understand or control
a love that wants to share life
more than it wants to possess it (A).

If the individual mind tried to rent this love,
if it offered in trade all its ideas and compulsions,
even if it extended its whole being to join it,
it would still be completely humiliated.
The self-centered mind cannot rise so far:
a love that grows from the inside
would still look down on it (B).

Meditation—Heart Awareness 9: Love and Death

For clarifying your love for another:

Return to the sensation of breathing, feeling the heart as a mirror. Allow it to be as clear as possible for the present moment. Then consciously bring into the mirror two reflections and impressions: first, your love for another and after that, the death of your individual body consciousness. Allow the feeling, sensation and energy raised by considering your own death to act upon the love you experience and meet it directly. Allow it to whirl and to clarify everything that is not the deepest love, *ahaba*. What happens to possessive desire, compulsion and envy? Some of these travelers with love may vanish, and some may not, but they will likely be more conscious after this practice than before. And that strengthens the love.

Thunder Speaks - Mind Embraces All Opposites, Part 5 (Coptic)

(from the Nag Hammadi Library text "Thunder, Perfect Mind")

(First lines of George W. MacRae translation: Hear me, you hearers, and learn of my words, you who know me. I am the hearing that is attainable to everything....)

The "I Am" Alone Exists

Listen, then, those who can hear.
Also you angels and those who
appear in visions or deliver messages,
you disembodied spirits still around.
The "I Am" of all these sayings alone exists.
I have no one who judges me:
I embrace all opposites.
You may fool yourselves with
contrary thoughts,
imaginations,
traditions,
theologies,
commentaries
and legal precedents
by which you break contact with me.
It may be forgetfulness,
a passion to acquire or
a temporary intoxication,
to all of which human beings
become addicted
until they sober up, lie down and die.

But you will find me there, too.
The way you have treated me is
the way you have treated your own soul.
And this time you will not die.
You will live with me until you learn.

Meditation—Depths of the Self 9: Facing the "I Am"

For clarifying what is really important in life right now:

In this last section of "Thunder," the voice of Sacred Sense and Wisdom leads us to contemplate the passing of our personal consciousness, that which holds our many selves together, including the aspects of our *nephesh* still learning and growing. This event separates the two sides of the mirror, so to speak, but both sides will have changed through their experiences together. This practice takes its theme from the old Sufi expression, attributed to Imam Ali or Prophet Muhammad, "die before you die" (*mutu qabla anta mutu*). This may have been based on an earlier, Aramaic Christian practice in which one felt oneself as Jesus in the grave, then being resurrected.

After beginning with a remembrance of the Source, allow your breath and awareness to touch with love and respect all the aspects of your subconscious soul-self that you have experienced so far through these meditations. As you breathe in communion with each, bring in the awareness of the passing of your physical body. How does this help clarify for each voice what is really important? What is essential for it to fulfill its purpose as part of your consciousness at this time? What will remain after individuality separates? Don't force anything. This process must be undertaken in the context of deep and abiding love for all aspects of yourself and for their courage. End this meditation with a breath of thanks for all aspects of self and for the Source.

Resurrection (Aramaic)

(a translation of John 11:25 from the Peshitta version of the Gospels)

'amar lah yeshuw' 'ena' 'na' nuwchama' wchaye' man damhaymen biy 'apen nmuwt niche'

KJV: Jesus said unto her, I am the resurrection, and the life: he that believeth in me, though he were dead, yet shall he live:

Yeshua said to her:
Connecting I to the Only I, Simple Presence,
is the only repose and refuge
after a journey of agitation.
The self conscious of its Self can then
change house, move to a new revivified life,
when the old habits and habitation fade away.
This "resurrection" is the point of pause,
the still point in the pendulum's swing,
energized by the Holy One's creative peace.
Whoever has the same faith that I do,
who trusts and believes as I do,
even if they have passed through the doorway
between this life and the next,
between this world and another,
between this small self and a new one,
they shall find both energized rest
and a renewed sense of purpose
to carry them further on the way.

Meditation—Simple Presence 7: The Presence of Impending Absence

For being in the presence of dying:

To breathe consciously in the heart in the presence of a dying person may be one of the most profound prayers or spiritual practices. When there is nothing more that can be done for a person except to be with her or him, then simple presence can become the gift of each to the other. The unfulfilled aspects of the self unravel, which clarifies, purifies and enlightens the "I" of the person. The idea of death seems to die, leaving only a life that continues. This opportunity may be sought out, but if not, it comes sooner or later to us all.

In the presence of death itself, or remembering the passage of a loved one, return to a place of simple presence, breathing with each feeling and sensation that arises and following each to its Source. Allow yourself to meet the other in the resting place of existence, the deep peace after the agitation of selves and desires has subsided. Meet in the center of Life.

The Gift of the Rose (Persian)

(from the "Diwan" of the Sufi poet Hafiz of Shiraz, 14th century Persia)

The breeze at dawn shines with a gentle breath of musk;
the old world has become young again!
The tulip opens its cup to the jasmine;
the narcissus flirts with the anemone.
Mourning spreads to the palace of the rose
as the nightingale says its painful farewells.
Yes, I left the mosque for the tavern yesterday,
but don't blame me too much.
The weekly sermon went on and on—
valuable time was slipping away!
My heart, if you delay collecting today's pleasure
until tomorrow, who will guarantee that
your life's account will still show a balance?
The month of daylight fasting gets closer—
don't let the wine cup leave your hand:
This sun disappears until Ramadan is ended.
Smell the rose's gift as it passes! Its presence is priceless.
It enters the garden one way and leaves by another.
Musician! We're all friends here—get on with your song!
Enough of the chorus "As it was, so shall it ever be."
Hafiz entered the garden of life for you—enjoy him now and
say good-bye, for he will soon be leaving!

Love After Death (Persian)

(From "The Diwan of Shams-i-Tabriz," by the Sufi poet Mevlana Jelaluddin Rumi, 13th century Anatolia)

This is Love: to fly without limits;
to cut through all the veils—now!
The first instant—to reject the life you knew.
The last step—to give up feet entirely.
To see right through appearances,
To refuse to see addiction as inevitable.
"My heart," I said, "be grateful that
you have entered the circle of lovers,
that you look beyond what the eye sees,
that you feel the heart's twists and turns.
My inner self—are you out of breath?
My heart—what's all this commotion?
My bird of a soul—speak in your own language:
I can understand what's behind your song."
My soul-self answered:
"I remember now:
I was in the pottery studio...clay and water are mixing...
a new body being made, which is...
another workshop, another studio, my new home...
then I feel fire, something's baking.... I am trying to escape!
But they grab me. When I can no longer resist,
they begin kneading and molding me into shape,
just like all the other lumps of clay."

12. Remembering the Void: Is the Mystery the Message?

Encounters with love and death lead to the ultimate communion: a return to and remembrance of how it all began—the original state of the cosmos. When we remember our beginnings, we rediscover a sense of wonder and honor for what has gone before. We also find awe for the powers of recovery, regeneration and healing in all their forms.

When life draws you to selections in this chapter, you might consider how the situation before you asks you to remember a bigger picture—life before your birth, life after your death. Does stopping to contemplate this put into perspective how you feel about "work" and "rest"? Or about your own goals?

There is a void, a mystery, at the beginning of existence, which only a large, sacred question mark can fill. That question also frees us to connect with the consciousness behind all creation, and to release the same creativity within ourselves. Ultimately, there is nothing more that words can clarify. We only recognize the taste of what we experience when we encounter the Friend behind and within all friends.

Returning - Day 7, Part 1 (Hebrew)

(a midrashic, or interpretive, translation of Genesis 2:1-3)

wayekhullu hashamayim weha'aretz wekhol-tzeba'am (1):
wayekhal 'elohim bayyom hashebi'i mela'khto 'asher 'asa wayyishbot bayyom hashebi'i mikkol-mela'khto 'asher 'asah(2):
wayebarekh 'elohim 'et-yom hashebi'i wayeqaddesh 'oto ki vo shabat mikkol-mela'khto 'asher-bara' 'elohim la'asot (3)
KJV: Thus the heavens and the earth were finished, and all the host of them (1). And on the seventh day God ended his work which he had made; and he rested on the seventh day from all his work which he had made (2). And God blessed the seventh day, and sanctified it: because that in it he had rested from all his work which God created and made (3).

The Storyteller continues:
As the caravan of creation continued,
the encouragement of the future—
that magnetic "shall become" urging
it all forward from behind—
had completely activated all the basic
wave and particle tendencies that
the Holy One had radiated from the
primordial "was" in the Beginning.

All the principle processes of the
trial-and-error experiment in consciousness
had been seeded and were growing.
You could say that the "character" and "habits"
of the universe were establishing themselves.
Of course, the unexpected could always happen.
One of the prime traits that the Universe Being
was expressing through itself was expectancy

and the desire to fulfill and complete itself,
in form and consciousness,
through the creative dreams of every being (1).

Spreading through the four directions,
filling heaven and earth,
what was left for the seventh
movement of the light symphony
of the Holy One?
It could only be the mysterious
movement of turning and returning.

A clear "I can!" was resounding
from the heart of the Universe,
responding to the questioning void
that began creation.
Nothing would return to the way it was,
no matter what happened.
So the Holy One permitted itself
the most mysterious creative movement of all.
It began restoring to itself
the remembrance and awareness
of all that was going on from the
start of caravan of creation until now.
With this connection of sacred "memory"
rippling through the wave of movement,
it seeded the possibility for humans to
remember, in awe and mystery,
what had been "before the beginning."
And riding that wave came
deep empathy with everything
that drops its form,

releases its visible journey,
returns to join the "ancestors"—
with all that "dies (2)."

But even that was not enough.
The Universe Being again sent out a breath
of magnetism and compassion toward
this new period of luminosity
in which it was remembering
its own original state.
This act of restoration,
returning to Source,
the Universe set aside as pivotal, holy.
To clear space in one's awareness,
to remember the primal "before"
with empathy and compassion,
became just as essential to creation's
development as all the other
previous movements of the symphony.
Before, creation had only been a
"what's next?"
Now, the cosmos contained the seed
that would allow human beings
to touch the void and remember that
everything they care about,
everything that seems so important,
at one point was not here,
and at another would not be.
This inner turning and returning,
the opportunity for pausing and taking stock
of one's connection to the Source,
became the archetype of

what is sacred, *Sabbath*:
a holy moment,
a holy "day (3)."

Meditation—Gratitude and Celebration 9: The Original State

After completing a creative act, project or relationship:

Allow yourself to take some time to breathe in the heart with a sense of peacefulness and accomplishment. Feel a breath of fullness and completion in unison with the breath of the universe and bring into the mirror of your heart a recollection of all the stages of the process that you have experienced right back to the original inspiration or impulse. Then go back even before this: what was there? As you embrace the blessing of the original void, release the form that this adventure in creation took for you. Then clear space in the heart to undertake the next step in your own story.

This type of clearing and recollection can also be done at the end of every day, week, or month. Consider the projects, relationships and actions that have come to fullness, as well as those that are yet incomplete. Take some time to remember your own original state, as well as that of the universe. Then allow this remembrance to revivify your energy and clarify what lies ahead. Make this period of remembrance your own Sabbath, a sacred space and time of renewal.

The New Order: Everyone Breathes Like Everyone Else (Egyptian)

(a version of coffin texts from the Middle Kingdom, around 2000 B.C.E.)

(First lines of John A. Wilson version: The All-Lord says in the presence of those stilled from tumult on the journey of the court: "Pray, be prosperous in peace! I repeat for you four good deeds which my heart did for me in the midst of the serpent-coil, in order to still evil....")

Ra, the Radiance, returns
in the daily journey of the sun-boat,
collecting the souls of the dead at twilight.
The Radiant One interrupts the passengers,
who are taking a rest
in between the noise and stress
of being in a fleshy body:

"Please be calm—enjoy the peace!
Let me tell you about four good things
my own heart created for me
when I was enmeshed in the struggles
and strains of creating the world.
At the dawn of existence,
I made the four winds so that
everyone could breathe like everyone else.
I made the great flood that creates fertile earth,
so that the poor might have the same rights as the rich.
I made every human being alike.
I did not give any orders for them
to violate this principle:
their own hearts did that.

I enabled all human hearts to remember death,
so that they would honor those
who had gone before.
From One Radiant Essence came
all the shining ones and human ones.
The gods were my sweat,
the humans my tears."

Wings of Healing in Diversity's Temple (Hebrew)

(an expanded translation of Isaiah 6:1-2)

bishnat-mot hammelekh 'uzziyyahu wa'er'eh 'et-'adonai yosheb 'al-kisse' ram wenisa' weshulaw mele'im 'et-hahekhal: (1)

KJV: In the year that king Uzziah died I saw also the Lord sitting upon a throne, high and lifted up, and his train filled the temple (1).

In the year that King Uzziah died,
suddenly, I was struck by a ray of power,
a vision of *Adonai*—
that aspect of primeval cosmic Unity
that emanates new life,
that creates diversity and complexity,
that gives and receives
unexpected gifts as well as
the results they unfold.

This Diversifying Universe appeared
as if returned to its original state—
the collection and meeting place of
all straight lines and all curving spirals.
At that pinnacle of reality
all strong movements,
expanding from a center
like a ray filling space,
were uniting with
all fragile movements,
spiraling wildly without a center.

A harmonious balance of
these two energies clothed
cosmic Diversity in power.
The edge of this "cloak,"
woven by a dynamic peace,
unfurled throughout space and time.
It embraced and sheltered
all individual beings.
Within the sacred temple of Diversity,
all life was gathering each moment in awe.

serafim 'omedim mimma'al lo shesh kenafayim shesh kenafayim le'echad bishtayim yekhasseh fanaw ubishtayim yekhasseh raglaw ubishtayim ye'ofef (2)
KJV: Above it stood the seraphims: each one had six wings; with twain he covered his face, and with twain he covered his feet, and with twain he did fly (2).

Around the original seat of Diversity
gathered all the healing powers of the cosmos,
those forces of regeneration and redemption
called seraphim or angels.

Each recovery power had six wings—
harmonious extensions from its core—
that could touch the inner soul-self of every being
like a mutual, interdependent skin.
These wings arose from the sacred desire
to embody souls in diversity
from the First Beginning.

12. Remembering the Void:

Contact with this angelic "skin"
could remind a being of its source
and repair the illusion of separation.
Each two wings,
recalling the first split in the cosmos,
satisfied a particular need:

Two wings could heal one's face and atmosphere—
the desire of the self to appear whole.
Their touch could return one's presence
to its original state.

Two could heal one's motion and emotions,
whatever stirs and agitates the feeling self.
Their touch could reconnect all movement
to the unfolding wheel of celestial joy.

Two could heal a soul's interior baggage,
burning away the unnecessary clinging.
Their touch could renew the instincts
and cause a being to fly.

Meditation—Depths of the Self 10: The Grace of What's Needed

Asking for healing from the power behind miracles:

After beginning with a remembrance of the Source, allow your breath and awareness to touch with love and respect all the aspects of your subconscious soul-self that you have experienced so far. Allow each aspect of the self to express what it feels most in need of at the moment. Some may or may not be cooperative; if not, give them time. For those who do make a request, ask the help of all the healing and recovery powers of the cosmos to provide what is needed.

Open to the possibility that these healing forces are present everywhere. Allow them to touch the presence, feelings and sensations of each self. If it feels appropriate in the moment, follow the healing powers back to the Source: catch hold of their wings and fly, perhaps even to the sacred temple of Diversity itself. To conclude this meditation, thank each aspect of the self and thank the Source.

About Work and Rest (Aramaic)

(an expanded translation of Matthew 11:28-29 from the Peshitta version of the Gospels)

taw lwoty kulkhuwn la'ya' washqiylay mawble' we'na' 'aniychkhuwn (28)
KJV: Come unto me, all ye that labor and are heavy laden, and I will give you rest (28).

Come to me,
all of you, all of yourself,
in your frenzied weariness,
your movement without end,
your action without purpose,
not caring in your fatigue
whether you live or die.

Come enmeshed by what you carry,
the cargo taken on by your soul,
the burdens you thought you desired,
which have constantly swollen
and are now exhausting you.

Come like lovers to your first tryst:
I will give you peace and
renewal after constant stress:
Your pendulum can pause
between here and there,
between being and not-being.

shquwlw niyry 'laykuwn wiylapw meny dniych 'na' wmakiykh 'na' bleby wmeshkchiyn 'ntuwn nyacha' lnapshatkhuwn (29)
KJV: Take my yoke upon you, and learn of me; for I am meek and lowly in heart: and ye shall find rest unto your souls (29).

Why not absorb yourself in my work—
here's newly plowed earth ready
for a crop of guidance and illumination.
Jump into the whirlpool of wisdom,
the impassioned spiral of understanding
your self.
Here's the peace you're looking for—
the softening of the heart's rigid
feelings and thoughts.
In my way, you will find a
refuge of renewable energy
within the struggle and grasping
of your subconscious soul.
In my way, when you
wrestle for the knowledge of your Self,
the self you find finds rest.

Meditation—Simple Presence 8: A Refuge of Renewable Energy

For developing a sense of rest and renewal:

Return to the place of simple presence, breathing with each feeling and sensation, following each to its source. To support this meditation, breathe in and out with the words *Alaha Nyach* (Unity is rest and renewal, "A-LA-HA NEE-ACH"), allowing the phrase to find its own rhythm with your breath. Open to as much peace as you are capable of feeling this moment and allow this peace to flood your self.

Sense the natural pause when the breath is either all in or all out. In this instant of stillness, enter a deeper communion with both your soul-self and the peace of existence from which it, and all beings, arose. Feel this breath as an ark of refuge on the sometimes troubled sea of mind. The biblical name *Noah* is derived from the same roots as *nyach*, the peace of existence. Could this breath be your own "Noah's ark," bearing you through the overwhelming flood of life's impressions? Once again, conclude this meditation with a breath of gratitude and thanks.

Speak Unity's Name (Arabic)

(A meditation on the Qur'an, Surah *al-Ikhlas*, 112:1-4)

Bismillahir rahmanir rahim qul huwa allahu ahad (1) 'allaahu (a)s-samad (2) lam yalid wa-lam yolad (3) wa-lam yaku(n) la-hu kufuw[an] 'ahad (4)

A. Yusuf Ali version: Say: He is Allah the One and Only (1) Allah the Eternal Absolute (2)

He begetteth not nor is He begotten (3) And there is none like unto Him (4).

We begin in the atmosphere of Sacred Unity,
the Reality behind all ideas, language and stories,
from which is being born
all compassion now being given and
all compassion now being received.

Speak Unity's Name:
Support the Oneness of existence.
Unity's sound, heard everywhere on the wind,
combines the "yes" and "no" of being—
all force extending toward a purpose,
together with the unimaginable abyss of emptiness.
Realize that every single and distinct object
arose only from the passion of this Mystery,
which cannot be enclosed or contained (1).

This ultimate Unity throughout the cosmos
envelops and surrounds all dimensions,
measurements, laws and tendencies.
It fulfills and completes the potentials
of all natural beings as they unfold in joy.
It is the Refuge and Support for every need (2).

Unity is Ground and Context of Being—
nothing is born from it and nothing produces it.
It is not confined to breeding, family,
lineage, race, nation or creed.
It is the Seed of both cause and effect (3).

There is no comparable existence.
No metaphor, word or sacred name
can match or explain this Mystery,
the source of all of our
personal and mutual dreams of being (4).

Meditation—Sound and Embodiment 11: The Mystery of Communion

For opening to a greater sense of inner sacredness and refuge:

As with the other meditations with sound, begin by breathing with awareness centered in the heart. Allow yourself to feel that you are calling on two living qualities of Unity seeded within you at the first Beginning. This is the medieval Sufi Ibn Arabi's view of the "99 Beautiful Names" of Unity. The two pathways of the heart mentioned in this surah, *al-Ahad* and *as-Samad*, can open us to a renewed sense of mystery and awe in life.

As you slowly intone "YA AH-HAD" in the heart, open to a feeling of the unity of all being in the cosmos, beyond names, forms and ideas. Open to a sense of mystery. Allow yourself to feel that there is a guiding consciousness behind all being that cannot be put into words. After a few repetitions, intone "YA SAH-MAD" in the heart. Allow this sound to open your heart to receive from the One being whatever is needed to fulfill the purpose of each aspect of your being. There is a part of your soul that recognizes this refuge for all the possible needs of life.

Then slowly alternate the sounds as you feel your connection to these energies of guidance and help. At the same time, a door to your whole subconscious soul-self, the *nafs*. The heart can hold all this. After some minutes, return to breathing both phrases silently, then releasing the words, and breathe only with the feeling that remains. Follow the feeling and conclude with thanks for whatever has been received.

Everyone Bows When the Friend Passes By (Persian)

(from the "Odes" of the Sufi poet Sa'adi of Shiraz, 13th century Persia)

The world is greening—that suits me!
For everything has greened because of the Friend.
I love all worlds now since the Friend owns them.
Companions! Breathe in Jesus' breath,
Wake up your dead hearts!
You will live again if the Friend breathes you.
Neither heaven nor the angels
own a truth that doesn't change.
But what you find in the core of
every human heart is from the Friend.
If my sweet one brings poison,
I am happy to consume it.
Pain and devotion come together.
Anyway, the Friend is also my medicine.
If the wound does not heal, all the better.
The Friend's glance relieves the rawness.
Is it wise to separate joy and sadness?
Bring wine! At least I know
my wound came from the Friend.
Rich, poor—it doesn't matter:
Everyone bows when the Friend passes by.
Sa'adi, if the flood of longing washes out
your house, make your heart stronger.
The Friend will lay a new foundation
that will last for eternity.

The Visit and the Gift (Persian)

(from "The Secret Rose Garden" by the Sufi poet Mahmud Shabistari, 13th century Persia)

At dawn, the moon,
like a creature of fantasy,
stole into my room
and woke me from some
lazy and unproductive sleep.
Her face quickly illuminated
the underside of my soul
and my own being stood
revealed in the naked light.
Sighing in wonder, I
faced my Self, which said:
"Your life so far has chased
the illusion of control:
You will not find me on that path.
One flash of my glance
is worth a thousand years of piety."

Overcome by waste and loss,
my soul endarkened itself with shame.
But my moon-faced Self,
whose radiance equaled the sun,
filled a cup of Direct Experience
and urged me to drown my despair:
"No bouquet, no flavor,
but this wine can wash away
your being's whole historical library."

12. Remembering the Void:

I finished the cup in one gulp,
and, intoxicated by its purity,
fell to the earth.
Since then I am not sure
whether I am here or not.
Neither sober nor drunk,
sometimes I feel the joy of
my soul's eyes looking through mine.
Other times I feel the curl of its hair
and my life bobs and weaves.
Sometimes, from sheer habit,
I'm back on the compost heap.
And sometimes,
when that glance finds me again,
I am back in the Rose Garden.

13. Journey's Pause: Is it Time For Thanks?

All journeys of diversity, interiority and communion pause now and then, taking a look backward and forward at the same time. Much has happened, much will happen.

When life draws you to selections in this chapter, you might consider how the situation before you asks you to realize yourself as part of a larger picture, something living, fragile, mysterious and sacred. To cultivate the quality of gratitude may be the greatest antidote to our habitual abuse of the natural world and of each other. The Native Middle Eastern tradition points toward a way to pray, praise, thank and bless what arises from our own wordless experience. Words can be used or not, but this way of devotion does not depend on repeating anything from the past. In fact, nothing is ever really repeated in a universe in which past, present and future are moving and changing together. If we are awake, we may catch the unique scent of a rose at dawn. Or we may hear the camel bell calling us to travel further in the caravan of creation.

A New Name for the Universe Being - Day 7, Part 2 (Hebrew)

(A midrashic, or interpretive, translation of Genesis 2:4)

'elleh toledot hashamayim weha'aretz behibbare'am beyom 'asot yhwh 'elohim 'eretz weshamayim

KJV: These are the generations of the heavens and of the earth when they were created, in the day that the Lord God made the earth and the heaven.

The Storyteller continues:
The whole story told so far may be
only a sign or symbol,
perhaps a family history,
of the way in which
the evolving desire of the Holy One
to experience consciousness in
wild and unexpected ways
is working through everything
we're aware of,
whether in wave and particle,
as it moves toward
its purpose in life.
The Universe Being is revealing
this story line through us
in what we may see as only
one luminous, intelligent activity,
one Cosmic Day
from *then* until *now.*

During this Day,
the Holy One has been irresistibly drawn
to realize itself as a Being/Process
that simultaneously was, is and will be.

This is not just a matter of
the past affecting the future,
but, as we have seen, of
the future affecting the past and
both affecting the present moment.
The unified field of "time,"
which we view only through
stories, metaphors and theories,
not through its sacred mystery as it is,
continues to be unaffected by our
limited awareness and construction of it.
Yet the awareness and consciousness of the
Holy One continued, and continues,
to expand and deepen as the experiment continues.

To mark this new, evolving awareness,
the Universe Being (*Elohim*)—
the Sacred One-And-Many,
realized and named
a new quality of its own essence:

Life Squared (HH)
interpenetrated with both
its own Power to Manifest (I)
as well as the awareness of its own
original Being and Nothingness (O-U):
IHO-UH.

We can also feel this
pure, open, resonant sound
more subtly,
in the whisper and feeling
of our own breath—

13. Journey's Pause:

yhwh...
connecting us to the
breath of Being.

And this Being of Beings,
another name for Unity,
continues to interpenetrate
the foundations of our existence—
all waves, all particles—
as the Seventh Day continues.

Meditation—Heart Awareness 10: One "Day" at a Time

For becoming part of creation's adventure:

Return to breathing with awareness in the heart and feel the heart as a mirror, as clear as possible for the moment. With a gentle breath, breathe in life from the universe, feeling the inner sound of the breath. Add to this the power of life to manifest, and remember all the life that has come into your body in the past. Finally open your sense of openness to the mysterious goal toward which the whole universe is moving. Breathe into the heart all the blessing you are capable of breathing in. Breathe out all the blessing you are capable of breathing out. Allow the mirror of your heart to contain the entire planet. Allow your own heart to be contained within the heart of the Universal One. And let the mirror disappear. When this meditation is ready to end, conclude with thankfulness.

The Power and Glory of Dark Matter (Hebrew)

(an expanded translation of Isaiah 6:3)

weqara' zeh 'el-zeh we'amar (A)

qadosh qadosh qadosh (B)

yhwh tzeba'ot (C)

melo' khol-ha'aretz kebodo (D)

KJV: And one cried unto another, and said (A), Holy, holy, holy (B), is the Lord of Hosts (C): the whole earth is full of his glory (D).

Then each Power of Recovery,
each angel of healing, called out to the others,
spontaneously and in unison
naming the essential medicine behind others,
engraving it upon their mutual reality, saying (A):

qadosh qadosh qadosh—
Clear Intelligent Spaciousness:
Matrix and Turning Point of the Cosmos:
Focused Illuminating Emptiness:
Holy Holy Holy (B)

yhhhhwwwwwwhhhhhh.....
the Breath inside all breaths,
iiiiiihhhhhuuuuuuuhhhh....
the Life Force squared—
past without beginning,
future without limit,
the Soul of all hands, claws, tendrils, pseudopodia, orbits,
the Self of all eyes, ears, antennae, protoplasm, atmospheres,
the Being of Beings behind Being:
Energizer of the Cosmic Story.

This Ultimate Energy to Be
is unfolding through harmony
the law-generating-and-revising habits of the cosmos.
A crowd of illuminating order travels with this Life,
just as the stars swirl through the silent void (C).

This Universe Energy fills
the entire form of all elements,
the whole of earthiness in all its
imagined and unimagined shapes.
It burnishes all substance from inside
with the force of the Intelligent Abyss,
the abundant Depth of Depths,
the power and glory of Dark Matter (D).

Meditation—Sound and Embodiment 12: The Turning Point

For reawakening the healthy ability to praise:

It is a human gift to be in awe of and praise the cosmos around us. To the extent that our culture has isolated us from both fear and awe, making praise unfashionable, it has prevented us from achieving the clarity about our place in the cosmos that older native traditions attained. Yet both mysticism and the recent findings of physics promote an experience of both fear and awe. In both arenas, what we do matters a great deal: No act is insignificant. Reawakening the ability to praise, even when not in words, is essential to real communion with the universe. Recognizing that we are part of something sacred is the matrix and turning point of the cosmos, and the source of all healing.

As before, begin by breathing in the heart. Then add the inner sound of the word *qadosh* ("QAH-DOHSH"), the sacred emptiness that brings healing. After some moments, intone the sounds slowly on one note. Focus your intention on opening a space for praise and devotion in your life. In many native traditions, one gives praise and thanks for things that one has not yet received, thereby creating a spaciousness that the Universe can fill. At the end, if you feel some sense of thankfulness, give thanks for this as well.

O Breathing Life (Aramaic)

(an expanded, then condensed translation of Matthew 6:9-13 and Luke 11:2-4 from the Peshitta version of the Gospels)

abwun dbashmaya' (A) netqadash shmakh (B) te'te' malkuwtakh (C) nehwe' tzeby-anakh 'aykana' dbashmaya' 'aph ba'r'a' (D) habwlan lachma' dsuwnqanan yawmana' (E) washbuwqlan chawbayn (wachtahayn) 'aykana' da'ph chnan shbaqn lchayabayn (F) wla' ta'lan lnesyuwna' 'ela' patzan men bisha' (G) metul diylakhihy malkuta' wchayla' wteshbuwchta' l'alam 'almiyn (H) ameyn (I)

KJV: Our Father which art in heaven (A). Hallowed be thy name (B). Thy kingdom come (C). Thy will be done in earth, as it is in heaven (D). Give us this day our daily bread (E). And forgive us our debts, as we forgive our debtors (F). And lead us not into temptation, but deliver us from evil (G). For thine is the kingdom, and the power, and the glory, forever (H). Amen (I).

O Breathing Life, your name shines everywhere (A)!
Release a space to plant your presence here (B).
Envision your "I Can" now (C).
Embody your desire in every light and form (D).
Grow through us this moment's bread and wisdom (E).
Untie the knots of failure binding us,
    as we release the strands we hold of others' faults (F).
Help us not forget our source,
    yet free us from not being in the present (G).
From you arises every vision, power and song
    from gathering to gathering (H).
Amen—May our future actions grow from here (I)!

Meditation—Simple Presence 9: A Prayer for the Cosmos

For developing a wordless sense of contemplative prayer:

Return again to a place of simple presence. Sitting comfortably, eyes closed, feel the rise and fall of the breath. With each breath, reach out to whatever feelings or sensations arise and feel the breath illuminating each with awareness. Without needing to add anything, feel each sensation that rises to awareness as already illuminated, already radiating with brilliance and remembering its own home in the wave and particle reality of the cosmos. Feel each sensation giving thanks, in its own language of feeling, offering a prayer of vision, power and song to the cosmos.

A Blessing of Lucid Fire and Loving Refuge (Hebrew)

(a translation of a blessing of the Qumran, Dead Sea Community, circa 100 B.C.E.-100 C.E., 1QS 2:2a-4a)

ybarekkhah bkhol tob (A)

wyshmorkhah mkhol r'wh (B)

wy'ayr libkhah bsekhl chayyim (C)

wyachonkhh bd'at 'olamym (D)

wysh' fney chasadyw lkhah lshlom 'olamym (E)

(A.M. Habermann translation: May He bless thee with all good (A) And keep thee from all evil (B). May He enlighten thy heart with immortal wisdom (C) And grace thee with eternal knowledge (D). May He Lift up His merciful countenance upon thee for eternal peace (E).

May the Being of the Universe
breathe into you
the light of blessing and ripeness,
the fulfillment of health and balance,
helping you fulfill your purpose in life (A);

May the Holy One protect you
with a sphere of lucid fire from
everything crooked and brittle,
distractions from your path (B);

May the Unnameable One enlighten
the heart of your passion
with the contemplation
of living energy in all life (C);

May the Universe Being uncover
hidden understanding within you,

insight into life's diversity
as it flows from the First Now (D).

and may the Holy One lift toward you
its face of secret grace and loving refuge,
wherever you may find it,
as it gathers every being in creation
in a communion of deep peace (E).

Road, Compass, Fuel (Aramaic)

(a translation of John 14:5-6 from the Peshitta version of the Gospels)

'amar leh ta'wma' maran la' yod'iynan la'yko' 'ozel 'ant wa'ykana meshkchiyn chnan 'uwrcha' lmeda'(5)
'amar leh yeshuw' 'ena' 'na' 'uwrcha' washrara' wchaye' la' 'nash 'ate' lwat 'aby 'ela' 'en biy (6)
KJV: Thomas saith unto him, Lord, we know not whither thou goest; and how can we know the way? Jesus saith unto him, I am the way, the truth, and the life: no man cometh unto the Father, but by me.

Thomas said to him,
You who remind us of the light of the One—
we can't grasp where you're going,
so how can we find the way to understand it?

Yeshua said to him:
The "I Am" is the path,
the sense of right direction
and the life force to travel.
The self conscious of its Self reveals the way,
solves the mystery of choice and
frees all the animal energy you need.
The ego fully aware of the Only "I"
shows the road,
provides a compass and
fuels the journey.
The depth of Identity
illuminates what's ahead,
liberates choice and
connects us to nature's power.

The eye of your I's momentary swirl is
the understanding, the confidence and the vigor.
No limited self travels any other way
back to the Source of Creation—
the breathing life of all—
except by traveling as I do.

The Open Road (Arabic)

(a meditation on Qur'an, Surah *al-Maida,* 5:48b)

Likullin ja`alnaa minkum shir-atanwwa minhaaj(an). Wa law shaa'a 'allaahu laja alakum 'ummatanw waahidahtanw walaakilli yab-luwa-kum fii maa 'aataakum fasta biqul khayraat. 'Ilal-laahi marjiukum jamii`an fayunabbi -ukum bimaa kuntum fiihi takh-talifuun

A. Yusuf Ali version: To each among you have We prescribed a Law and an Open Way. If Allah had so willed He would have made you a single people but (His plan is) to test you in what He hath given you: so strive as in a race in all virtues. The goal of you all is to Allah; it is He that will show you the truth of the matters in which ye dispute.

For all peoples we have prescribed two medicines:
the first, a clear pointer to the watering place of Unity,
liberating ways and laws modeled on natural harmony;
the second, an open, well-travelled road,
allowing you to track, footstep by footstep,
the impulse seeded in you at creation.
If desired, the One could have created you
as a monoculture, one identical community,
like Roman numeral I's lined up together.
But in order to honor you as a test experiment,
the One bestowed on you the blessing of diversity.
So compete with each other in this race:
The first one wins who creates the
most good for others, helping them embody
the original life force gifted
within as their purpose in life.
Towards the One you are all returning together,
as one gathering of all creatures.
By bringing what is inside you into the light,

the One will prophesy through you
the actual state of affairs,
giving news of the race results
and repairing the breaks, wounds and
delaying disagreements
that have arisen along the way
toward your shared Home.

A Song About a Journey (Persian)

(From "The Diwan of Shams-i-Tabriz," by the Sufi poet Mevlana Jelaluddin Rumi, 13th century Anatolia)

Calling all lovers! It is time to break camp in this material world!
From the Universe, I hear the drum of departure calling me.
The driver was up long ago and prepared the camels.
He says it's not his fault we are still asleep—wake up!
The hubbub of departure surrounds us—camel bells behind and ahead.
Every moment a soul leaves on a journey to the unknown.
Look! From these upside-down candles in the night sky bowl
magnificent beings arose so that the mystery could unfold.
This whirling of planets and stars brought you a sound sleep.
For a life so light, be careful of a sleep so heavy!
My inner self—seek the Self of love!
My inner friend, seek the Friend!
Inner witness, stay alert! It's not your job to fall asleep.
The streets are full of torches—chaos and din are everywhere!
Tonight this grasping-getting world
gives birth to an eternal one.
It's simple:
You thought you were dust
and now find you are breath.
Before you were ignorant,
and now you know more.
The One who led you this far
will guide you further on as well.

Meditation—Gratitude and Celebration 10: Guidance

For asking for what to ask:

In most native traditions, there is a prayer that asks the Sacred to choose the right prayer. This affirms that we don't always know what to ask for or how to ask, but want to open ourselves to guidance anyway.

In the Hebrew language, the Biblical prophets often used the phrase *hinneni* ("HI-NAY-NEE," for instance, in Genesis 22:1), meaning "see, here I am, use me." In Aramaic, the fourth line of Jesus' prayer asks that the desire of the universe come through us, equally in form and vibration, wave and particle, heaven and earth. In Arabic, the Beautiful Name of the One often used is *"al-Hadi,"* the One who guides ("YAH HA-DEE," a form of this word also used in Surah *Fatiha*, line 6)

Using any or all of these prayers, one of your own choosing, or a wordless one, open yourself to the next step in guidance. If you are willing to allow the heart of the Universe to change your life, let it speak to and through you for the benefit of all beings. Allow it to lead you "further on."

Gaze Gently on These Blossoms (Persian)

(from "The Secret Rose Garden" by the Sufi poet Mahmud Shabistari, 13th century Persia)

I have plucked this bouquet of scent
from a place I have called
"The Secret Rose Garden."
There roses bloom that reveal
the mysteries of the human heart.
There the lilies' tongues really sing,
and the narcissus sees everything perfectly.
With your heart's eyes,
gaze gently on these blossoms
until all your doubts fade away.
Hopefully, you will find some wisdom,
both practical and mystical,
all detailed and arranged clearly.
Don't use cold eyes to find my mistakes:
The roses may turn to thorns.
Ingratitude usually reveals ignorance,
and the friends of truth are thankful.
If you remember me, please
send a little breath of mercy my way.
As the tradition goes, I sign off with my own name,
Mahmud, which means
"May all I do and am return to praise the One."

Acknowledgments

Many thanks to the Kalliopeia Foundation, which made the publication of this new, revised edition possible. Its ongoing dedication to promoting the awareness of global unity continues to fuel "what's fresh and verdant."

The original work was undertaken and completed in a nomadic fashion in Northern California, Germany, Austria, Jordan, Israel, Syria, and England and back to Northern California, between 1992-1994, a time during which I had no fixed home. My thanks go to all my friends and hosts who provided hospitality and a place to spread innumerable papers and a laptop computer, including Kamae A. Miller, my partner during the initial writing.

This revision was completed between 2009 and early 2011 primarily at home in Edinburgh, Scotland. My deepest gratitude to my wife Natalia Lapteva for her love and insight, sustaining me through this re-vision of the visions of another time and another place.

For helping draw out and support the wisdom necessary for this time, my thanks also go to the many friends and supporters of the Abwoon Study Circle, the students and faculty at the Institute in Culture and Creation Spirituality in Oakland, California from 1986-1994 and the worldwide circles of the International Center for the Dances of Universal Peace. For introducing me to and helping me maintain a living practice that touches the depths of self, my special thanks to my Sufi guide, Hazrat Murshid Moineddin Jablonski as well as the late Rev. Frida Waterhouse.

For their deeply ecumenical wisdom and example over the years, my thanks go to Dr. Matthew Fox, Br. Joseph Kilikevice, O.P., Marlene DeNardo, S.N.D., Joanna Macy, Rabbi Zalman Schachter-Shalomi and Brian Swimme. For their guidance and example on the Sufi path, I thank Hazrat Sufi Ahmed Murad Chisti, Hazrat Murshid Shamcher Beorse, Hazrat Murshida Vera Corda, Hazrat Pir Vilayat Inayat Khan, Hazrat Shemseddin Ahmed, Murshid Wali Ali Meyer, Murshid Saul Barodofskly, Murshida Fatima Lassar, Pir Hidayat Inayat Khan, Murshid Karimbaksh Witteween, Dr. Ali Kianfar and Dr. Nahid Angha.

As my first spiritual teachers, I thank my mother and father, the late Frieda and Verner Klotz, who introduced me from childhood to their own particular "holy trinity" of the three "c's": chiropractic, (Edgar) Cayce and (Rachel) Carson.

For help in preparing the final manuscript, my thanks go to Elizabeth Ferrio, Sharon Mijares, Alan Heeks, MJ Maraffa, Elizabeth Reed and Alice Saunders.

Special thanks also to Tom Grady, my former editor at HarperSanFrancisco (and later my literary agent) for his patience and help in bringing the first journey of this caravan-project to its appropriate destination. Likewise, my gratitude goes to the Rev. Elizabeth Reed, director of the Abwoon Resource Center, who helped shepherd this new flock of desert voices to other, greener pastures.

Appendix: A Mystic's Peace Plan

While lecturing and teaching on Middle Eastern spirituality, I am often asked whether I have any special insights on political peace in the region. I have mentioned some of my thoughts about this in the Preface; namely, that the West's interventions in the Middle East in the last century, and so far in this one, have been at best ignorant of the Middle Eastern mind and at worst manipulative for its own benefit. The West needs to do less until it understands more. In addition, the recent history of violence and human tragedy on all sides has produced an extreme climate of fear and mistrust. Any peace efforts must deal with this climate of fear before effective agreements can be made.

A plan that addresses these points was offered by Samuel L. Lewis (1896-1971), the American Sufi mystic who studied the spirituality of the region extensively and lived there for a number of years. Lewis was born into a Jewish family and studied Jewish mysticism and Kabbala in depth along with his Sufi work. His ideas arose from discussions with Muslim and Jewish spiritual leaders in the 1960s and reflect an attempt to change the atmosphere (or "wave-reality") of the region as a preparation for any specific political changes in the "particle-reality." Lewis felt that only careful confidence-building efforts focused on spiritual, semantic, economic, ecological and cultural fronts would effectively prepare for long-term, political solutions. Several former U.N. officials including Gunnar Jarring and Robert Muller endorsed the basis of the plan. The main points of Lewis's skeleton radical yet simple plan follow:

1. **Spiritual:** Place all religious holy places in the entire region under international protection, including the entire Old City of Jerusalem. All people should be protected in their worship and spiritual practice. This part of the plan also involves setting up "safe corridors" so that devotees of all traditions and religions feel safe to travel between all shrines and places of worship. Lewis felt that this would establish a spiritual network of prayer and peace, much like the "cities of refuge" in medieval Europe. Because the spiritual life is so important in the Middle East, one must denationalize holy places to both stop arguments about them and secure them for worshipers. Since the publication of the first edition of this book, one part of this approach is currently being pursued by the "Abraham Path" project (see www.abrahampath.org).

2. **Semantic**: Obtain agreement from all parties in all peace processes to use terms consistently or not at all. For instance, one side's "security" cannot be another side's "terrorism." One side's "dispossessed persons" must be judged equally with another side's. The use of words like "home" and "historic homeland" must be judged by objective criteria and applied equally to all sides or else eliminated from the discussion. Lewis felt that using words as emotionally laden weapons to escalate wars of public relations prevented all sides from dealing seriously with each other at the bargaining table. As a student of Korzybski's "general semantics," Lewis also felt strongly that these unhealthy linguistic habits, usually associated with politicians, obscured

the real problems at hand under a cloud of fuzzy meaning and thinking. "The reason we often don't solve problems," said Lewis, "is that their answers get in the way of our concepts." (For more on this "general semantic" approach to peace, see my paper on Lewis published in the Journal of the Traditional Cosmology Society of the University of Edinburgh, referenced in the Bibliography).

3. **Ecological and Economic:** Regional conferences must be held to resolve the fair use and trade of natural resources in the entire "Holy Land" bioregion. This would include honest discussions about the use and conservation of water, minerals and oil. From the end of World War I and the breakup of the Ottoman Empire, the strategic interests of Europe and the USA have largely imposed the political borders and boundaries in the present-day Middle East. They do not serve the people of the region, who have been divided artificially into haves and have-nots by outside forces wanting to exploit the resources for their own use. When the people of the Middle East can meet to decide the best use of the earth's resources in their area, then the ground will be prepared for just determinations about land and borders. "I shall continue in desert reclamation research," wrote Lewis in 1967, "knowing that sooner or later Israelis and Arabs will both have to drink from the same well."

4. **Cultural**. The West should officially sponsor cultural exchange on all levels with the Middle East, including sponsorship of Middle Eastern tours of music, dance and art. It should seek to educate its own people as much as possible about Middle Eastern culture in order to diminish racism and anti-Semitism. With the same goal, it should sponsor exchanges of citizen diplomats between the West and the Middle East

(much as was done in the former Soviet Union). At the same time, the West should support tours of the best of its own folk arts, music and dance to the Middle East. It should ban the export of the worst aspects of Western pseudoculture to the Middle East, including pornography and films that exploit violence and fear. Lewis supported all means whereby ordinary people could come together simply to recognize their mutual humanity. Only this recognition would prove stronger than the modern economic and political forces that drive the many apart for the benefit of the few. "My main peace theme is: eat, pray and dance together," he said.

On the ground, I have attempted to pursue most of these initiatives through my own citizen diplomacy work, including co-founding, with Mr. Neill Walker, the annual Edinburgh International Festival of Middle Eastern Spirituality and Peace, now in its eighth year (see www.mesp.org.uk).

Textual Notes

Chapter One

1. Particle and Wave - Genesis 1:1.

Translations influenced by a mechanistic, dualistic worldview artificially widen the gulf between "heaven" and "earth." In the mystical sense of the Hebrew words, both realities exist simultaneously: one as vibration, one as form. Most people in modern Western culture have heard that scientists now view light as both wave and particle, that energy and matter are convertible. If we were to substitute these close equivalents for the Middle Eastern mystical rendition of "heaven" and "earth," we might begin to recover the cosmology of the storyteller of Genesis 1:1.

This version of Genesis 1:1 combines several literal translations of the key ancient Hebrew words to give some of the multileveled sense of the verse. For a more extensive discussion of this approach to Genesis, please see my later book *The Genesis Meditations* (2003) as well as the work of Hebrew scholar and mystic Fabre D'Olivet (1815).

The initial word *bere'shit* combines the primary Hebrew letters R and Sh to denote something happening in principle, that is, involving the *power to be* but not yet actual manifestation. In Middle Eastern mystical cosmology, this power to envision a new reality precedes the reality itself, whether that reality is seen or unseen. *Bere'shit* can also mean "before anything else," "in the beginning-ness" or at the head or start of a process. The roots themselves show a central point or dot that unfolds itself into a circle, surrounded by wings or flames.

The entire first verse may be compared to the musical overture of a performance, which summarizes the themes that will follow.

The "actor" in this unfolding process is *Elohim*, which I have translated as the "Being of Beings," the Ultimate Pronoun. While singular in meaning, the word has a plural ending, which leads to the difficult translation "It-They-Who Are." *Elohim* is the answer that the storyteller of Genesis gives to the question physicists now ask: "What existed before the beginning of the universe?" This sacred name could also be translated "the inherent intelligence of the divine That-ness," which includes both the One and the Many.

In Hebrew, the roots of the verb *bara'* mean not only "create," but also to draw from an unknown element or to render "same" what was "other." The centuries-old argument by some scholars as to whether the verb means "to create something from nothing" or "to create something from something" misses the point from a Middle Eastern mystical view. "Some-thing" and "no-thing" are not words that make sense at this stage of consciousness or existence. The process described concerns a change of state from unknown to known, from non-being to being. Although not very elegant, D'Olivet proposes that to translate *bara'*, one must coin a new verb: "to thing."

In principle, what the Being of Beings created before anything else was *shamayim* and *aretz*. As I have pointed out elsewhere (1990, 2003), the difficulty of translating *shamayim* as "heaven" is that, to the Western mind, conditioned by Platonic philosophy, this word has come to mean something separate from and specifically above "earth." One can also translate *shamayim* as the "world of vibration"—life seen as the furthest extent of light, sound, name, atmosphere, time and space, all of which are vibration or wave phenomena. To the Middle Eastern mystic, even the sound of our own name can link us to the source of all names, the sound of the universe heard as one sound. The "sky," as seen from the viewpoint of ancient Middle Eastern cosmology, is a graphic example of *shamayim*, but this greater vibratory reality is in no way limited to what is "above" us.

The strict division of matter from spirit, cause from effect, inner from outer results from a worldview inherited from Greek and Latin abstract philosophy. This "way of knowing," which drives modern Western consciousness, is only one of many in the world, although it is gradually swamping the cosmologies of various indigenous traditions. The exaggeration inherent in this type of dualistic thinking has brought the modern world to the brink of destruction by turning nonhuman reality into objects for our use. Similar to other ancient cosmologies, the Native Middle Eastern tradition (as expressed through what is recorded in the visionary writings in Hebrew, Aramaic, Arabic, Ugaritic, and other languages) rejects dualistic, pseudo-objective categories in favor of mutually coexisting paradoxes and symmetries (like wave and particle, *shamayim* and *aretz*).

We can translate the word *aretz* as "earth," but from its roots, it includes all ideas of a power that is stable, defined by relative limits or boundaries and yet continues to move. From the Middle Eastern mystical view, this defines life seen as discrete entities or particles. The earth, in this view, is not exclusively female any more than *shamayim* is exclusively male. According to D'Olivet, *aretz* also indicates the primary divisions of embodiment into earth, water, fire, air, ether (the combination of the first four) and light (in its individual or particle form). As expressed by the roots of *aretz*, particles and individuals move toward limits, solutions, ends and goals. By comparison, the wave reality shows no such movement toward boundaries and purposes. It is ultimate communion.

2. Character Development.

This poetic version is based on reading #17 from a Sumerian account of creation included in a collection of transliterated Sumerian language texts compiled by C. J. Gadd (1924), pp. 133-137. His literal translation of this text is based on Ebeling,

Zeitschrift der deutschen morgenländischen Gesellschaft, 1916, 532ff, and Langdon, *Le poème sumérien du paradis*, pp 42ff.

3. Binding and Letting Go - Matthew 18:18-20.

This translation of Matthew 18:18-20 from the Syriac Aramaic, is taken from the Bible used by Assyrian and Syrian Orthodox Christians, the Peshitta version (meaning pure, straight and unadulterated). For further background on this text and my approach in rendering it, please see the introduction as well as my other work, especially, *Prayers of the Cosmos* (1990), *The Hidden Gospel* (1995), *The Genesis Meditations* (2003) and *Blessings of the Cosmos* (2006).

Greek translators of the words of Jesus experienced considerable difficulty in translating Aramaic idioms, Middle Eastern cultural expressions, and Semitic language psychology and cosmology into a more abstract, metaphysical language, which by the time of the translations had been heavily influenced by Platonic philosophy. This resulted in the greater part of the spiritual and mystical expression of Jesus being strained out and left on the other side of the linguistic and epistemological sieve. The resulting Greek-based texts were ripe for theological formulations and political manipulation that separated "heaven" and "earth" and helped create the impression of an exclusive religious and priestly elite that had the sole power to "bind" and "loose."

When Christianity became institutionalized as the official religion of the Roman Empire in the fourth century C.E., the link between theology and politics became even stronger. The Greek scriptures were declared the "original" versions of the words of Jesus. This is still taught in most seminaries even though scholars find it impossible to defend the position that Jesus taught in Greek.

In the first passage (verse 18), the Aramaic words translated as "bind" and "loose" are linked in a very sublime wordplay. The first word, *'asiyr* (based on the root ASR) can mean: to bind, tie, engage or enmesh oneself in something; to harness one's energies, and symbolically to enclose one's directed passion in a closed circle. The energy that is enclosed is the "straight-line" variety: it is meant to flow through conditions back to its Source and not ultimately to be held onto by any one form. We shall see the appearance of this straight-line energy again later as the Genesis story unfolds.

The second word, *shre'*, (based on the root ShR) shows in symbolic form this same closed circle opening up. This leads to the additional meanings of liberation, loosening and solution. The root also suggests the image of the severing of the umbilical cord after birth, a graphic image of the letting go that follows a natural act of creation.

In verse 19, the Aramaic word *neshtwuwn*, translated as "agree," may also mean: to be worthy by being in harmony or equilibrium, to be fitting or qualified because of a balance of the forces between movement and stillness, or between any other two coextensive but paradoxical realities, like individuality and communion. The root of the Aramaic word for "ask," *dneshe'luwn*, is the same word as *pray* in Jesus' language. The word points to a direct, straightforward, passionate energy, like a line traced from one object to another, or like birds going to their watering place. We shall encounter this word again in chapter 10 in one of Jesus' sayings (see also *Prayers of the Cosmos*, p. 86ff).

As mentioned in my earlier work, the word translated as "father," *'aby*, may also indicate the "breathing life of all" and ultimately the archetype of all parenting, which is the active emanation of *ruha*, the sacred breath or spirit coming into form. The Aramaic version clearly shows that it is the quality of "wholeheartedness," in harmony with the intention of the universe, that empowers the energy of a prayer to be answered. The "answer" is really the resonance of the group heart (*leba*) affecting events that follow, rather than some inherent privilege of membership in a particular group.

In the final verse (verse 20), the Aramaic word *kniyshiyn* can mean to gather, hide or wrap oneself in something. In this case,

Jesus suggests wrapping oneself "with or within my *shem*" (*bshemy*), an expression that the Greek translation limited to the meaning: "in my name." An Aramaic view shows the variety of meanings that the root ShM holds. Like the creation described in Genesis 1:1, this root points to all wave- and vibration-related reality, the realm of communion that connects seeming individuals through light, sound, vibration and atmosphere. The Aramaic word *baynathuwn*, usually translated as "in the midst of" or "among," can also mean "alongside of," "inside" and "available for" whatever happens next.

4. The Next Thing, Part 1 - Surah Fatiha – Bismillah.

Sacred use of the *bismillah* phrase continues today as a practice throughout the many Sufi esoteric schools in the world. Murshid Samuel L. Lewis (Sufi Ahmed Murad Chisti), the Western Sufi and spiritual teacher who began the Dances of Universal Peace, wrote that seemingly impossible and unimaginable things could, with devotion, be accomplished through the use of this practice. Ultimately, the intention of this word of power calls us to remember our Source before we approach "the next thing."

By comparison, Christian theologian Matthew Fox (1986) has named the seminal spiritual reality of the Judeo-Christian tradition "original blessing" (in contradistinction to the nonbiblical theology of "original sin" later developed by St. Augustine). Using the sound of either the Aramaic phrase *bshemy* or the Arabic phrase *bismillah* as a meditation may remind us of our real origin and potential in a way that may lead us beyond concepts into an actual experience of blessing.

Every surah or chapter of the Qur'an except one begins with the Arabic formula *bismillah ar-rahman ar-rahim*, often translated "In the name of Allah, most Gracious, most Merciful." Some Islamic mystics have said that the essence of the Qur'an is contained in its first surah. In even more powerful fashion, this essence condenses in its first phrase and, most powerfully, in its first word.

Many Sufi mystics breathe or say *bismillah* as a word of power in order to begin the day, or a project or relationship, with the name, light and sound of Cosmic Unity. Like the Hebrew and Aramaic root *shm*, the equivalent Arabic root *sm* also points to the entire sphere of a being, its connections and atmosphere, the sign by which it is known. The prefixed preposition *b-* indicates whatever comes next or along with something, what advances or opens, an instrument or means, in addition to the usual meanings of "by," "with" or "in."

The word *Allah* (whose form is shortened in the second half of *bismillah*) is not a proprietary name of the divinity invented by Muslims, but a continued use of the same root/word of power existing for at least 6000 years in the Middle East, beginning with the Old Canaanite *Elat* and extending through the Hebrew *Elohim* and *Eloha* to the Aramaic *Alaha*. All of these words point to the reality of Cosmic Unity and Oneness, the ultimate force behind being and nothingness, which includes the most mysterious concept: Holy Absence, the "No" (LA) that balances the Holy Presence, "Yes" (AL, considered as the definite article, some "thing" differentiated from something else).

The word *bismillah* takes the same linguistic form as the statement Jesus makes in Matthew 18 about how to pray and come together in communion. In the Qur'an, the mystical formula for all beginnings affirms the same reality: "with the name, light, sound, experience, atmosphere of Unity." In the teaching of Jesus, one touches the *shem* of the One by attuning first to the atmosphere of another human being ("in *my shem...*") and then by following that atmosphere to the Source. In other words, there is a bridge between the particle and wave realities through the atmosphere of a mystic who could be at the center of both. The Qur'an, instead of pointing to Muhammad, affirms a direct connection to the sound and light of the Only Being.

The difference may have to do with six centuries of history between Jesus and Muhammad. Relying on dualistic translations that could not catch the nuances of Aramaic words like *shmaya* and *a'r'a'*, the church, at the time of Emperor Constantine in the 4th century, began to create creeds that transformed mystical experiences into concretized beliefs. It began to insist on the particular person of Jesus (not simply his *shem*) as standing between humanity and the Holy One.

With some knowledge of this, Muhammad insisted that no pictures or statues of himself should ever be made. Interestingly, none were made of Jesus either until after Constantine made Christianity the Roman imperial religion and the formulation of various Western Christian creeds created "heresy." Yet even in Islam, after the death of Muhammad, the prophet's personal way of life, prayer and conversation took on increasing importance, and his sayings were collected as *hadith*, or traditions. By doing so, Muhammad's followers also built a human bridge to the direct experience of Allah, especially by emulating the Prophet's personal way of prayer. Even though Muhammad had outlawed a separate priestly class, his recorded example became a legal precedent that has spurred discussion and argument (similar to those within Christian theology) between the legal experts of the various branches of the House of Islam.

5. I Am Not

This version is based on the literal translation of #31 in the collection by R.A. Nicholson (1898: 124-127).

Chapter Two

1. Before the Fireball - Genesis 1:2.

The Hebrew expression *tohu wabohu* (translated "without form and void" by the King James Version, KJV) refers to a potential germ of being contained within another such potential existence, revealing the layered idea of the abyss of being that is essential to Native Middle Eastern cosmology. Here the writer of Genesis describes the primordial state of the universe as being a seed of possibility enclosed within the shell of circumstance. Shell and seed coexist like problem and solution, question and answer. Does what is inside push its way through to the outside, or does what is outside call forth the latent potential of what is inside? This question helped begin the Universe, says the storyteller of these passages.

The story continues when a disturbance occurs on the "surface" of these potentials. The Hebrew word *choshekh* (pronounced at the beginning with an aspirated "h" sound), which is translated as "darkness" by the KJV, actually refers to a violent, disordered movement caused by an inner ardor that seeks to extend itself out of harmony with its surroundings. *Choshekh* is simultaneously a compression and a contraction, a tightening as well as a force trying to liberate itself—perhaps a graphic image of stress, whether healthy or unhealthy. This type of action shows an imbalance of the individual (particle) and communal (wave) realities of life. Yet, most importantly, this imbalance itself helps further the unfoldment of the cosmos.

The Hebrew says *wechoshekh 'al-penei tehom,* which the KJV translates "darkness was upon the face of the deep." *Penei* can mean the surface or the edge of something, or what first appears as phenomena, the initial aspect or countenance of anything. It can also mean the manner in which anything becomes present or enters the world of phenomena, or the idea of presence itself. We shall see some form of this word used throughout the Native Middle Eastern tradition, linking as it does with the later Sufi term *fana*, usually translated *effacement*. *Tehom* refers to the layered, seemingly bottomless, depths of existence. The collective sign *m* collects and unites all this "depth" into the absolute abyss of existence, which also paradoxically contains its most vital power.

Ruach (usually translated "spirit") is the force here that reminds stressful self-involvement—*choshekh*—of its place in the evolution of the universe. *Ruach* is the animating power of breathing that can also be variously translated as "soul," "wind," "ethereal breath" or a "force of expansion." As this passage closes, the breath of the Source touches the *mayim*. Much more than just "the waters," the latter word refers to the primordial, unawakened womb of existence, a fluid reality associated with the female principle of generation, the intimate essence of which, according to this cosmology, remains forever unknown. The KJV talks about *ruach* "moving" on the face of the waters. The biblical Hebrew *merachefet* can also mean to agitate, expand, dilate or actively generate something.

As the primordial womb (which combines the roots MH and IM) is impregnated by the divine breath *ruach* (RH), it becomes RHM or *rahm*—the activated womb, a raying forth of creativity, heat, compassion and mercy. Although the word *rahm* is not mentioned here, it is implied by the burst of light and energy that follows in the next verse. As we shall see, in its various forms in Hebrew, Aramaic and Arabic, *rahm* is the principle archetype of what we call unconditional love.

2. The Mother Womb Creates the Human.

This version is based partially on the translation of E. A. Speiser from the Old Babylonian and Assyrian as contained in James B. Pritchard's collection (1955: 99-100). In certain instances, I have retranslated some of the Old Babylonian (also a Semitic language) for greater clarity, including the following:

Speiser renders the Old Babylonian word *suq* in my lines 3-5 as the "burden of creation," which he says is a "pure guess." From the later

Semitic roots this word is similar to *shq*, which in the latter, related Semitic language Assyrian means both a burden, something carried, as well as any inclination to possess, or to be enveloped or absorbed by a task. This impulse to envelope can be seen as self-absorption, or in its more profound sense, reflexive consciousness, which is pictured as a layered state, like the skin of an onion.

The name for primal humanity, *lullu*, refers to a contradictory movement of two opposing forces—one drawing itself to a center and the other drawing away—linked by the vowel *u* which in sound meaning is the link between being and nothingness, the universal connector, the archetypal *and/or.*

The incantation first names the Great One, the goddess Inanna, who is first named *Mami.* Here we can see the original Semitic mother-root AM, which indicates all sources of maternity, creative possibility and the matrix of life. Or as a compound root, MA plus MI shows a being that embraces both generative power and energized fluidity. Further, as a combination of the sign of water doubled, MM, enlivened by the creative principle (A) and energizing life (I), we find yet another image of one of humanity's first, and most enduring, names for the Mother.

The latter two names of the Great One in the text (*Nintu* and *Ninhursag*) are variations of the root NN. This root indicates the continuity of existence through the continuance of generations, families and lineages: the new replaces, yet is linked to, the old. The word *Ninhursag* adds to this basic root the image of a circle gradually expanding from its center to embrace and augment new growth. In Babylonian mythology, Ninhursag was also associated with mountains, the breasts of the earth, similar to the original meaning of the Hebrew word *Shaddai.*

3. From Their Inner Wombs - Matthew 3:7.

These translations of one of the Beatitudes in Aramaic center on the key words *lamrachmane'* and *rachme'*, which are usually translated as "mercy" or "compassion." Following the older roots back to their source gives the additional meanings associated with the Hebrew *rahm*, the archetype of the original Sacred Womb: a long, heartfelt breath, shining from deep within a body, the sensation of all prayers answered, radiance of warmth, heat and ardor.

I have translated the initial word *tubwayhuwn* as "ripe" in distinction from the Aramaic word *bisha*, "unripe." Jesus often contrasts these two words in his teachings, but Greek-based translations usually render them as "good" and "evil." The earth-based, planting image revealed by the Aramaic text opens up the meaning considerably. *Tubwayhuwn* may also be translated as "happy" or "blessed" (because in tune with the sacred), "aligned with the One," "healthy" or "healed," "integrated" or "resisting the effects of entropy and deterioration," and "tuned to the Source." For further translations of sayings Jesus in Aramaic connected with "good" and "evil," see chapter nine of my book *The Hidden Gospel* (1999). For a complete translation of the Beatitudes in Matthew, see *Prayers of the Cosmos* (1990) and of those in Luke, see *Blessings of the Cosmos* (2006).

4. The Womb is a Great World.

The Mandaeans are a surviving offshoot of first century C.E. gnostics and heterodox Jewish sects, living today mostly in Iran. Their complex cosmology emphasizes knowledge (which is the meaning, in eastern Aramaic, of their name) as the solution to the usual states of "drunkenness," "oblivion" or "sleep" in which most people wander through life. Despite this ascetic-sounding philosophy, the Mandaeans take an interest in penetrating the mysterious depths of embodiment. Isolated from the theological developments of mainstream Christianity and Judaism, they continue to celebrate the sacred power of flesh, soul (pictured as an individualized ray of divine light, *nishimta*), breath (*ruha*) and womb (*marba* - the emanation of birth from within).

This version is based on a selection from Book I, Part 2 of Lady E.S. Drower's (1960) collection of Mandaean literature, *The Thousand and One Questions,* pp. 162-164. Additionally I have retranslated various qualities and concepts based on the Mandaean Aramaic transliteration she provides.

5. A Conversation About Rebirth - John 3:2-8.

In verse two, the word *'ameyn* can mean firmly, truly and in faithfulness. It can also mean to stand firmly or to assert something by what is firm underneath. At the time of Jesus, people regularly used this word as an affirmation either before or after making an important statement. George Lamsa (1939) comments about the place of this word in his native Aramaic-Assyrian culture: "When a priest or prince makes a statement the people generally respond by saying 'Amen' to indicate their ready acceptance and belief. When oral laws are enacted and proclaimed, the people raise their hands and say 'Amen' as a mark of approval and loyalty" (214).

The older roots of the word combine AM, indicating the "mother" or matrix of things with IN, indicating manifested, individual existence. No doubt there is a relationship here to the ancient Egyptian sacred word *ament,* which could be translated as "the ground of being." As in many surviving Neolithic cosmologies, some Egyptian stories tell of the "Lady of the Ament" who presided over this "underworld," a land of death and rebirth, which was the destination of the souls of the departed.

The phrase *metiyled men driysh,* usually translated "born again" literally reads "born from the source" or from the primary origin of all life in light and fire. The word *riysh* is related to the main Hebrew root in *bere'shit,* the first word of Genesis 1:1. The word *nechze'* in verse three points to an inner vision or contemplation (just as in Matthew 5:8, the sixth Beatitude, which mentions "seeing God"). The roots of the word point to being illuminated instantly, as by a flash of lightening.

The phrase *malkuwteh da'laha'*, used in many forms by Jesus, could best be translated as the "I Can" of the cosmos, a combined sense of creative fire and willingness to take responsibility for an idea or vision. The word also points to all ruling visions that can dominate the collective mind of humanity. When queens, and later kings, became part of Middle Eastern political scene, this same word-root was used to name them, thereby leading to the translations "queen" or "king." Here the "I Can" is that of *Alaha*, the One behind all beings. For more on this phrase, please see *The Hidden Gospel* (1999, especially chapter six).

In his response (3:4), Nicodemus clearly misunderstands Jesus' reference to returning to the source of existence, since he uses the construction *lkharsa' ... lme'al wnetiyled*, an expression that means to enter the space created by womb or belly, or the opening of the vagina.

In verse 5, the words *maya'* and *ruwcha'* are the same primordial waters and breath that we encountered in Genesis 1:2. Yeshua uses the word *dne'uwl*, indicating that entering the "I Can" of the cosmos can be experienced through one's embodied senses.

In verse 6, Yeshua plays with *besra'*, the word for "density" and "earthiness," both to contrast it with *ruwcha'*—breath, wind or inspiration—and to show Nicodemus his mistake in trying to apply particle-reality rules to wave-reality wisdom.

In verse 8, Yeshua continues this theme by pointing to the mysteries involved in the breath and winds. There were then—and still are now—many things we do not understand about why air masses around the planet move as they do. The weather is barely more predictable now than it was at the time of Yeshua. These mysterious movements—the coming together and bonding with which the entire universe embraces itself, the search for a harmonious relationship to the earth and embodiment—still drive most of our lives. The person who has returned to contemplate the Source moves in unison with the movements of the whole natural cosmos.

6. The Next Thing, Part 2 - Surah Fatiha.

The Arabic words *rahman* and *rahim* are both derived from the primitive Semitic root *rahm* or womb (*rahmat* in Arabic), previously discussed. Here the primordial womb of Sacred Unity emanates the first two qualities of the essence of the One: the active and receptive sides of warmth, heat, compassion, mercy and love. *Rahman* is the active, solar side, radiating regardless of its reception. It is, in Jesus' words, the sun that shines on the just and unjust. *Rahim* is the receptive, lunar side, responding without limit to all needs. Shakespeare expressed this energy of the universe in *The Merchant of Venice* when he wrote: "The quality of mercy is not strained. It droppeth as the gentle rain from heaven."

This important sacred phrase affirms that whenever we remember our true origins, we can begin our lives anew with the same sacred energy that began the cosmos. *ar-Rahman* and *ar-Rahim* are the first two of what are called the "99 Beautiful Names of Allah" in the Sufi tradition. For more on the Sufi tradition as well as a retranslation of these "pathways of the heart" from the Arabic, see my later work, *The Sufi Book of Life* (2005).

Chapter Three

1. Light Shall Be - Genesis 1:3.

The key word here, *aor*, refers to all varieties of light, intelligence and elemental energy, everything that is enlightening, or that produces joy, happiness and grace. It is a direct, straight-line energy, not whirling or spiraling like its counterpart *ash* (which appears later). The mysterious phrase *yehi 'aor wa yehi 'aor* (usually translated "let there be light, and there was light") presents an essential feature of this native mysticism: That which is created initially in principle, archetype or vision draws present reality into manifestation and embodied existence in accordance with the original vision. There is, so to speak, a "pull" from the past on the present that causes tendencies to unfold now.

The view of time in ancient Semitic languages is similar to a large caravan of which we are a part, with the past moving ahead of us, drawing us onward. There is likewise a "push" from the future which, using the same way of looking, is moving "behind us," willing us to fulfill our purpose in the present, in unison with the Holy One. In this synchronic view of time, both past potential and future possibility exert a real influence on the present. For more on this, see *The Genesis Meditations (2003)* as well as my work for Traditional Cosmology Society of the University of Edinburgh (2002). The notion that ancient Semitic peoples lived in a static, spatial universe is a major mistake in both language and epistemology by various scholars.

This view of the universe is also supported by recent research in scientific cosmology. Some scientists now regard the action of both the past and the future on the present as a fundamental principle of the development of the universe. To bring us to where we are today, they say, required more than a random series of developmental changes. The tendency or texture of the universe was toward a type of complexity that predisposed its entire development to the unique conditions that brought life as we know it into being on this planet, including human self-reflexive consciousness.

The Hebrew word *yo'mer,* usually translated as "said," also has several, more expansive, meanings. It points to a power that declares, manifests and reflects its own inner nature outside. In this tradition, to declare something with such power is a step in manifestation—its reality becomes engraved on the vibratory slate of the cosmos, so to speak.

In verse 4, the word *yar',* usually translated as "saw," may also mean to direct a straight ray of intelligence toward something. This word is closely related to the one for light. That is, the quality of the One itself that recognized the light was, in fact, drawn forth by the new existence of light. The word *tob,* usually translated as "good," means more exactly ripe or appropriate for the moment and thereby healthy, integrated, capable of conserving energy and setting aside corruption (same root as the Aramaic *tubwayhuwn* used to begin each of the Beatitudes in Matthew). The word *yabdel,* usually translated as "divided," refers to an interior activity that causes things to become distinct or individual. For notes on *choshekh,* the primordial dark, please see the textual notes on the preceding Genesis passage in chapter two.

2. Your Radiance Suckles Every Blade of Grass.

This excerpted version is based on earlier literal translations of an El-Amarnah tomb text by John A. Wilson in James B. Pritchard's collection (1955: 370-371) and by Adolf Erman (1927: 289-291). In the first stanza, I have re-translated and given an expanded version of the sacred names Re, Har-akhti, Shu and Aton based on their underlying roots and meanings using the studies of E.A. Wallis Budge (1895, 1911a, 1911b), an early Egyptologist, and the Hebrew-Egyptian etymological comparisons of Fabre D'Olivet (1815).

3. The "I Am" Illuminates - John 8:12.

About twenty years ago, most biblical studies scholars felt that John's Gospel was written first in Greek. That opinion has gradually changed, as many scholars have re-evaluated the relationship between the community that produced the Gospel of John, and that which produced the Gospel of Thomas. Now, a leading point of view is that both John and Thomas may have been originally composed in Syriac Aramaic. For more on this, see *The Genesis Meditations* (2003). To make things simpler, we can say that if Jesus spoke these words, he said them in Aramaic, since all of his listeners were native Aramaic speakers. In addition, an Aramaic view is the most helpful for discerning the native spirituality and way of prayer behind the words, before they came to be considered through the lens of Platonic philosophy and later theological overlays.

In the Aramaic subtext of Jesus' "I Am" statements, we have the Native Middle Eastern approach to the question of individuality. If everything is linked in communion with the Holy One, why do we have individuality and how does it serve the universe's unfolding? In the Aramaic expression Jesus uses here, *'ena' 'na'*, we have an intensification of the word for "I," literally the "I-I" or "the I of I." This is not an abstraction of the "I" but a distillation of its essence, as the alternate meanings of the roots show.

As mentioned in textual note three in chapter one, the "wave reality" or *shem* of an individual is a bridge to her or his consciousness of the Only Individual ("God," so to speak). So in using "I-I" as he does here, Jesus is both including and pointing beyond his personal awareness of cosmic Unity. He is the bridge for those who attune to him in this way. A number of scholars have noted that speaking in this "I am" formula linked Jesus to the tradition of Holy Wisdom, who united various "voices," inner and outer into a greater unity (again see *Genesis Meditations,* 2003).

Here Jesus points out that a deep, evolving, sense of "I" or interiority illuminates and guides all primal matter. The source of this "I" is not personal egotism, but the Only Self—the Holy One. This sense of unfolding is built into every atom of the cosmos, not only the so-called "organic" life.

The Aramaic word *nuwhreh* is directly related to the Hebrew *aor*. The addition of N to the root adds a sense of newness and youth to the illumination, yielding light which leads or guides somewhere, like a lamp or beacon. The word *alma'*, usually translated "world" refers to all primal matter, vegetation, development and the collection of them into masses, unions and conjunctions, each being a "world" (similar to the sense we saw in the Mandaean hymn in chapter two). The word *cheshuwkha'* is the Aramaic form of the Hebrew word *choshekh*, which we saw in the Genesis 1:2 passage: darkness, unknowing. This non-linear, seemingly chaotic reality is necessary for creation to come forth, for when holy breath (*ruach*) makes love with darkness (*choshekh*), light or knowing (*aor*) is born. This is a brief gloss on the entire beginning of Genesis as well as on this saying of Yeshua. The Aramaic word *haye'* means life energy, embodied in the forms of creation, but with its origin in the divine Life. As we shall see later, the roots of this word in Hebrew compose the most sacred (and "unnameable") name in Judaism.

4. Metaphors of Light - Surah 24:35.

Whole books have been written on the spiritual significance of this one *ayat* or verse of the Qur'an, and no translation or interpretation can completely do it justice. My expanded version includes some of the alternate meanings of the Arabic text, but the mystery to which the verse points is a matter of experience rather than mental understanding.

The word *masalu* (in line C) can be a parable or a symbol, a line of meaning drawn between one thing and another. The word usually translated "niche," *mishkat*, can be any space that envelopes energy or consciousness, that sculpts and focuses it as a lamp shade does light. It also points to the image of shrouds or veils within veils, or the skin of an onion. The lamp itself, *misbah*, also indicates other, more physical layers of the veils. The glass, *zujajah* (line D) is the exterior of this dynamic form, both protecting the light inside as well as obscuring it, depending upon one's personal history or development through life.

As the verse's metaphor continues to develop and expand in all directions (like light itself), it leaps across the cosmos: We are taken in line E from the glass to the stars (*kawkabun*), a word based on a root pointing to burning and combustion. This burning radiates both a fragrance and an ethereal atmosphere (*durriyyuny*). The light of the stars also comes from somewhere, and following the metaphor of fragrance, we come to the blessed tree (*shajaratim*) in line F. The roots of this word point to any combination of movement and growth that brings a being back to face its original Self.

At this point (line G) the image of the olive tree (*zaytuha*) enters. The roots of the word also point to a luminous ray, flash of light, grace or brightness. We are reminded of the illuminated essence of every being that one can see at moments when its purpose in life shines out. This "tree of life" is neither of "East nor West": in an alternative meaning, it has nothing to do with either liberation or bondage—it shines because of its nature to shine. It does not need to be ignited from the outside.

Then comes the beautiful phrase in line H, *nurun ala nur*—light from (or upon) light. The only place the metaphor can end is in the end of metaphor, that is, in the Only Reality, the One (*Allah*, embedded in the word *yahdillahu*, line I). Ultimately the One provides the only context for all metaphors: the Being behind the Universe has a clear desire (*yashaa*—usually translated as "whom he wills") that unfolds its ongoing story. This desire is heard as a call by those who are receptive to it (as Jesus also pointed out: "those with ears to hear").

The signs of the call are everywhere, all of manifestation serves to connect us to it. The last word *alim,* usually translated as "know" may also mean to comprehend or embrace a thing. What Oneness embraces here is *kulli shayim,* the entire particle reality of the cosmos.

5. Unity's Disguises – Hadith.

The collected sayings of Muhammad, while not considered in the same class of sacredness as the Qur'an, nevertheless have become an important source of guidance and precedent for Muslims. This saying complements the verse of light by noting that a metaphor can reveal or hide truth, just like a veil (*hijaba*). The latter word can mean anything which covers, wraps, screens, obscures, outshines, eclipses or shelters. The number seventy thousand may relate to a sense of endlessness. The word contrasted here with *nur* is *zulmatin,* the ultimate extinction of light, the deepest darkness imaginable, the vanishing, cessation or disappearance of intelligence. It can also refer to a shadow that moves or reflects some ultimate source. In this connection, it is directly related to the Hebrew root *tzlm,* which refers to the divine image or shadow in which humanity is created in Genesis 1:26. The same Arabic word (and it's implications) is used in the "zikr of Jonah," rendered in chapter nine. The Being of Beings itself is beyond both brilliance and eclipse, both glare and shadow. To think that the Only Being is only in light and not darkness is also a veil. Both are needed for complete creation.

6. The Back of the Mirror.

The Sufi poet Mevlana Jelaluddin Rumi is renowned throughout the Middle East as the greatest mystical poet of all time. He met his teacher and beloved friend, Shams-i-Tabriz unexpectedly. Shams (whose name also means "the sun") appeared suddenly one day while Rumi was studying. The raggedy dervish seized all of Rumi's scholarly writings and according to one account, threw them down a well. Shams offered to make them reappear if Rumi wanted, or he could help him open his heart. Rumi chose the heart. This collection of poems bears Shams' name because Mevlana felt that they were the result of his guidance, or, even more intimately, the voice of Shams coming through him.

This version is based on a literal translation of number 4 in the collection by R.A. Nicholson (1898: 14-17). I have added the titles for this and all selections from Rumi, Hafiz, Shabistari and Sa'adi. Classical Persian poetry has no titles, only numbers related to the volumes in which they were collected.

The saying of Allah in the second stanza, "I was a hidden treasure, and I created the universe so that I might be known" is from a "Hadith Qudsi," that is a "sacred saying" of Allah through Prophet Muhammad, but which is not in the Qur'an. It is often quoted in Sufi literature.

Chapter Four

1. The First Day - Genesis 1:5.

The Hebrew word *yiqra'*, usually translated "called," can also mean to engrave a sign or character, to compress something into a firm course or fate, and also to name. To the extent that the *shem* (vibration, atmosphere, light) of every being was beyond one particular name, this act of engraving by the Cosmos compressed the more expansive energies of Light and Dark, considered in the last chapter, into their more particular characters of Day and Night, *yom* and *layela.*

It should be clear that the "day" and "night," *yom* and *layela,* talked about here are not, in the cosmological sense, periods that add up to twenty-four of our hours. The addition of M to the root IO in Semitic languages means a gathering or massing of this intelligence, illumination and straight, radiant energy. The latter root is related to *aor,* the light. The word *layela,* from the root LL or LIL, points to all circular, swirling movement that draws toward and away from a center, as well as any force that binds or envelopes things in such a vortex.

The Genesis 1 story alludes to at least two aspects of this opening and closing. First, the entire primordial cosmos opened with a period of spontaneous lucid creation—the fireball, "singularity" or other event that began the universe we know—and is closing during a period in which such radiant creation is being consolidated. For instance, the birth of galaxies was a one-time event that happened ten to fourteen billion years ago. The conditions for this creation cannot, as far as we know, be recreated (although some scientists are attempting it). From the standpoint of the galaxies, we are still in the period of consolidating and using the energy and elements that the fireball or "singularity" at the beginning of the universe seeded. We are still in the first "night."

Second, according to this Native Middle Eastern story, the process of opening and closing, of radiating and consolidating, continues to repeat itself with each new creation. The first "day" on earth might have begun as the planet attained a fixed orbit and rotation in relation to the sun. Our journey toward and away from light began to repeat itself regularly rather than constantly create itself anew. The regular pulse of light for a certain period created a way to measure duration and to create the perceptions that various cultures have called *time.*

The phrase *wayehi-'ereb wayehi-boqer,* usually translated "there was evening, there was morning" refers to two further refinements of this opening and closing. The root of *'ereb* points to a process whereby things and energy congeal, become denser and move toward a purpose. Correspondingly, *boqer* points to an expansion, renewal and new beginnings.

2. The Right Time and Place.

Starting around 1700 B.C.E, the Persian prophet Zarathustra Spitama brought a universal message of One Being based on freedom and tolerance, which influenced the development of Hinduism, Buddhism, Judaism, Christianity and Islam. For almost a thousand years, Zoroastrianism was the dominant religion of the Iranian plateau, and while there was a brief interruption during the Alexandrian conquests, the Zoroastrian Parthian Empire rivaled that of Rome during the time of Jesus. The Parthians gave way to the Sassanians, who were also Zoroastrians, in the third century C.E. and lasted until the Arab Islamic conquest in the seventh century.

From this time, the number of Zoroastrians declined drastically. A large remnant resettled in India in the ninth century. This group is usually called the Parsis (people from *Pars* or Persia). Today there are between 125,000 and 200,000 Zoroastrians in the world (the number living in Iran is disputed). Many who had lived in Iran up until the twentieth century have moved to Europe or North America because of persecution from Islamic fundamentalists.

The *Ashem Vohu* is one of the central daily prayers of Zoroastrianism and affirms the wisdom that to be in right relationship with the natural world, as a face of the Only Being, is the true source of happiness. The word *ashem* (based on *asha*) points to the sense of timeliness, right direction and ripeness that guides the universe. The word *vohu*, usually translated as "good," points to the source of universal guidance and blessing, the heart of the cosmos.

My version retranslates the key sacred term (*asha*) and is based on comparisons with several previous literal translations including Jafarey (1988: 42-43), Boyce (1979: 38) and Dhalla (1942: 2). Zoroastrian scholar Ali A. Jafarey comments on this prayer:

> Righteousness [*asha*] is the universal law that stands for order, evolution, progress and the perfection as ordained by God for the cosmos. One becomes righteous by doing the right thing at the right time, in the right place and with the right means to obtain the right result. It means precision in every thought, word and deed. It means constant improvement and continuous renovation. It brings enlightenment, true happiness, provided that happiness is shared by others (43).

3. Tomorrow Means Things Depart - Matthew 6: 33-34.

The word *b'aw*, usually translated "seek," can indicate any rushing, harsh, anxious movement including searching and boiling. The word *luwqdam*, usually translated "first," comes from the root QDM, which points to the primordial, originating time of the universe, the earliest "before." *Malkuwteh* is another form of the "I Can" energy of the cosmos—the ruling principles, ideals and visions of the One being, *Alaha*.

The Aramaic word *zadiyquwteh* is based on an old Hebrew word, *tzadak*, which, like the Ashem Vohu prayer, refers to a sense of straightness, faithfulness, mercy and honesty—all attained by restoration of a right relationship with the cosmos. It is related to Arabic names like *Sadiq* and *Siddiq*.

The phrase *khulheyn haleyn*, usually translated "all these things," literally refers to the sum total of universal "thing-ness," including all vessels, vehicles, tools, accomplishments, mental and emotional states—anything one might attempt to possess.

The word *mettawspan*, usually translated "shall be added unto you," is based on an important Middle Eastern mystical root SPh, which points to whatever is added to complete, perfect or achieve consummation in a thing or being. This quality represents a dynamic wholeness, an ability to embrace all points of view and states of feeling. It also points to one who becomes a threshold or an open doorway, or one who pours out or prostrates the small sense of self in order to receive the Self of the One. Later this same root may have become part of the name *sufi* in Arabic. Here Jesus says that when we pursue a right relationship with the depth of Being, or the universal One, and allow this relationship to realign our life, we produce a condition of receptivity in which we will receive anything we need to help complete our purpose in life.

In verse 34, the Aramaic *hakhiyl ti'tzpuwn*, usually translated "take thought," points to a tortured state of watching over and trying to hold on to things. The word *mchar* (first used in the form *damchar*) is usually translated as "tomorrow." It comes from a root that points to what passes away or into disuse due to the effects of time and the elements. In Aramaic, "tomorrow" literally means "what passes away" or "things depart." And, according to Jesus, tomorrow watches while time and the elements cleanse each new day of what no longer belongs.

Following this theme, Jesus again uses a word with the SPh root, the one for completeness, but turns the metaphor inside out. Each illuminated period (*yawma'*), or each day, carries its perfect complement (*sapeq*) of unripeness or inappropriate action (*biyshteh*). This last word is usually translated as "evil" but really refers in Aramaic to any action that is not done in its right time, that is, either too early or too late. The implication here is that even unripe action has its place in the broader sense of all-embracing wholeness, which the universe's developmental creation produces each day.

4. The Day is Nearly Over - Surah 103.

Surah Al 'Asr is a short, early Meccan surah sometimes used in the Islamic daily prayers. It reminds us that loss is a function of the cosmos. No forms, including human ones, are intended to last forever or to think themselves omnipotent.

In the second line, the Arabic word *'asr,* usually translated as "time" or "time through the ages" also means what is pressed down, sold, compressed as though from the outside, bounded, limited or restricted. As we have already seen, all of these are naturally associated with the effects of time in Native Middle Eastern cosmology. There was no sense of "unlimited natural resources" or denial of mortality, both of which have plagued modern consciousness. The sense of "eternal time" is Platonic, not ancient Semitic.

In the third line, the word *insana* refers to humanity or human existence. It is made up of two older roots: IN, which points to an individual existence created by a vortex of contracting energy and SN, which points to the light given off by a polished gemstone. The word *khusr,* usually translated as "loss," also refers to anything that is only temporary or that diminishes in volume, like a shelter or momentary refuge.

In the next section, the word *'amanu* comes from *iman,* a central concept usually translated as "faith." The word also points to a matrix of meaning, a mother-principle that includes all determined, unshakable and beneficent actions, energy that gives without expecting to receive. The words *'amilus sallihati,* usually translated as "righteous deeds," refer to all effects that spread from a soft, open connection to the Only Being and that are fully formed, complete from beginning to end. Developing both of these qualities of being—beneficence and openness—mitigates the wearing effects of time, says the Qur'an, because they focus on giving rather than grasping.

In the last section, the Qur'an says that coming together in community (*tawasaw*) to cultivate and share wisdom with each other helps counteract the stress of time. In particular, the Qur'an mentions two sacred qualities that can be named and celebrated. The first is *haqqi*, (based on *haqq*), usually translated as "truth" but deriving from an older Semitic root meaning "the breath of wisdom from underneath." In its Egyptian form this is *hek* (used in the sacred name Hek Mat); in its Hebrew form this is *Hokhmah*, holy wisdom, who reappears later in chapter 6. One could translate *haqq* as the sacred knowing within us that recognizes the truth in and of the moment, the reality here and now. The second quality is *sabr* (derived from *sabur*), which is usually translated as "patience." It also refers to all fixed boundaries, limits and disciplines that serve as useful channels to focus the fire and flow of the cosmos. These two are also numbered among the "99 Beautiful Names." For more on them, see *The Sufi Book of Life (2005).*

5. The Past Flies Away.

Little is known about the life of Sa'duddin Mahmud Shabistari. He was born near Tabriz, northwest Persia, in about 1250 C.E., the same town noted as the birthplace of Mevlana Rumi's teacher, Shams. Shabistari is said to have written "The Secret Rose Garden" in reply to questions asked him by a Sufi doctor of Herat. This version is based on previous literal translations by Florence Lederer (1920), E.H. Whinfield (1880) and Johnson Pasha (1903).

6. Time, Patience and Love.

Hafiz lived about a century after Shabistari and Rumi. Born in about 1320 in Shiraz, Persia (the same birthplace as Sa'adi), he is said to have died about 1390 C.E. He suffered the loss of both his wife and his son, whom he mourns in his poems. According to some writers, he was a closet Zoroastrian mystic, and his references to wine, taverns and cupbearers have coded meanings.

According to others, he was an Islamic Sufi, albeit very unorthodox. According to this opinion, all his images have references to the wine of divine ecstasy, the meeting house for sacred practices and the spiritual guide. No matter which opinion (or both) is correct, it seems clear that Hafiz was a free spirit who embarrassed everyone. He uses metaphors based on his own experience of love, disappointment, inebriation, ecstasy and the natural world. His emotional life itself became a guide to the spiritual path, one that led him to connect ever more deeply with the Feeling behind all feeling. Even confusion, impatience and boredom became his teachers, as we shall see in subsequent selections.

This version is based on literal translations of number 48 from the "Diwan" of Hafiz translated by Justin Huntly McCarthy (unpublished manuscript) and H. Wilberforce Clarke (1891). While I am not able to capture either the rhyme or poetic form of Hafiz's poetry, I attempt to remain faithful to the actual words he uses and their meaning in a Sufi sense.

Chapter Five

1. The Earth's Personal Space - Genesis 1:6-8.

To contemplate the wisdom embedded in the Hebrew text of Genesis brings up the questions: were its authors passing down very ancient stories reworked from oral tradition? If so, on what were these stories based, considering that no humans were around during the "beginning times" described? Was it pure imagination, and if so, how does one account for the fact that there are clear correspondences to habits of the universe that scientists have only recently discovered and articulated?

The most compelling explanation might be that some cellular memory of early storytellers gave them access to images for the broad sweep of how the universe evolved. In William Blake's words, perhaps they really did "see eternity in a blade of grass and the universe in a wildflower." Since humans are not simply self-contained particles inhabiting an inert universe but are intimately interlaced with its evolving story, long periods of communion with the natural world can evoke a knowledge of the universe's basic habits and tendencies. Isolated from such communion, we tend to see such knowledge as special "wisdom." We enshrine it in sacred scriptures, which then often become the basis of disputes. However, all sacred texts and stories are inspired by the human relationship to the cosmos and nature. According to the modern Sufi, Hazrat Inayat Khan (1978), "There is only one sacred manuscript, the sacred manuscript of Nature, which alone can enlighten the reader."

In this portion of the Genesis story, we confront immediately the mysterious word usually translated as "firmament." In the Hebrew text, this is *raqia'*, a process that rarifies or attenuates things and makes them more expansive. All its meanings center on what we call space, in particular, an emptiness that is creative. The addition of this spaciousness to the dark wave-matter of the primordial universe created the density differences we usually call our atmosphere.

The words *mabdil* (verse six) and *yabdel* (verse seven) are usually translated as "divide." They are based on a root (BD) that means to separate the natures of a being in order to create diversity, individuality or peculiarity. The word *mittachat,* usually translated as "below," refers in this relation to what is less spacious, denser or more closed. Its opposite is *me'al,* usually translated as "above,"—a sense of exaltation, breaking the bounds of confinement. This latter word is still used in its Arabic form (*hal*) to describe temporary states of ecstasy that Sufi mystics experience from spiritual practice.

In verse 8, we see the primordial archetype of "wave reality," or ShM (root of *shamayim*) becoming embodied as the personal space and vibratory atmosphere surrounding our planet. Neither infinite contraction nor infinite expansion, this atmosphere makes possible not only life but also sound. The density difference created by *raqia'* serves as a sort of dome that allows sound to resonate and be heard. Our ears and vocal cords were ultimately shaped by this earlier development of wave reality in our region. Sky embodies the archetype of freedom, expansiveness and choice. At the same time, it presents an obvious but often overlooked message about the communion of all species: There is only one sky, we all breathe one breath. It is difficult to get around this point without completely denying a interdependent relationship with nature. Unfortunately, this is generally what modern Western culture has done.

2. The Depths of Shamash.

This version is based on a fragmentary text translated by Ferris J. Stephens from the Akkadian manuscripts in the library of Ashurbanipal, 668-633 B.C.E. as collected in James B. Pritchard's collection (1955: 389).

The name *Shamash* is related to the Semitic root *shem,* the vibratory wave reality of the cosmos. Although most scholars consider the Babylonian Shamash to be male, there is equally good evidence that she was part of a long Middle Eastern tradition that embodied the sun and sky as female. For a thorough discussion of sun-sky goddesses in many traditions, see Janet McCrickland's (1990) study *Eclipse of the Sun.*

3. Hear the Sound - Deuteronomy 6:4.

This passage is one of the most sacred in Judaism and contains worlds of meaning. My expanded translation can at best be called a meditation for that reason. The first stanza elaborates on themes contained in the word *shema',* which is derived from the root ShM that we saw in the previous selection.

Many Jewish mystics have noted that the word *israel* points not only to a name for the Jewish people but to all humanity. It is composed of multiple roots that show all beings as streaks or rays (RA) of manifestation (I) from Oneness, the Sacred "That" or *El.* The same root also expresses itself in a verb that can mean to struggle, persevere or exert oneself. The second stanza works with these alternate meanings.

The sacred name used here, *yhwh,* is the nameless or "unnameable" name, which is usually not pronounced in Jewish prayers. The four letters YHWH can be rendered as roots multiple ways, which lead to a variety of meanings. I have focused here on rendering the root HH as primary. Modified by the other letters it expresses ever-living Life, in the past, present and future. Really the roots express action rather than a state of being, an action pre-existing, existing and post-existing simultaneously. In ancient Hebrew, one finds no strict separation between what we normally call past, present and future. I have elaborated on this in my fourth book *The Genesis Meditations* (2003), which reviews the long, usually buried, tradition of creation mysticism in Judaism, Christianity and Islam.

For this translation of *yhwh*, I am also indebted to my good friend Rabbi Arthur Waskow, who has pointed out that arguments over how the name may have been originally pronounced are moot. Perhaps the four letters, he says, read as consonants, never had vowels attached. In that case, they could only be heard or expressed as emulating the sound of one's own breath, the sacred name of the One unique to each person. The reader will find other possible meanings of *yhwh* in the translation of Isaiah's vision in chapter thirteen.

The life energy behind the universe, expressed in our own breath, points to *'Elohenu*, which can be seen as the "that" (*el*) and "not that" (*lo*) of existence. Viewed in this way, we can see the sacred name as the unity of all opposites, the "yes/no" of reality. The name is also connected to *Elohim*, the One that is Many. It may be a struggle to find Ever-Living Life, the one mystery behind the cosmos, in the diversity of situations, beings and relationships we face each day. When we do, however, the same Ever-Living Life leads us to sacred communion. There is a center where all lines meet (*'echad*). Being conscious of the divine breath in our own breathing allows us to follow any "one" to its depth, bringing us back to the One.

4. By the Heart and by the Tongue.

This hymn to Ptah reveals an essential feature of the way Native Middle Eastern cosmology sees life coming into form. The process described has become the basis for several versions of a "law of manifestation." Whether or not what the text describes is a "law," we can say that the universe demonstrates certain habits that support the creative process that the Egyptian "technicians of the sacred" told about almost 5000 years ago. The essence is contained in the final statement: space unfurls / heart reveals / voice clarifies / life creates.

This version is based on literal translations of the Egyptian text, dated between 2700 and 700 B.C.E., by John A. Wilson as contained in James B. Pritchard's collection (1955:5) and by J.H. Breasted (1933:

35). I have retranslated and given expanded meanings for the key sacred names based on their underlying Semitic roots and meanings, also using the works of E.A. Wallis Budge (1895, 1911a, 1911b), an early Egyptologist, and the Hebrew-Egyptian etymological comparisons of Fabre D'Olivet (1815) as references.

5. Ethphatah—Be Opened! - Matthew 7:32-35.

One of the arguments for an original Aramaic text of the Gospels, according to the Aramaic-speaking churches (which include the Syrian Orthodox and Assyrian Church of the East) is that even the so-called original Greek version contains several Aramaic words. We see one example here. Other Aramaic expressions rendered literally include idioms such as "poor in spirit," and "meek...inherit the earth." The latter are clearly based on a lack of understanding of the original Aramaic expression, much like the American expression "to buy a pig in a poke" does not translate literally.

This version is based on an expansion of the Aramaic word of power "*ethphatah*," which seems clearly based on the older Egyptian word *ptah*. This invocation of the space-clearing dimension of the universe, which is also connected with name, hearing and sound, continued to be used by the desert mystics in the Middle East. It reappears as the Arabic *al-Fatah*, "the opener of the way," which is another of the "99 Beautiful Names of Allah." Chanting this word in the same fashion that Jesus used with the deaf man continues to this day.

6. The Opening - Surah Fatiha 1.

Just as the *bismillah* phrase contains the essence of Qur'an, so does its first surah, in more expanded fashion. One version or commentary cannot do it justice. Here, the Surah helps summarize the first stage of our journey through sacred diversity and prepare us for the one into the depth of interiority.

After beginning with the *bismillah* phrase, affirming the positive and receptive sides of divine love, the surah emphasizes praise. The second stanza focuses on the multiple meanings of the word *alhamdulillahi,* which points beyond mere verbal praise to the way in which the essential purpose or *hamd* of every being is constantly dedicating itself to the One Being. The third stanza focuses on the words *rabbi-l'alamin,* sometimes translated "cherisher and sustainer of the worlds." The root RB points to all action that gathers, grows and brings something to fruition. The word *alamin* indicates not only material worlds, but all collections of matter, meaning, learning and knowledge.

Then, as though to emphasize their central position, the surah repeats the words *rahman* and *rahim,* reminding us of the Womb from which all life has come. The phrase *maliki yaumadin,* usually translated "Master of the Day of Judgment" is based on the same Semitic root we encountered earlier (MLK), which points to the "I Can" of the cosmos. The "day" (*yaum*) is also related to the word we saw used in both Genesis and the saying of Jesus. It is an illuminated period of time. Here what the surah spotlights is an archetypal unraveling of causes and effects, the return of all elements to their source. From this standpoint, the One Being is "backing out" of time in the same way it is "coming in," as described in Genesis. On another level, this sense of timelessness, the unraveling of complexity, a pristine sense of discrimination, is an experience that many people have had. It is cultivated by mystical practice in the Middle East. In this sense, the words *maliki yaumadin* are about an awareness *now* more than they are an eschatological statement about the proverbial *later. Later* and *before* are always connected due the synchronic nature of ancient Semitic languages.

The next half of the surah offers a prayer that One Being use us in whatever way it chooses. The phrase *iyyaka n'abudu wa iyyaka nastain* affirms the intention to cut through all distractions, diversions and clinging patterns of mind, to serve and receive sustenance only from the Source. The next phrase, *ihdinas siratal mustaqim,* contains several words of power. The word *ihdinas,* usually translated as "show" comes from another of the "99 Beautiful Names" in Arabic—*al-Hadi,* which also means to guide, show a path, or hear a voice that gives direction. The word *mustaqim,* usually translated as "straight," is related to the sacred Name *al-Qayyum,* which points to all energy that rises, wakes up, stands up and continues to do way repeatedly. It is the One's repeated "wake-up call" that cuts through mental and emotional muddles. Both *qayyum* and its related word *qiyama* have Aramaic predecessors.

Finally, the path of the Universe Being (which we have just asked to follow) is described further. The path is filled with delight and abundance (*ladhina*) as well as a sense of wonder and grace (*an'amta*), which every being carries from the Source. The path is not about frustration or annoyance (*maghdubi*); it is not, in fact, about losing our way (*dhalin*). The way is not meant to be difficult or obscure; it becomes that only when we wander too far from the heart of the matter, from *rahman* and *rahim,* the Wellspring of Love with which we began.

Chapter Six

1. The Essence of Seed - Genesis 1:9-13.

In verse nine, the Universe Being again "speaks," that is, it engraves its purpose by manifesting a development that leads to increased diversity, interiority and communion. The Hebrew word *yiqqawu*, which is not translated in the KJV, indicates that this calling forth by the Universe was tending toward a purpose or driving toward a goal. The phrase *hammayim mittachat hashamayim*, usually translated "waters under the heavens," refers to a vibratory state of flow that was less than that of the primordial manifested atmosphere.

As each part of the flow found its own optimum level, the settling process created relative stability, pointed to by the Hebrew words *'el-maqom 'echad*, usually translated as "one place." This "place" is the counterpart of the word *me'al* in verse 7 (a state of expansion that is unstable). Just as *me'al* is related to the Arabic *hal*, used by the Sufis to indicate a temporary state of ecstasy, so *maqom* becomes in Arabic *makam*, the embodiment of a mystical state as a "station," a way that one lives everyday life. According to scientists, all the planets in our system went through this process of "settling down" into a more embodied state with a center or core.

The word *yabbasha*, usually translated as "dry land," actually carries no reference to "land" at all. The word refers to an inner burning and continuous combustion, a radiant ferment that empowers the next step in the process. This inner fire results when the expanded wave energy finds a way to live in form—the pulsation of the fireball within a body. On one level we could see this as the earth's molten, magnetic core. On a psychological level, the embodiment of an expanded spiritual experience or state can, if worked with in a conscious fashion, lead to a more integrated sense of one's real self or interiority—of one's heart's purpose.

Again, without looking for exact correspondences, there seems to be a relation here to the earth's own process:

> When Earth reached the state where the heaviest elements were at the center and the lightest at the surface, the geological ordering would have ended had it been guided by the gravitational attraction alone. But breaking up this static order was the radioactive energy. The unstable elements created by the stellar explosion broke apart and released their energy. This heat, arising throughout the planets, kept them in a boil. (Swimme and Berry, 1992, p. 82)

Previously, we saw the universal wave reality of *shamayim* embodied in the primordial atmosphere of the planet. In verse 10, we now see evolving the more embodied characters of particle reality (*aretz*) and flow (*yammim*), the latter based on the same root as *mayim*.

The key words in verse 11, *tadshe'* and *deshe' 'eseb*, usually translated as "bring forth" and "grass" are both based on the root DSh, which points to everything that gives seed or germinates. The root is related to RSh, which we saw earlier in the first word of this story *bere'shit*. The words here point to an embodied center that unfolds movement, a seed that sprouts and grows from an inner self or origin. According to this tradition, each seed, each primordial living cell, unfolded from a centralized interiority that mirrored the one-time unfolding of the whole universe.

The phrase *mazria' zera'* in verses 11 and 12, usually translated as "herb yielding seed," refers to something that leaves a material enclosure and spreads, disperses and radiates, that diverges from a previously set pattern. The process of unfolding from a center involves built-in spontaneity in this universe, it seems. Similarly, some scientists now see that the self-organizing quality of a being (and some other natural phenomena, like flocks of birds and clouds) is related to its unpredictability (part of the so-called "chaos theory"). The word *'etz*, usually translated "tree," refers to any vegetable substance offered to the senses of another being. It represents the entire principle of vegetation and instinctual growth, rather than a specific tree. This distinction has profound implications for a later phase of the Genesis story.

Even the first living cells on this planet, the prokaryotes of four billion years ago, which did not exchange genetic material with others, showed this spontaneity from their own interior depth. Swimme and Berry comment:

> Throughout the whole of the early seas, cells gave birth to new versions of themselves, but they did so in a way that produced offspring slightly different than themselves. Once every million births, a cell was created that was new.... This phenomenon—*genetic mutation*—is a primal act of life. Mutation explains a great deal of life's story in much the same way that gravitation explains a great deal of the galactic story. (1992, p. 88)

2. Sacred Power and Sacred Sense - Proverbs 1:7.

The word *yir'at,* usually translated as "fear" can also mean terror, reverence, awe, veneration and respect. The next word is the most sacred name in Judaism, so sacred that for many centuries it has not been pronounced. As noted in note two in chapter five, there are many traditions behind this. One, according to D'Olivet, is that the name originally was not pronounced with any consonants at all. To make compressed and limited what was meant to be expanded and unlimited (as in pronouncing the name "Jehovah" or "Yahweh," as many Christians do) constitutes a curse and not a blessing. A certain knowledge of the mysticism of sound is necessary to pronounce the name at all. As I wrote in the note in the previous chapter, another point of view is that originally the name had no vowels at all, making its "pronunciation," the natural expression of a person's breath.

Be that as it may, the meaning of the word is sublime and multilayered. A few meanings are given in this translation, and more will appear in later translations. Suffice it to say here that the roots of the word can be rendered several different ways, starting with HH, indicating the life behind all elementary life. To this is added the action of life manifested (I) and the power that shuttles back and forth between being and nothingness (U). Here I use the transliteration YHWH to mark the place of the name. It could also be transliterated IHUH or IHOH.

The third word of the verse, *re'shit,* again returns us to the beginning-ness, the primal origins of Genesis 1. Conscious interiority begins with a sense of awe for the force behind the Universe, says this passage. Holy Wisdom or *Hokhmah* is not only an archetypal quality (worthy of being capitalized) but also the first voice within our own sense of "depth," our inner self. Her name may be translated in perhaps as many ways as YHWW, but we can start with the breath of manifested Life (the first H, the letter *heth*), which enters the middle of collected manifestation (KhM) and leaves as pure, intelligent Life (the second H, the letter *hey*). One could also say that Hokhmah is the breath of life and the perception of sensation that is embedded underneath, or in the middle of being. It is Sacred Sense, or *Sensing.*

The word *musar,* usually translated as "instruction," carries the sense of correction, discipline, self-control and even punishment. It points to anything that gives a proper outline, direction or training to something or that allows its true nature to develop. It is related to the later sacred word in Arabic, *al-Musawwir,* another of the "99 Beautiful Names of Allah." The word *'ewilim,* usually translated as "fools," refers specifically to any being that suffers from an excess of expansion and that surrenders its movement to an inflated sense of its own perceived desire, disconnected from the desire behind the Universe. The word also points to the grandiosity of a being that overextends itself and refuses to recognize a universe whose creative power is based on limits.

3. For All Time Wisdom Rules.

This is part of a much longer text that contains the story of Ahiqar, who appears to have been an oracle or priestly counselor in the reign of Sennacherib (704-681 B.C.E.). After he retires, Ahiqar sets up his nephew as his successor, who unfortunately turns the new Assyrian king Esarhaddon against Ahiqar and attempts to have him killed. However, Ahiqar asks for a favor owed him by one of the king's high ministers, whom Ahiqar had earlier hid during a similar intrigue. The minister hides Ahiqar until the king misses his counsel, Ahiqar is "rehabilitated" and the ungrateful nephew gets his comeuppance. Ahiqar's proverbs reflect his seventh-century B.C.E. Assyrian street sense combined with a praise of Wisdom, which here, as in Proverbs, is personified as a female archetype who has existed from the beginning.

Another recurring theme associated with Holy Wisdom is the warning against telling secrets, or "loose tongues." Wisdom's name in Hebrew or Aramaic can be rendered "the wise breath of interiority." So various traditions emphasize her non-intellectual, intuitive dimension, which feeds all beings with "sacred sense," not concepts or words. Perhaps because her secrets cannot be spoken, keeping a secret became associated with her wisdom.

This version is based on a much longer Aramaic text of "The Words of Ahiqar," translated by H.L. Ginsberg from a fifth century B.C.E. palimpsest papyrus discovered in the debris of Elephantine, Upper Egypt in 1906-7, as contained in James B. Pritchard, ed. 1955. *Ancient Near Eastern Texts.* Second edition. Princeton: Princeton University Press. pp. 427-428.

4. Thunder Speaks, Part 1.

The text usually called "Thunder, Perfect Mind" was part of collection of more than fifty scrolls from an ancient library found in Nag Hammadi, Egypt in 1945. It is written in Coptic, a language derived from ancient Egyptian. Without going into an extensive background on this find, which is available in other works, one can say that the books discovered show a variety of cosmologies, beliefs and spiritual practices, much of them related to the early "Jesus movement." By the fifth century C.E., after a form of "orthodox" Christianity became the official religion of the Roman Empire, most of these beliefs and practices were banned as unorthodox and heretical.

As Elaine Pagels demonstrates convincingly (1979), what these books exhibit and what was purged from the development of orthodox Christianity, were: (1) a more collaborative approach to authority in early Jesus movement circles (the position of bishop or priest was often shared or rotated); (2) an interpretation of Middle Eastern cosmology which emphasized God the Mother as much as God the Father and (3) alternative definitions of the "true church" that had more to do with personal spiritual experience than with correct religious belief.

Past commentaries on "Thunder, Perfect Mind" have emphasized its beautiful, paradoxical "I am" statements ("I am the first and last, honored and dishonored..."). Some scholars initially tried to infer the text's relation to Greek philosophy. In this version I have emphasized its perfect expression as the Native Middle Eastern voice of Holy Wisdom or *Hokhmah*—the breath of interiority and "I-ness" from the core of all beings. In this regard, the use of paradox and antithesis clearly connects to statements by the voice of Holy Wisdom in Proverbs. More recently, many scholars have now agreed with my assessment of the text in 1995. As important as the presence of an early Semitic feminine archetype of the divine may be, I find even more important the text's expression of the voice of our own interiority, the seed at the center of our inner self. This "community model" of the self connects the post-exilic Hebrew themes associated with Hokhmah to Jesus' ministry and practice uniting rich and poor, male and female in a new vision of *malkuta*, the queen-kingdom of the Holy One. See also my paper for the Society of Biblical Literature's Psychology Group in 2003,

"Reading Wisdom with Reich: Proverbs 8-9 as Interpreted through the Psychotherapy of Wilhelm Reich." For more on research linking Holy Wisdom with early Jesus movement views of Jesus as Hokhmah, see Schroer (2002).

This version is based on the previous literal translations of George W. MacRae (1979: 231-255) and Bentley Layton (1987: 77-85) from the Coptic manuscript.

5. Wisdom's Gift - Matthew 26:26.

To say that there are many interpretations of what happened when Jesus broke bread at his last Passover celebration is an understatement. My expanded recreation of this event from the Aramaic is based on a translation of several key words in Matthew's report.

The Aramaic word *shqal*, usually translated as "took" (as in "took bread") also means to poise, to weigh, to embrace or envelop, to absorb oneself into something in a special gesture of unification. The word *lachma'*, is related by its roots to Hokhmah as the embodiment of the breath of wisdom, understanding and nurturance. It is also the word for "bread"—food for all aspects of life, not simply the physical. (For more on this, see my previous discussion of the fourth line of the Lord's Prayer (1990) where *lachma'* also appears.)

To bless something in Aramaic (here *barekh*) means to breathe into it with energy and feeling. The word *qtza'*, usually simply translated as "brake" points to a very special sort of breaking or dividing, one which was associated with the action a seer uses to divine or prophesy based on the shapes which the pieces made.

Jesus' own words are very enigmatic. The phrase *sabw 'akhuwlw*, usually translated "take, eat," has several alternative meanings, which I have included in this version. The word *pagry*, usually translated as "body," refers specifically to a dead body or corpse, a form that has lost its inner strength and heat. Aramaic does not have a word for what we call a "living body." So in this sense we are enfleshed, not embodied. The flesh is connected with the Holy One, and as long as it is fulfilling the divine purpose, it is just as sacred as the breath/spirit. Only when the breath leaves the body is it considered as a separate thing, a corpse. For more on the differences between Semitic and Greek language on these points, see *The Genesis Meditations* (2003) and the texts cited there.

6. Wisdom's Bread - John 6:35.

The Aramaic word *haye'*, usually translated as "life," refers to life force, energy, the power which feeds our animal existence, the fuel for our human passion. Generally we are taught by our culture to look outside for this life-energy, to fill an inner void with things that never really satisfy. At the same time, it is the life force, the presence, the freshness in food, relationships and work that feeds us—a connection to what feels energized in our psyche. When we connect with the "I am" within ourselves, we go directly to the source of our life force. This is the presence within us that can enter, renew or leave any outer relationship from a place of abundance rather than scarcity.

The words usually translated "hunger" (*nekhpan*) and "thirst" (*netzhe'*) are forms of the same words used by Jesus in the fourth Beatitude reported in Matthew (See *Prayers of the Cosmos*). Aramaic words like these never refer only to physical hunger and thirst, because ancient Semitic languages never divided life into the categories of body, mind, emotions and spirit that Western culture does. The latter categories, which we take for granted, all derive from Platonic Greek philosophy.

For further information on the background to the "I Am" statements in John, see textual note three in chapter three.

7. Like Seed and Fruit.

This version is based on previous literal translations by Florence Lederer (1920), E.H. Whinfield (1880) and Johnson Pasha (1903).

Chapter Seven

1. How to Organize a Self - Genesis 1:14-19.

Many of the words in these verses have already been the subject of textual notes in the previous two chapters. In verse 14, the word *me'orot,* usually translated as "lights," is based on the word *aor* used in verse 3, but modified to mean that which embodies the sensation of light, or that which organizes the perception of light into bundles of light. Toward the end of the verse, the word *'otot,* usually translated as "signs," also points to any character, type or symbol—essentially whatever establishes a relationship between an "I" and something outside, a "Thou." Some part of our consciousness, a "Sacred Sense" or "Holy Wisdom," constantly organizes and creates a "self" so that we are not overwhelmed by the enormous wealth of sensation that the universe presents.

At the end of verse 14, the phrase *lemo'adim uleyamim weshanim,* usually translated as "for seasons, days and years," also points to the way in which the storyteller sees consciousness becoming organized. *Mo'adim* (root Y`WD) points to the kinesthetic or body sensation of time's passage. The periodic pulsation of fluids within us conveys a feeling of being in a regular rhythm, the basis of our sense of time. *Yamim,* based on the same root as *iom,* points to the effect of light on the mind or nervous system of a being. *Shanim* points to an inner sensation of change over time, the sense one may have that one is not the same as yesterday. The way that light organizes our consciousness, and vice versa, according to Genesis, produces a change in the very nature of our existence.

2. The "I" Joins the Journey - Proverbs 8:22-24.

The word *qanani,* translated in the KJV as "possess," can also mean to create, absorb, assimilate into oneself, redeem and acquire. This variety of seemingly disparate meanings coalesces around the root

QN, which points to the power of ardor with density, compression and tension, a centralizing force, a nest or enclosed home of awareness. The word *re'shit* again returns us to that archetypal "beginningness," the primordial origin of mystery that is the object of so much contemplation in this tradition.

The word *darko*, translated as "way" in the King James, can also mean a journey, course or path—that is, something that unfolds gradually rather than is pre-ordained. The phrase *qedem mif'alaw me'az*, usually translated as "works of old," points to a pivotal moment, a point on which everything turns, at which time something wonderful, mysterious and miraculous happened. This mystery is hidden in the germ of everything, according to the root PhL. The word *me'az* points to a definite, fixed point in space or time, one that never recurs in the same way. It is related to another of the "99 Beautiful Names" in Arabic, *al-Aziz*.

In verse 23, the word *olam*, translated as "everlasting" in the KJV, refers to another archetypal moment—the ancient first gathering of sensing and feeling that enabled a sense of "past" to arise. What was before we could feel a "before"? For life itself, and for our own lives, this is *olam*. Related meanings come into Arabic words like *alam* and another of the "99 Beautiful Names," *al-Alim*. The word *nissakhti*, usually translated as "set up," can also mean to pour out, appoint or consecrate, pointing to a sacred flow that initiates awareness and that is likely mirrored in all baptismal rites.

In verse 24, the word *be'en*, usually translated "when no," could literally be translated "before being" or "when there was nothingness." The word *tehomot*, usually translated as "depths," can also be translated as abyss, flow, chaos or the depths of universal existence. The word *cholaleti*, usually translated "brought forth," can also mean to turn in a circle, whirl, twist, reel or be in the labor of childbirth. The Hebrew word for circle dance, *cholla*, is based on this and can also mean to bear a child. Behind this is the Semitic root CHL, which refers to any effort to extend the self, to develop or stretch. As an interior reality, this is also hope and expectation.

The word *ma'yanot,* usually translated as "fountains" derives from the root `WYN, which indicates the manifested source or "eye" of something living. *Nikhbaddei,* usually translated "abounding," also points to a sufficient amount, whatever is necessary for the moment. Combined with the word *mayim,* the primordial flow, the whole phrase points to the point of origin from which even chaos pours out and pulses in the appropriate amount for the unfoldment of the cosmos, just like the pulse of fluids within us.

3. Thunder Speaks, Part 2.

This version is based on the previous literal translations of George W. MacRae (1979: 231-255) and Bentley Layton (1987: 77-85) from the Coptic manuscript.

4. The Door Between the Worlds – John 10:9.

For further information on the background to the "I Am" statements in John, see textual note three in chapter three.

The Aramaic word *thara,* usually translated as "door," also points to everything that makes a transition from one form of reality to another, which turns us from one mode of being to another, which converts, distills or infuses something into something else. Earlier uses of this ancient Semitic root, ThR, probably includes the Egyptian sacred name *Ha-Thor,* she who presides over death and rebirth, as well as the later, somewhat mutated, word *dervish* in the Sufi tradition—the one who sits in the doorway between realities.

The Aramaic word *'nash,* human being, also refers to any being that comes into form or embodiment for a limited period of time. The word *ne'uwli,* based on the root 'WL, conveys not only the word "enter," but mystically the whole process of coming into material form, the alchemical *chul.* The word *niche',* translated "be saved" in the KJV, is based on the root for life energy (HH or HA), found throughout the Semitic language tradition as the Hebrew *hayye* and the Arabic *al-Hayy* (another of the "99 Beautiful Names"). The word *nepuwq,* translated in the KJV as "go out," refers by its primary root NPh to a process of scattering or dispersing a solid object, and so of leaving form. The word translated as pasture, *re'ya'* is based on the same root (R`W) as "shepherd," which is used in another "I Am" saying later in the same chapter (and translated here in chapter 8, "The Creator of Ripeness"). This root refers to all the cares and sorrows of material existence, to one who shares these same cares and who can manage the needs and desires expressed by the whole flock of voices that make up our inner "I am." This "shepherd" is in many ways our conscious self, the connection of small self to Only Self. It is also the door that allows us to pass freely from one reality or world to another.

5. In the Doorway.

This version is based on a portion of the literal translation of #36 in the collection by R.A. Nicholson (1898: 145).

6. Drops and Specks.

This version is based on previous literal translations by Florence Lederer (1920), E.H. Whinfield (1880) and Johnson Pasha (1903).

7. The Soul's Three Faces.

This version of a small selection of the Zohar is based on the literal translation of Gershom Scholem (1949: 44, 96). In addition, I have re-translated the meanings of the key terms from the original Hebrew roots and hopefully clarified the meaning of the rest of the passage in relationship to them.

Chapter Eight

1. The Preferential Option for a Soul - Genesis 1:20-23.

In verse 20, the word *yishretzu*, usually translated as "bring forth abundantly," points through its roots to a circular movement that causes new generation to occur by a process of separation or individuation. What individuates first from the cosmic flow (*mayim*) is *nephesh chayya*, usually translated "creature that hath life," but a clear reference to the living subconscious or soul-self, which is the subject of so much attention in Hebrew, Aramaic and Arabic sacred scripture. The roots of the word *nephesh* can be rendered in at least three ways: NPh, that which breathes in, can be inspired or infused from the outside; PH, the reaction to the in-breath, the sense of expansion and effusion moving from inside to outside, and ASh, the primordial embodied fire, which generates ardor and passion for a goal. This three-part nature of the soul-self in the Native Middle Eastern tradition causes it to act as a living being in its own right.

The second new creation in the interiority of living beings is *we'of ye'ofef*, usually translated as "fowl that may fly." The roots of this word also point to an interior activity of material sentience and sensation that is quick, unbounded by particle reality (*'al-ha'aretz*) and whose natural element is wave reality and atmosphere (*reqia' hashamayim*). I have translated this as the instinctual self, an intelligence that operates at the level of our so-called involuntary nervous system. This instinctual self, when we don't block out its action with mental chatter, is extremely sensitive to atmosphere, vibration and sound. It reacts quickly, and with support (like training in the Eastern martial arts) can become astonishingly fast.

In verses 21-23, the new soul-selves multiply and diversify, and one could say that the interiority and consciousness of living beings becomes much more complex as more differentiation occurs. On the outer level, the larger "swimming" beings (usually translated "great whales") can, of course, include many early sea creatures no longer in existence. The Genesis story also relates that early winged creatures also came from the waters, which accords with some views of evolution. The "whales" and "flocks" can also represent the "scale" of different experiments in consciousness that the Holy One created, as well as "communities" of inner, psychic beings or realities. While some have attempted to limit these images to various systems of archetypes, disembodied beings and so forth, the Genesis storyteller clearly indicates that they are more diverse than one limited construct of metaphysical reality. They are all "stories" being told by the Divine Mind to itself, so to speak.

The words that the Universe Being speaks to these new beings are: *pheru urebu umil'u* (usually translated "be fruitful and multiply and fill.") These words point respectively to the actions of producing offspring and becoming fertile (*pheru*), of creating great numbers of beings through an interior process (*rebu*), and of filling any gaps, extending until each being is entirely formed (*mil'u*). The Holy One offers another form of this blessing to the first human being a few verses later, which as I shall note there, led to one of the most tragic mistranslations in the history of the transmission of this story.

2. Wisdom's Dinner Party - Proverbs 9:1-6.

The word *baneta* usually translated "hath builded" refers to an interior activity that creates a boundary or circumference around the self and that forms, embodies or constructs something from the "me." What is created by this enclosure is *betah*, usually translated "house," but also any container or separate inside space, an interior or a "within." The word *chatzeba*, usually translated as "hewn," comes from the root H`W, which points to any division that occurs by pushing from the outside until a split occurs. The phrase *ammudeha shib'ah*, usually translated as "seven pillars," refers to parts which come together and bond in a way that satisfies or fulfills a purpose—in this case to form the "I am" of an individual. Why seven? Probably for the same reason that the Genesis 1 creation story happens in seven days. According to some Rabbis (including my friend Rabbi Arthur Waskow), the seven can stand for seven modes of locating the human in creation: above, below, north, south, east, west and the most mysterious "location": the process of "returning" from outer to inner, the latter of which is enshrined and remembered in the seventh or Sabbath day (based on the same root as *shib'ah*).

The phrase *tabecha tibchah* in verse two, usually translated "killed her beasts," actually says "slaughtered her slaughter" or "resisted her resistance." Both words have the same root (TB): a force of resistance from the inside that conserves the central integrity of a being or that sets aside any corruption. Using the basic root meaning, we could also translate the phrase "ripened her ripeness." The phrase *masekha yenah,* usually translated "mingled her wine," can also mean to fuse or compress (*masekha*) the intoxicating, spiritual power of pure mind or intelligence (*yenah*). The phrase *arekha shulchanah,* usually translated "furnished her table," can also mean to spread out, order or move into physical reality a harmonious (ShL) fixed extension of time and space (ChN) that supports the growth of the self.

The phrase *shalecha na'aroteha* in verse three, usually translated "sent forth her maidens," can also mean to stretch out, extend or sprout a new impulse or desire. The word *tiqra',* usually translated as "cried," can also mean to proclaim, plead, summon, celebrate or praise. This is related to the Hebrew *iqra',* to engrave, which we saw in Genesis 1:5 (chapter four). The phrase *'al-gappei meromei qaret,* usually translated "upon the highest places in the city," can also mean an enclosure that protects and fills space around something centralized and sacred. The word *meromei,* from the root RWM, pictures a stream or a ray of light rising and filling space.

The word *mi-feti* in verse four, usually translated as "simple," may also mean open, susceptible or accessible. It is based on the root PhTh, opening, which we encountered several times in chapter four. The phrase *yasur henna*, usually translated "let him turn in hither," points to turning aside in order to be instructed or corrected, to take a new direction in the present moment, right now. The phrase *chasar-leb,* usually translated "as for him that wanteth understanding," actually talks about someone diminished or blocked in heart, courage, force or passion.

In verse five, the words *lachamu belachami,* are both derived from *lechem,* the elemental food that includes sustenance for all levels of being. *Lechem* offers for the soul's consumption all natural vigor, radical moisture, everything verdant, young or fresh.

The phrase *'izbu feta'yim* in verse six, usually translated as "forsake the foolish," can be read various ways. *'Izbu* may mean also mean to set free, release or loosen. *Feta'yim* is the same simplicity, openness and susceptibility mentioned in verse four. The word *wichu,* usually translated "and live" is related to *chyh,* elemental power and life force, which we have encountered previously. The final phrase, *'ishru bederekh binah,* usually translated "go in the way of understanding," is repeated many times in Hebrew scriptures. The word *'ishru,* means to walk straight and directly, to go in the way that leads to ultimate happiness for the soul. It is based on the root ASh that we encountered previously as the fire that empowers the basic soul-self (*nephesh*). The word *derekh* points to any journey, path, course, manner or way. The word *binah,* which later becomes important as a quality on the Kabbalistic Tree of Life, points to the understanding or intelligence that educates a soul from within.

3. Thunder Speaks, Part 3.

This version is based on the previous literal translations from the Coptic of George W. MacRae (1979: 231-255) and Bentley Layton (1987: 77-85).

4. The Creator of Ripeness - John 10:14-15.

For further information on the background to the "I Am" statements in John, see textual note three in chapter three.

In the "good shepherd" passages of John 10:11-16, Yeshua plays with several Aramaic words that are related by root or meaning to each other. As we have seen, the word *taba'*, usually translated "good," points to all ideas of ripeness and right timing. As in the similar Hebrew word we saw in Proverbs 9:2 above, it also conveys the idea of a force that resists corruption, conserves a central integrity and leads to healthy, timely action or ripe "fruit." It is the opposite of *bisha*, or unripeness, which we encountered in the saying by Jesus about timeliness in chapter four ("Tomorrow Means Things Depart," Matthew 6:33-34). It is a variation of the same word that begins all of the Beatitudes in Aramaic (see chapter two). The Aramaic word *ra'ya'*, usually translated as "shepherd," may also mean anyone who shares the same cares, pains or anxieties as another, who rules or leads but is at the same time a comrade or neighbor.

The Aramaic word *yoda'*, usually translated "know," is based on the ancient Semitic root for "hand." From this comes all ideas of knowing, grasping, understanding and gathering, that is, bringing many impressions into a "knowable" unity. The word for "sheep" (*'erbe'*, verse 12), and "flock" (*'ono'*, verses 12, 13, 15, 16) both have the initial root letter 'W (the Hebrew *ayin*), which mystically is the most materialized form of the letter-sounds of the breath (*hey, heth, koph, ayin*). In this sense "sheep" also point to a still "endarkened" sense of growing life within, the wandering aspects of our inner being that have yet to know themselves in the light of the One. Similarly, the word for "flock" (*'ono'*) is an obscured, endarkened form of *'ena' 'na*, the I-I of simple presence, one to One.

An important word included in neighboring verses to the ones translated in John 10 is "hireling" (for instance,"The hireling fleeth, because he is an hireling, and careth not for the sheep," verse 13). This is the Aramaic *'agiyra,'* which shows from its roots a hoarding action, and means anyone who is paid for work. This self-aggrandizement contrasts with the self-giveaway necessary to allow the One Self to be mirrored through the small one. The true guide, according to Yeshua, is not one you pay, or who gains from your "following," but one who, sacrifices his or her own *naphsha* (small self) in order to lead you to your own inner Guide, the I-I within. I have included this sense in the parenthetical just before the last stanza of the translation.

5. Find a Self, Lose a Self - Matthew 10:39.

In these few words, Jesus gives some very profound and subtle teachings about the *naphsha*, the small self, which can be seen as a collection of voices becoming one in "ripeness" with divine Unity. First, in working with the *naphsha*, it is important to realize that, while its voice is very important, it is not the voice of guidance or the voice of the Source of the whole cosmos. Its needs and demands, even when very powerfully expressed, are material to work with creatively, not to blindly obey. The true heart of feeling does not come from a place of compulsion.

The Aramaic words *de'shkach* and *neshkchiyh*, different forms of the word usually translated as "find," also mean to follow a direction or inclination, to possess something material, to accomplish a duty, to pursue a desire that has no end to its layers, or figuratively to peel something which has no core (like an onion). The Aramaic words *nawbdiyh* and *dnawbed*, usually translated as "lose," may also mean to separate, isolate, individualize or sprout something through an interior activity of division.

Using the more physical "following" energy (*de'shkach*) to obey the demands of the *naphsha* can only lead to its isolation. Its real desires have to do with fulfilling its purpose, not possessing objects or people. One's compulsive needs for outward stimulus, possessing things, and even people, are layered on top of the self's deeper needs for contact, love and inclusion in the purpose of its whole being. These needs can only be fulfilled by oneself together with the One Self.

As Yeshua says, the other path is more fruitful: when the voice of Inner Guidance (the I-I of the previous passage) separates and clearly hears all the voices of the *naphsha*, its needs for contact, love and inclusion begin to be met. When the voices of the *naphsha* are heard in connection with sacred Unity, they do not need to shout or imitate the voice of Source. When included in this sacred psychology, the small self's needs are fulfilled and followed in that they are integrated with the purpose of the whole being.

Contrary to what some voices in modern psychology advocate, the individual subconscious and its needs are not "God," nor are they a reliable source of guidance. For instance, the extreme emphasis on individual, *human* needs has led Western culture to devastate the planetary ecology in ways unknown in previous eons. According to the tradition of ancient Semitic psychology out of which Yeshua comes, our work is not so much to "follow our feelings," but to have our feelings follow us, a process that involves slowly developing better internal communication, so that we know who "us" is in relation to the real "I am."

6. The Self of Nature and the Nature of Self - Surah 91:1-10.

Like Surah *Fatiha,* this is another early Surah, from the time that the Muslim community was very small and living in Mecca under persecution. Many of the early Surahs are short cosmological hymns or psalms, pointing out the wonders of creation, as well as its order and proportion, and asking its listeners to consider whether there could *not* be One Being behind it all. Surah *ash-Shams* ("the Sun") moves from a consideration of the balance of light in nature, similar to Genesis 1, to that of the balance and purpose created in the soul-self, *nafs* in Arabic. Its warnings about the dangers of burying the richness of the soul resonate with those of Jesus in the Gospels about "burying one's talent."

In the Gospel of Thomas, another manuscript in the Nag Hammadi collection, Jesus is quoted as saying, "If you bring forth that which is within you, that which is within you will save you. If you fail to bring forth that which is within you, that which is within you will kill you" (Logion 70). This is a succinct comment on all forms of addictive and compulsive consumption and behavior. Generally we need to shift from thinking that the presence of unwanted, self-defeating behavior in us is "bad" to looking at it as an opportunity to communicate with our soul-self. However, this opportunity will continue to present itself with more and more urgency for us humans, as individuals and as a whole species, if we continue to ignore it.

In the first verse, the word *shams,* from the ancient Semitic root ShM that we saw in chapter one, can mean "sun" or anything that shines and connects in sound or light. The word *zuhaahaa,* from *zahiya,* translated by Yusuf Ali as "glorious splendor," means to experience heat, become uncovered or revealed. From the old Semitic root DwH, to appear or expose the self. In verse two, the word for moon, *qamar,* comes from an Arabic root that means to be white. The old Semitic root (QM) means something whose nature is undefined and reflective. The word translated "conceals," *talaahaa,* comes from a verb (*tala*) that means to follow, imitate or walk behind. Its Semitic root counterpart (TL) indicates something that veils or moves like a shadow.

In verse three, the word translated "day" *nahaari,* is from the verb *nahara,* to stream or flow abundantly, which came to mean to do something in the daytime. The word translated "glory" here is *jallaahaa,* from *jalla,* to be imposing, great or clear. It comes from the ancient Semitic root GL, any expansive force that unfolds itself, like a wheel, or a being that shows joy in its movement. In verse four, the word for "night" *layli,* is from the ancient Semitic root LYL, to bind things together or envelop them. We saw its Hebrew equivalent *layela* in the Genesis 1 portion in chapter four. The word translated by Yusuf Ali as "conceal" is *yaghshaahaa,* from the verb *ghashiya,* to cover or come upon. It stems from the ancient Semitic root GSh, to touch or contract.

In verse five the word translated "firmament" is *samaa'i*, from *sama*, name or attribute, the same root as the word *bismillah*, which we saw in the first section. The word can also mean to be high or raised. The ancient Semitic root SM refers to any sphere of activity. So as "name" this word points to the sign that distinguishes the activity or function of something. It also connects to the ShM root in its meanings of sound and vibration as above. The word translated "structure" is really a verb *bana*, to build or erect, related to the Semitic root BN, any birth, emanation or embodiment. In verse six, *'arzi* is the word for earth, related to the Hebrew *aretz* and the Aramaic *arha'*. The word translated "spread out" is *tahaahaa*, from *taha*, to spread out or extend.

Coming to the section on the soul-self, *nafs*, in verse seven, we find again the equivalent of the Hebrew *nephesh* and Aramaic *naphsha*, which we considered in the Genesis note above. The word translated "proportion and order" is again a verb *sawiya*, to fashion something in balance and sound health, fit for a particular purpose. It links to the Semitic root ShU, something qualified for and leaning toward a goal. Reading the root as SHA, it can indicate both tranquil water and the whirlpool, something able to be either calm or wild. In verse eight, the word *'alhamahaa*, translated "enlightenment" by Yusuf Ali, is from the verb *lahima*, to swallow or gulp down food. *Ilham* is animal instinct or inspiration, what human beings receive from the One via the divine breath. The word translated "wrong" is *fujuurahaa*, from a verb meaning to break up, dig up or go off the right path. Its Semitic root parent is PhG, which means to extend too far or to separate, and so lose strength and heat. The word translated "right" is *taqwaahaa*, from a verb meaning to protect, save or preserve. It can also be linked to the verb *qawiya*, to be strong or to blow with a strong wind, related to *al-Qawi*, one of the "99 Beautiful Names."

The word translated "succeed" in line nine is *aflaha*, from the key Arabic verb *falaha*, to cultivate the earth, to unfold or reveal inner qualities, to bring something planted in one to realization. The ancient Semitic equivalent root is PhL, something miraculous, precious and mysterious. The word translated "purifies" is *zakkaahaa*, from *zaka*, to clean and thrive. It forms the basis of the Arabic word *zakat*, used to indicate the purification of giving a percentage of one's income to the poor. The ancient Semitic root ZCh unites these various meanings together with the image of pruning a plant or tree so that it can bear more. We will see the same image in the next chapter in a saying of Yeshua. In line ten, the word translated as "fails" is *khaaba*, from a verb meaning to be undone or fail. Its Semitic root predecessors are ChB, to centralize and HB, to remain secret or enclosed. Finally, the word translated as "corrupts" is *dassaahaa*, from the verb *dassa*, to hide, bury or conceal.

7. Gambling the Self.

This version is based on previous literal translations by Florence Lederer (1920), E.H. Whinfield (1880) and Johnson Pasha (1903).

8. The Moon and the Sea.

This version is based on the literal translation of #19 in the collection by R.A. Nicholson (1898: 76-79).

Chapter Nine

1. An Experiment in Independence - Genesis 1:24-26.

In verse 24, the word *totze'*, usually translated "bring forth," refers to an action that sets a certain character or choice in motion. That choice then grows, matures and follows its own course. The word *behema*, usually translated as "cattle" or "beast," refers to a movement and noise that occur when a being is raised from or extended away from the earth. The word *remes*, usually translated as "creeping thing," refers to contractile movements that gather or pile up things. The phrase *leminah wayehi-khen*, which occurs in various forms throughout this account and is usually translated "after his kind," points to an exterior result that follows and develops from the original definition of a living interior reality or idea, literally "toward-within-among-(its)-kind-living-in-this-way."

In verse 25, the important word *adamah*, which is not translated in the KJV, means the universal, immortal and powerful (A) assimilation, collection and whole aggregation (DM) of primordial creative life (AH). In one of the main renditions of the root as DAM, it can be a being of "juice, wine, sap or essence." According to this cosmology, nothing in our cosmic evolution came from anywhere but the Universe Being itself.

Several words in verse 26 deserve closer attention. The word *'adam*, usually translated as "man," connects closely with *adamah*. It does not refer to a masculine-gendered person or even one particular human. It means the collective assimilation of the Universe's activity so far in a stable form—the experiment in consciousness or "soul" embracing all that had gone before it. This was in order to solve the challenge of individual souls losing awareness of the whole sacred community of being, which had occurred in the previous experiment (verse 25).

The word *betzalmenu,* usually translated "in our image," also means "in the universal shadow of" or "in the veil of." It does not mean a visual image, but rather the moving, breathing likeness of universal consciousness embodied. It also points to a moving form projected by means of light. The word *kidmutenu,* usually translated "after our likeness," is linked to the root DM above and points to something that is assimilated, mingled with or identified with the whole. It is a "blood-bond" between humanity and the Universe Being, including the way it conceives, thinks and imagines. (For more on ancient Semitic ideas of "image," see my later work *The Genesis Meditations,* 2003).

The word *yirdu,* usually translated "have dominion" points to a power to radiate the remembrance of diversity and differentiation, a power that spreads out, unfolds and occupies space by its very nature, that moves with firmness and perseveres in its own will. However this power is not given "over" the beings created before us, but "along with," "in," or "within" them (the meaning of the Hebrew preposition "b," *beth*). There is no evidence for this preposition ever meaning "over," in the sense of domination, within the entire Hebrew scripture. The power given to the interiority developed by the human had all these qualities, again for better and for worse, but it was also given the power to remember what had gone before as well as the sacred ground of Being from which everything came. Could it remember both at the same time? This was the challenge that the Universe set for itself.

As the interiority of human beings continued to develop and become more complex, the tendency increased for the small "I" to forget its Source. This, in short, is the entire history of humanity's psychic evolution up until now, and in accelerated form, in the modern era. Yet the potential for the deeper remembrance remains, according to the storytellers and mystics of this tradition.

2. The Old Order: Every Mouth is Crammed with "Love Me!"

Version extracted from and based on Papyrus Leningrad 1116B, from literal translations by John A. Wilson as contained in the collection of James B. Pritchard (1955: 445) and Adolf Erman (1927: 112-114).

3. Thunder Speaks, Part 4.

This version is also based on the previous literal translations from the Coptic of George W. MacRae (1979: 231-255) and Bentley Layton (1987: 77-85).

4. Like Vine and Branches - John 15:1-5.

Like the other "I Am" sayings in John, this one also forms part of Yeshua's preparation of his students for his departure. The "vine and branches" section occurs as part of his final talk with them, just after the blessing of "greater works" and the "peace I give to you" portions. For more on this final talk, see *Blessings of the Cosmos* (2006).

Here Yeshua weaves his sayings around the multiple meanings of *gpeta'* and *shbishta'*, the words usually translated as "vine" and "branches." *Gpeta'* refers to any channel or canal, any object hollowed out in order to allow something to flow through or in order to protect, enclose or defend life. It is related by Semitic root (PhT) to the "opening" power (see "By the Heart and by The Tongue" in chapter five). *Shbishta'* refers to that which receives something and passes it on, in order to return a flow of energy to its original state. So the impulse that begins with sacred Creation, and which expresses itself through the whole developmental history of the universe, also expresses itself in the actions of every being. When a person acts with the consciousness of this, it expresses the harmony of the Holy One, of the whole. When a person acts with only a limited consciousness of the self (*naphsha*, found in verse 4), says Yeshua, nothing can happen that carries on the healing and teaching transmission he has brought.

Other key words include: In verse one, the "true" vine is *dashrara*, based on the root ShR, which expresses the sense of right direction, at the right time and place. A form of this word also occurs in the saying, "I am the way, the truth and the life," which is translated in chapter 13. The word usually translated "fruit" throughout the passage is *pi're'*, based on the root PhR, expressing the old Semitic idea of emphatic (Ph) outward movement or activity (R). A form of the word is used in Genesis 1:22 and 1:28 in the expression *pheru urebu* ("be abundant and become nurturing"). It is also indirectly related to the old Egyptian word from which we get "pharaoh." The word usually translated "husbandman" is *palocha'*, the root of which can also refer to the germ of a seed, or something unique, miraculous or mysterious.

In verse two, the word usually translated "bear fruit" is *yohba'* (based on the root YHB), which is connected to all of the main creation words in Aramaic, including *abwun* (the Cosmic Parent of the Lord's Prayer) as well as forms of *aheb* (the creative love that Yeshua uses in his saying "love one another as I have loved you"). The phase "he taketh away" in the KJV is *shoqel lah* in the Aramaic, which actually means to "take up or away into itself," an image of pruning that expresses its function. The word translated as "purgeth" is *mdake'*, which means to purify something so that it can fulfill its purpose.

In verse three, Yeshua says that he has "purified" his disciples through his whole teaching and conversations with them (*metul melta'*). This enables them to realise that the limited part of themselves is not doing the acting.

In verse four, he emphasises this point. The word usually translated "abide" is *qawaw*, which from its root QW, refers to the sacred force that moves all of existence in unpredictable ways. This Aramaic word is also related to one of the "99 Beautiful Names," the Arabic *al-Qawi*. The words translated "cannot bear fruit of itself" is in the Aramaic *la' meshkcha' dtetel pi're' men napshah*, which literally means "cannot find fruit to give of its own self-ness." The final word is one we have considered extensively through this book.

In verse five, Yeshua beautifully sums up this poetic teaching using all of the main words and features of the metaphor he has previously introduced.

5. Communion's Gift - Matthew 26:27-28.

As in the previous passage from Matthew 26, the Aramaic word *shqal*, usually translated as "took" (as in "took the cup") also means to poise, to weigh, to embrace or envelop, to absorb oneself into in a special gesture of unification. In Aramaic, the word *kasa'*, used for "cup," may also mean any temporary cover, accommodation, clothing or physical shelter. By inference it points to the body. (It's also related to the later Arabic word *khusr* we encountered in the Qur'anic surah about Time; see chapter four, textual note four.) The word *'wdiy*, usually translated "gave thanks," can also mean to praise or confess or profess something. From its roots AWD, the word indicates a desire that expresses itself outwardly.

The word *sabw*, usually translated "take," may also mean to surround, envelop or convert. The word *'eshtaw*, usually translated "drink," may also mean to enjoy, consume or undergo a movement which takes one to the depths or foundations of something.

Coming to the key word, *demy*, usually translated "blood," it is important to emphasize, as noted in the textual note on the Genesis passage above, that the word refers literally to any red wine, juice or sap, including blood. Its roots are directly related to the *adamah* found in Genesis 1, the assimilated essence of the Universe out of which all life came. These roots point to a bond which brings together what was previously separate, which allows parts to mingle into a whole or which assimilates individuality into the universal essence. It also points to our human heritage given at the first Beginning, to nurture and sustain ourselves along with and alongside all of the rest of creation. The words *ddiyatiqi' chadta'*, usually translated "new testament," may also refer to any renewing, abundant or effusive command, prescription or law, one that satisfies all needs or reconciles all opposites. The human heritage of forgiving and releasing was one of our primary "job descriptions" given by the Holy One in Genesis. For more on this interpretation of the Last Supper, see chapter eleven of *The Hidden Gospel* (1999).

The word *sagiye*, usually translated as "for many," may also mean "in a way which continues to grow or extend itself," as in the circumference of a circle opening. The word *mete'shed*, usually translated "shed," may also mean to flow out or pour out, as from a reservoir. The word *shuwbqana'*, usually translated as "forgive," may also mean to return something to its original state, untie or embrace with emptiness. The word *chtahe'*, usually translated as "sins," may also mean tangled threads, failures, mistakes or hopes frustrated in the past. These last two words are the same as those used in Luke's version of the Lord's Prayer. (For more on this, see the discussion in my earlier work, 1990, 1999).

6. From the Depths of Divine Shadow - Surah 21:87.

This ayat of the Qur'an appears within a much longer surah (*al-Anbiya*, meaning "the prophets"), which names and describes many of the other historical messengers before Prophet Muhammad, including Moses, Abraham, Jacob, David, Solomon, Ishmael, Idris and Mariam (Jesus' mother). Summarizing the message of all these prophets, the surah says (verse 24): "In actual fact, every Messenger We sent revealed the same message: 'There is no being except the Only Being, so bow only to this." Emphasizing that different messengers came to different people at various times and places in various languages, the surah calls them all (verse 92), one *'ummah*, a word often translated "community" or even "religion," but which clearly points to a unity that goes beyond the usual ideas of race, culture, language or human religious organization. "There is only one Nurturer and Sustainer behind all" (verse 92). A Turkish Sufi colleague of mine once wrote a book emphasizing this point entitled "Allah is Not God," meaning by "God" a human conception, theology or ideal of something that actually is beyond words, language and culture, that is, the Reality.

The name *Zan-Nunni* (usually translated DhuNun) literally means "he of the great fish." The Islamic story of the Jonah is very similar to the biblical one. Jonah receives a mission to Nineveh to try to get people there to acknowledge the One Being. He threatens them with divine punishment if they don't. Some actually do turn their hearts, and so the whole city is spared, but in Jonah's mind, if everyone didn't repent, Allah should have destroyed them all. Essentially he felt he had lost face, so he abandoned his mission and went on a long boat ride. The rest proceeds as in the Bible.

The word *zahaba* is from a root that means both to "depart" and to "hold a belief," that is, a belief that leads one away from the Source. The word *ghaza* can mean anger, irritation or confusion. It comes from an old Semitic root ('WTz) that presents images of rigidity and biting. The word *zanna* can mean to think, believe, imagine, be sure about or conjecture. By old Semitic root, it refers to the capacity of the mind to divide things, but in doing so, to lose the thread of unity.

The phrase *'allan-naqdira*, translated by Yusuf Ali as "had no power over," is from the root QD, which we have seen several times. The word for power here is one of the "99 Beautiful Names," *al-Qadir*, the sacred power (QA) that applies itself to individual forms by centering on a point (D) and then radiating this power outward (R). It is an image of the divine working through nature, in this case the storm and fish, to bring a person back to Reality. The word *fanaadaa* can mean to call, proclaim, invite or cry out. It comes from a Semitic root (ND) that refers to exile and flight from oneself, that is a result of becoming too "divided."

The word *zulumat*, usually translated "darkness," can also mean hardship, affliction or obscurity. It clearly connects with the old Semitic root (TzL) meaning shadow or image. We found the Hebrew form, *tzalm,* earlier in this chapter in Genesis 1:26. The same root is used in the final word of the ayat, *minaz-zaalimiin,* which translated by Yusuf Ali as "wrong." Literally it means "from or within the dense shadow or darkness." The "wrongness" here comes from the breath of the One becoming so materialized in its "shadow," part of the experiment in independence, that it forgets it is part of the divine experiment. The word *innii,* usually translated "indeed" or sometimes "behold," also refers to individuality and by old Semitic root (IN) whatever deprives others for one's own interest. The word *kuntu,* translated by Yusuf Ali as "was" is from the Arabic *kana,* to exist happen or occur. It is related to the imperative *Kun!* that the One uses to create. By its old Semitic root KN, the word means to bring something into action through nature, that is, material existence. Classical Arabic does not seem to preserve the word for living and existing that is made up of the "life" root (HH) as it is in Hebrew (for instance, see textual note one in chapter twelve).

The word "zikr" (also transliterated *dhikr*) in the title refers to the Sufi practice of remembrance that usually includes some form of the "*La ilaha illa 'llahu*" phrase, either chanted, spoken, sung, breathed or simply felt. Here Jonah's zikr uses the form "There is no being except you, the One unpolluted and pure, the only one to be praised." The final expression here is *subhaanaka,* related directly to *Subhan Allah,* a principle sacred phrase in Sufism. The old Semitic root of *subhan* is SB, which connects to Yeshua's *saba* and *sebyanach,* the willingness and desire of the One. When we touch the place of *Subhan Allah* within us, we touch that original divine image, pure and polluted, which was given us at the First Beginning.

In 1980, when I was visiting Sufis in Pakistan with a group of other students, a sheikh shared the "zikr of Jonah" with us, which was done in an unusual form. Upstairs in his coffee shop, we counted coffee beans with each repetition of the phrase, instead of using prayer beads. All of the beans began in the center of a circle of us sitting together. When they were all gone, we pushed them back into the center and began again. It was as good an image of trying to work out one's "divine image," slogging along in the depths of one's humanity, as one could imagine. Jonah chanting in the belly of a whale also presents a graphic image of a fully human being "from the depths" turning his heart back to the Source, away from a rigid idea of what "fulfilling a mission" is.

7. I and You.

This version is based on the previous literal translations from the Persian by Florence Lederer (1920) and E.H. Whinfield (1880).

Chapter Ten

1. Two Habits of Being Human - Genesis 1:27-28.

As mentioned in the previous chapter, the word *betzelem* in verse 27, usually translated "in the image," also points to a veil, shadow or projection of the totality of the Being who is One-and-Many (*Elohim*) into and onto the assimilated "stuff" of the universe (*adamah*). That the expression is repeated twice shows how important the storyteller of Genesis considered this concept of veiling and layers.

The relentless use of the masculine gender for the first human by various translators contradicts the clear assertion that this veil or projection happened from the beginning in two modes: *zakhar* and *neqeba*. The word *zakhar*, usually translated "male," points by its roots to everything which has to do with memory and remembrance, with action that grows, rises, engraves or hollows out, with what is apparent and obvious. It is related to the later Arabic sacred phrase, *al-Zahir*, one of the "99 Beautiful Names." The word *neqeba*, usually translated "female," refers to that which has to do with nurturance of the new, spaciousness and the creative void, with everything which is hollowed or cavernous. This is related to the later Arabic sacred word *an-Naqib*, the quality of keeping or maintaining a sacred space or community.

Both words emphasize that the ways of consciousness to which they point are innocent, pure and free of interference by other modes of being or doing, that is other acculturation. According to this story, these were the first species-level qualities of "male" and "female." These "ways of knowing" were present within each human (or human consciousness) and could appear in various combinations in the form of an actual individual. They have nothing to do with which sex is dominant or what roles are appropriate to each. They have everything to do with a sensory feeling for what the differences in consciousness and embodiment mean for fulfilling the purpose of the universe.

In verse 28, the word *barekh*, usually translated as "blessed," points to the sacred breath (*ruach*) and can also mean to breathe compassionately or to bend toward something with compassion. Emphasizing what is to follow, the storyteller also repeats the previously used word for "said" (*yo'mer*), which can also mean to radiate with sound and energy toward something.

The next words refer to the attraction of the Universe toward a principle that could embody the complete awareness of its consciousness. The controversial word *khibshuha*, usually translated "subdue," refers to a centralizing and internalizing (KhB) fire, heat and light (ASh), thereby empowering something through the force of compression. By another reading of its roots (ShU), it also points to redeeming something, helping it to fulfill its purpose in life (similar to the name Yah-Shua, "Yah, the Holy One, redeems").

The phrase *uredu bi-*, usually translated "and have dominion over," clearly says, "have dominion with, along with or alongside of." As noted previously, there is no evidence for the Hebrew (or Semitic preposition) *b* (the letter *beth*) meaning "over," in the sense of ruling over. This seems to have been simply assumed, when the Hebrew scriptures were translated into Western languages (Greek and Latin), by those aligned to the "imperial" Christianity established by Constantine. The ecological and human damage done historically by the ignorant or deliberate misunderstanding of this point cannot be overestimated.

The nature of the human "experiment," its ability to hold the consciousness of what had gone before, plus its ability to operate with a "shadow" of the "free will" that the Universe Being itself possessed was, of course, a dangerous course of development. Self-reflexive human consciousness can override its own subconscious self, instincts and other interior abilities that are a heritage from the interiority of older beings—including plants, fish, birds and animals. Herein lies perhaps the source of all physical and psychological "illnesses," as well as their possible remedy. As we shall see in the next chapter, despite the potential difficulties, the voice of the Holy One related by the storyteller of Genesis still calls this development "ripe (that is, blessed) enough."

2. Birds, Crocodiles, Ecstasy, Longing.

Versions based on Papyrus Harris 500 (British Museum 10060, recto iv 1-7, recto v 6-8), Cairo Ostracon 25218, lines 6-10 and Papyrus Beatty I, verso C iv 6-v 2 with literal translations by Adolf Erman (1927: 243-248) and John A Wilson as contained in the collection of James B. Pritchard (1955: 467-469).

3. A Song About Love - Song of Songs 8:4-5.

In verse four, the word *hishba'ti,* usually translated "charge you," may also mean to swear or confirm with an oath, or to captivate. The phrase *ma-ta'iru uma-te'oreru,* usually translated "stir not up nor awake," both come from the same root 'WR, which points to a blind passion, an inner ardor and fire that produces disorder and leads to the loss of light and rational intelligence. It also points to nakedness or naked skin.

The word *ahaba* points to a mysterious force of life-giving love or friendship that grows gradually from the inside and then spreads out to others. It expands from a desire to possess into a desire to share unselfishly. We found an Aramaic form of this word, *aheb,* in Yeshua's "vine and branches" saying in chapter nine. The roots of this word also appear later in the Arabic sacred phrases *ma'abud Allah* and *ma'abud lil-lah:* the One is the process of loving, or all loving is for or returning to the One.

The word *shettechpatz,* usually translated "until he pleases," could better be translated "until it chooses," or "until its foundations and depths are securely laid." The roots of the word also point to bending and bowing, to finding the pleasure or desire of another. The phrase *benot yerushalaim,* usually translated "daughters of Jerusalem," also has other layers of meaning. *Benot* may be any child, future descendant or pupil. It is linked to the word for the embodiment of interior intelligence *(bina)* that we encountered earlier in Proverbs. Besides being the name of the city, the word *yerushalaim* also points to fear or respect for the flow of peace or harmony (*shalom*).

The word *'ola* in verse five, usually translated "cometh up," may refer to any action of ascending, mounting, rising or being lifted up, also to foliage or leaves that rise in the same way. The word *midbar*, usually translated as "wilderness," also refers to any open space of grassland or pasture that spreads without restriction. The word *mitrappeqet*, usually translated as "leaning upon," can also mean to rest, restore, heal, mend or recover. The roots (RPh) point to a regenerating movement that acts as a medicine or remedy. The same root is used in the name of the angel Raphael, as well as the one of the "99 Beautiful Names of Allah," *ar-Rafi*. The word *dodah*, usually translated "beloved," can also mean a chosen vessel of love or a flower.

The phrase *tachat hattappuach*, usually translated "under the apple tree," may also be translated as below, down in or under the depths of the self. The word for apple *tappuach*, comes from a root (NphH) related to the word for individual breath, or self, from which we have the Hebrew *nephesh*. The word *'orartikha*, translated in the KJV as "raised thee up," is the same word mentioned above in verse four, which means to arouse, excite or inflame with blinding passion. The word *shamma*, usually translated "there," carries the sense of "within," "inside there" and more emphatically, "in that very place." It is related to the word that means to astonish or desolate. The word *chibbelatkha*, usually translated "brought thee forth," carries a number of meanings: to bind or link, to labor in childbirth, to bring forth with pain, to destroy or ravage.

4. A Prayer for Seed, Bread and Water.

Sumer was located in the extreme southeast of what is present-day Iraq. As a political force, its greatest impact lasted from approximately 3100-2100 B.C.E., although its science, economics, political organization and religion continued to influence the Middle East for a much longer period of time.

Inanna and Damuzi are the archetypal lovers of the Middle East whose passionate love and separation, including Damuzi's death and (sometimes) rebirth, influence later myths like that of the Egyptian Ast and Usari (Isis and Osiris by their Greek names). As we have seen, Sumerians also identified Inanna with creation, planting and growth. The identified Damuzi with herds and shepherding. Their sacred marriage united these two modes of living in relationship to nature. This small portion of a much longer hymn would have been chanted as part of a "sacred marriage" ceremony. Perhaps this was also the way the Song of Songs was used, according to some Jewish scholars. The literal translation on which my version is based is from S.N. Kramer as contained in J.B. Pritchard's collection (1955: 642).

5. As the Cosmos Opens and Closes - Matthew 7:7.

The word *sha'lu*, usually translated as "ask," may also mean to pray intensely or interrogate. The roots point to a stroke that unites or a straight line traced from one object to another. The word *netiyheb*, usually translated "receive," also refers to the action of bearing fruit from an inner, generative force. This is the same mysterious, growing love and sympathy, related to the Hebrew word *ahaba*, that we encountered in the Song of Songs. This force becomes progressively deeper—from respect to friendship, from friendship to love, from love to the sacred source of Love.

In the next phrase, the word *b'aw*, usually translated "seek," points to an anxious searching or inquiry, one that figuratively boils over with impatience. It is an interior action that seeks to complete itself in a material sense. The word *teshkchuwn*, usually translated "find," refers to nature's power of regeneration, to the embodied form of the sympathetic fire (ASh) that we have encountered many times previously. Here the action, which begins by looking outward, finds stillness and fulfillment through connection with what is behind appearances, the inner fire of life in all beings. One of the roots (ShCh) points to the image of a force that reaches stillness after being uncoiled or unbound.

In the last phrase, the word *quwshw*, usually translated "knock," may also mean to pitch a tent, or strike the strings of a musical instrument. The roots point to a sense of innocence, a willingness to be a beginner. They also point to a spacious, unconfused state inside that allows any decision made, action taken or note struck to be done with simplicity as well as strength. The word *netptach*, usually translated "opened," is related to the one we encountered in chapter five as a word of healing ("Ethphatah—Be Opened").

6. Her Eyebrows Have Kidnapped My Heart.

This version is based on selections from the Odes of Sa'adi from a literal translation from the Persian by R.M. Rehder in James Kritzeck's collection (1964: 236).

7. Cups and Wine.

This version is based on #72 from "Ghazals from the Divan of Hafiz," translated by Justin Huntly McCarthy, unpublished manuscript and by H. Wilberforce Clarke (1891).

Chapter Eleven

1. Eating and Being Eaten - Genesis 1:29-31.

The developing human self could assimilate the personality and character of other beings—both their new tendencies and the stronger memories of what they had been. According to our Genesis storyteller, other interior soul-selves could only assimilate the life-giving newness, the personality of other beings. While they might have their own character, they could not "eat" that of another and incorporate it into their psyche. In this way, the human came to contain the interiority and character of all previous selves, according to this story.

The word *lakhem,* translated "meat" in the KJV, is the same archetype of food, bread, and understanding, the "daughter" of *Hokhmah,* that we encountered earlier. It points to any food, not necessarily material, that can be assimilated by living beings directly into themselves from Holy Wisdom. It is not specifically an animal product. We found its Aramaic equivalent, *lachma,* in chapter six.

We also previously encountered the word *'eseb,* usually translated "herb" in verse 11. It also means all creations, work, labors, sacrifices or offers of the whole vegetable world. In verse 11, we also previously saw the phrase *zoreha zera,* usually translated "bearing seed." These are the primal mutations, the departures from what had gone before, which seem to be completely foreign or strange in comparison to the beings that bore them. Here we encounter the principle of lavish diversity in the universe: no two blades of grass are alike—one could not be considered the exact duplicate or clone of another, much less its "child." In other words, according to the storyteller, this type of bond does not exist in these beings. As a quality of human consciousness, this could be compared with *personality,* that which can excel in diversity and newness with only a slender hold on the past.

In comparison to this is the word *hetz* (also returning from verse 11), which is usually translated "tree." Its roots point to a growing substance that has stronger and harder boundaries and for this reason works to assemble elements into beings that express its essence more closely, either as fruit or children. According to the Genesis storyteller, both are in a closer, more bonded relationship with their "parents" than those beings that simply bear more newness. As a quality of human consciousness, this could be compared with *character,* which remains more stable and establishes a certain strength and reliability that makes more bonded relationships possible.

In verse 31, we find a departure from the usual formula that ends the other "days." Instead of finding everything *tob* (ripe, appropriate for the moment), we find them *tob me'od,* which the KJV translates as "very good." The word *me'od,* however, could also mean "as much as possible," "to a high degree" or "filling its whole extent," that is, "enough." It points to an action or process that, once chosen from multiple possibilities, must follow its course. The roots also point to a smoking fire—the smoke cannot be called back. Creation was, so to speak, "good enough for now."

2. Create Again the Rising Waters.

This expanded version from the Sumerian and Akkadian transcriptions is based on the text transcribed, transliterated and literally translated by Stephen Langdon in his collection of Babylonian liturgies (1913: 99-102).

The reference to the rising waters indicates that Damuzi has descended beneath the flood of death and lies sleeping in the submerged grain. In this version of the story, Damuzi descends into the underworld at the summer solstice and rises again at the winter solstice. In other versions of the story, he betrays Inanna, and she leaves him in the underworld.

3. A Song About Love, Part 2 - Song of Songs 8:6-7.

The word *shimeni*, usually translated "set me," is derived from the same root ShM that we have encountered previously (particularly in chapter five, "Hear the Sound"). As a verb, it can mean to engrave, to vibrate or resound, to set as a memorial or outward sign. The word *khachotam*, usually translated "seal," can also indicate the sign of an impression made or a symbol that declares that a much greater being or power is hidden and acting behind it. It also refers to a guarantee, that is, something that proves the truthfulness or integrity of that to which it refers. It is related to the Arabic *khatim,* used in the Qur'anic expression *Khatim an-Nabiyin*, "seal of the prophets," referring to Prophet Muhammad as the guarantee or proof of all the prophetic messages brought by his predecessors. The word *libbekha*, usually translated "heart," should also be familiar by now. It is the center of courage, passion, audacity, desire, affection or sense. It is also what always stays "at home," so to speak. The word *zero'ekha*, usually translated as "arm," also means strength or power, anything which leaves the center, spreads and disperses. It is what "leaves home" and everything that implies.

The word *'azza*, usually translated "strong," also means fierce, violent, bold and firm. The roots point to the sensuous, material force of nature that is doubled by being added to itself, through two beings becoming one. The word is also associated with the vigor and fertility of nature. The Arabic equivalent of this word also becomes one of the "99 Beautiful Names"—*al-Aziz*. The word *mawet*, usually translated "death," also means to wither, decay and return through an action of reciprocity to the sameness of universal existence from which a being came (Arabic equivalent in the "99 Beautiful Names," *al-Mumit*). We previously encountered the word for love, *ahaba*, as the mysterious power that grows and unites from within, that wants to share itself more than possess something.

In the next phrase, the word *qasha*, usually translated "cruel," can also mean heavy, difficult, confusing, obstinate, hardened and inextricable. The word *sh'ol,* usually translated "grave," also means the netherworld, the realm of the dead, depths or abyss. Its roots point to a whirlpool, a place where calm and delirium alternate, as well as place of questions and answers. The word *qin'a,* usually translated "jealousy," refers to yet another of side of the desire for communion in the universe. This desire can be eager and envious, it wants to possess and redeem, it is a confusing, tense ardor that often travels with *ahaba,* the deeper love.

In the last phrase of verse six, the words *reshafeha rishpei,* usually translated "coals of fire," both come from the same roots meaning a spark, flame, lightning, fever or plague. They are related, in a more material sense, to the primordial unfolding (RSh) in light and heat that began the cosmos. So is the next word *'esh,* not translated in the KJV, which refers to the fire as a growing, energizing life force in every living being (related to the words *asher* and *asherah*). Finally, yet another side of this image is shown in *shalhebetyah,* usually translated "flame." From its roots, this word points to the radiance, fire and love (HB) that is contained inside any form (BTh), for instance, in the accommodation before the fire that began the cosmos.

In verse seven, the word *mayim,* usually translated "waters," directly points to the primal waters of flow in Genesis 1. The word *rabbim,* usually translated as "many" can also mean great, abundant, strong or sufficient. The root RB can also refer to that which nurtures anything, for instance, in the Hebrew *rabbi* (nurturing through teaching) or the Arabic *rabbi-l'alamin,* which we saw in Surah *Fatiha* in chapter five. The phrase *yukhelu lekhabbot,* usually translated "quench," means to comprehend, apprehend, prevail over or assimilate something to the extent that it is restrained, contained, repressed or extinguished. The word *neharot,* usually translated "floods," refers to a different flow from *mayim*: it is a stream, river or current of light, that which guides, shines and enlightens in a direct path. It is related to the Aramaic *nuhra,* often used by Yeshua, as well as the Arabic "Beautiful

Name" *an-Nur.* The word *yishtefuha,* usually translated "drown," can also mean to pour out abundantly, overflow, wash away, overwhelm or persist without stopping.

In the final part of the verse, the word *yitten,* usually translated "give," can also mean hire, as in renting a dwelling. The word *'aish,* usually translated "man," refers more exactly to the intellectual individuality and possessions of a human being. The word *aish* combines the roots AI and ASh, an individual center that grows, grasps and apprehends for itself, so the human with a developing sense of individuality. It is used as a word for the human in the Genesis 2 story, after the "rib" is removed from *adamah,* and the human becomes an *aish* as well as an *aisha* (the creative initiative), usually translated "woman." For more on this, see my 2003 book *The Genesis Meditations.*

4. Thunder Speaks, Part 5.

This version is also based on the previous literal translations from the Coptic of George W. MacRae (1979: 231-255) and Bentley Layton (1987: 77-85).

5. Resurrection – John 11:25.

The word *nuwchama',* usually translated as "resurrection," may also mean repose, rest, a dwelling or abode of peace or tranquility. Specifically, the roots point to an experience of deep, creative peace that occurs after a long period of agitation (NUH) and that stems from the Sacred Sense residing in the "I" of every being (ChMA). The roots can also be read to point to renewed life, to changing one's dwelling, or finding a new flock. We also find this paradoxical set of meanings in the related word that Yeshua uses for "live," later in the passage: *niche'.* The word usually translated "dead" is *muwt,* which is another form of the Hebrew *mawet,* found in the Songs of Songs passage above. We can read the roots MWT as passing from one formed existence (M) through a mysterious doorway (W) toward a goal (Th) that is the origin of creation.

6. The Gift of the Rose.

This version is based on #98 from "Ghazals from the Divan of Hafiz," translated by Justin Huntly McCarthy, unpublished manuscript and by H. Wilberforce Clarke (1891).

7. Love After Death.

This version is based on the literal translation of #35 in the collection by R.A. Nicholson (1898: 136-139).

Chapter Twelve

1. Returning - Genesis 2:1-3.

In verse one, the word *ikhulou,* usually translated "finished," means literally "shall become/were wholly finished," and is based on the root KL, meaning completeness. As we have seen previously (for instance, in the creation of light), this form of a verb indicates that, through a progressive development, something has shifted from potential to action, that the future has activated a tendency in the here-and-now, making it an accomplished fact. The Universe's "call of encouragement from the future" causes its story to unfold in a way that never exactly repeats itself. The word *tzeba'am,* usually translated "host," refers to an order or direction that tends toward a purpose.

In verse two, the word *yekhal,* usually translated "ended," means more specifically "completely activated" and is related to the other KL word in verse one. The phrase *mela'khto 'asher 'asa,* translated in the KJV as "his work which he had made," describes a composition or creation (*'asa*) that embodies the primordial fire of life (*'asher*) through the vision, ideals, ruling principles and "I can" (*mela'kht*) of the cosmos.

The word *yishbot,* usually translated "rested," means to restore itself or return to its original state or point of departure (ShUB) in a way that completes and consummates something with sympathy (Th). This word becomes the name for any period of remembrance and return to the source. It forms the basis for the word *shabbat,* often anglicized as "sabbath." It is related by root to the word for "seven." As mentioned in a previous note, I owe to my good friend Rabbi Arthur Waskow, the understanding of "seven" as a sacred number, not as a direction (like north, south, east, west, above, below), but as a movement of returning, moving from "outside" to "inside."

In verse three, the word *yebarekh,* usually translated "blessed," also means, as we have seen previously, to breathe with compassion, to invigorate with spirit. The word *yeqaddesh,* usually translated "sanctified," points to setting apart or separating something for a specific purpose, to focusing or preparing the ground for something and to establishing a central point, pivot or motive upon which everything turns.

2. The New Order: Everyone Breathes Like Everyone Else.

Version extracted from several Egyptian coffin texts (Cairo Museum 28083, 28085 and 28094) from literal translations by John A. Wilson as contained in the collection of James B. Pritchard (1955: 7-8) and J.H.Breasted (1933: 221).

3. Wings of Healing in Diversity's Temple - Isaiah 6:1-2.

This text, and others like it, for instance in Ezekiel 1, were associated with an early Jewish mystical practice that aimed to ascend to the *merkabah,* or throne-chariot of the Holy One. Some readings of these texts describe a paradoxical descent before one can ascend, a reference that has confused some scholars. To me, this seems to clearly refer to the need to "go down" into the *nephesh,* the individual soul-self in all its diversity, before one can "go up" connecting all of the individuality in one's divine image to the soul-self (*neshemah*) in willing surrender to Unity. For a comparison, see "The Soul's Three Faces," in chapter eight.

In verse one, the word *'er'eh* usually translated "saw," can also mean being impressed by a ray of power, particularly to a visionary state. The word *adonai,* usually vaguely translated "Lord," points through its roots to the elementary power of unity (A) that divides itself (DN) in order to give life and energy (I), in other words, Sacred Diversity. The word *yosheb,* usually translated "sitting," connects to the same word we saw in Genesis: to return to its original state. The word *kisse',* usually translated "throne," can also mean the top, pinnacle, summation or accumulation of everything or anything. The word *ram,* usually translated "high," points to any straight movement that rises from a center and fills space in a very direct way. The word *nisa'*, usually translated "lifted up," points to any unstable, transient, whirling movement or to something, which by being weak and unstable, needs to be carried and lifted.

The word *shulaw,* usually translated "train," refers to a being that is in equilibrium, with all parts in proportion and following harmonious laws, like the edge of a robe that follows the center from which its movement arises. The word *mele'im,* usually translated "filled," also means to overflow, satisfy or complete. Images related to the roots of this word include: setting a gemstone in its bezel so that it fits perfectly as well as the consecration of a person in a holy office. The word *hekhal,* usually translated "temple," refers also to any place or way of doing things that assimilates power, compresses life and causes that life to come to fruition.

The word *serafim* in verse two, translated "seraphims" in the KJV, refers by its roots (ShRPh) to all powers of healing, reparation, recovery, redemption and regeneration, to the source of all medicine and remedies. This gift of the universe is the province of what the ancient Hebrew mind calls angels. The word *'omedim,* usually translated "above," can also mean gathered near, around or in union with something. The word *mimma'al,* not translated in the KJV, means to grow, extend or be filled out with something, as though a natural development.

Each healing power extended *shesh kenafayim,* usually translated "six wings." *Shesh* refers to a number that is in proportion, measure or harmony with what is needed. *Kenafayim* can mean any extremity, edge or border that, like a skin, extends and spreads out from a primal central force. The word is related by root (NPh) to that for the soul-self, *nephesh.* The word *shtayim,* usually translated "twain," also refers to that which leads to change and variation, to passing from one state to another, or to the initial divisions in the universe. The word *yekhasseh,* usually translated as "covered," can also mean to hide, clothe, conceal a fault and forgive, or to fill in any gaps necessary. It is related to the word used for "throne," the place where all opposites are reconciled. The word *fanaw*, usually translated as "face," also means the presence, countenance, atmosphere or outer aspect of a being. It is related to the Arabic word *fana*, the spiritual practice of "effacement." By filling in what is necessary in their own beings, the recovery powers show how healing works.

The word *raglaw*, usually translated "feet," also means all organs of motion and emotion, anything that moves a being (RG) and that connects with the orbiting, revolving movements in the whole cosmos. The word *'ofef*, usually translated "fly," also refers to any rising, expanding, soaring movements, either inner or outer. These result from the instincts being enlightened and purified, as if by fire, cleansed of excess weight.

4. About Work and Rest - Matthew 11:28-29.

In verse 28, the word *taw*, usually translated "come," also carries the sense of lovers coming together for the first time. The word *la'ya'*, usually translated "labor," also means to be tired, weary or exhausted. The phrase *shqiylay mawble'*, usually translated "heavy laden," means more exactly to be enmeshed and enveloped by a desire (the same root we encountered in the Song of Songs). This desire has turned out to be a burden, one that keeps swelling and expanding. The word *'aniychkhuwn*, usually translated "give you rest," is another form of the same word (*nuwchama*) that we encountered in Yeshua's "I am the resurrection" saying in the previous chapter. It is the repose of existence, a point of equilibrium, a rest and tranquility after constant agitation. It is also a peace that moves toward a goal, one of guidance and health. The basic form of this word is *nyach*, which is used in the meditation.

In verse 29, Jesus continues with a play on the words of the previous verse. Instead of being enmeshed in burdens created by a desire to possess something, he recommends absorbing oneself in *niyry*, a word usually translated "yoke," but which also means any labor linked to illumination and light (related to the Hebrew *aor*) as well as to preparing a field to be ready for planting. The word *iylapw*, usually translated "learn," points by its roots to a wheel or vortex of mental energy that seeks to comprehend or understand existence.

The expression *makiykh 'no' bleby*, usually translated "lowly in heart," is an Aramaic idiom which means to soften inner rigidities and blocks to feeling. The same word for "meek" is used in the third Beatitude in Matthew 5:5. The word *napshatkhuwn*, usually translated "your souls," is another form of the word *naphsha*, the subconscious soul-self which we encountered extensively throughout section two.

5. Speak Unity's Name - Surah 112.

The transliteration here uses ( ) for sounds elided (deleted) or [ ] for sounds added when the surah is chanted traditionally.

The word *qul*, usually translated "say," also means to profess, teach, advocate or support. Its roots point to the sound and voice of nature, especially that of the wind. The word and particle *hu*, usually translated "he," relates to the older Semitic root (U) pointing to the breath of existence that takes us from being to nothingness. This ending becomes defined as the masculine singular pronoun by the time Arabic is formalized as a language; it was not so earlier.

The word *Allah*, which we have seen in its various forms elsewhere, connects directly to its predecessors *Alaha* (Aramaic), *Elohim* and *Eloha* (Hebrew) and *Elat* (Ugaritic, Old Canaanite). All are centered on the root EL or AL, which points to the oneness of existence. This word becomes used as the definite article (equivalent to our word *the*) to indicate that every diverse being finds its distinct character in cosmic unity. There is no ultimate individuality outside of this larger, interconnected Unity. In the seed root AL, one finds power with extensive movement that tends toward a purpose. Balancing this is the root LA, which refers to absolute non-existence. It is movement without a goal, a line stretched out to infinity, to no-thingness. Even in the "no" of being, Unity exists.

The word *ahad,* usually translated "one," refers to every single, distinct object that is drawn or extracted from many. Its older compound roots refer to the passionate life and will in the universe (AH) which lead to the power of differentiation and diversity (AD). In other words, the Being and the Unity about which the surah is speaking is both the One and the one. The distinction between immanence and transcendence collapses at this point. As one of the "99 Beautiful Names," *al-Ahad* expresses that aspect of the sacred in which we feel part of the unknowable, mysterious oneness of Reality. This is not "our One" as opposed to anyone else's "One." We are in the heart of this Unity. The complementary quality of Oneness, *al-Wahid,* expresses the experience that "God is in our heart." For more on this, see my work on the "99 Beautiful Names," *The Sufi Book of Life* (2005).

In the second phrase, the word *samad,* often translated by Yusuf Ali as the "Eternal Absolute," comes from a root that means to defy, withstand, save, extend, supply whatever is needed or fulfill the whole extent of any rules, customs or measures. The medieval Andalusian Sufi Ibn Arabi called this quality, also one of the "99 Beautiful Names," the "universal refuge and support."

In verse three, the words *yalid* and *yolad,* usually translated "begetteth" and "begotten," are both based on an older Semitic root for bearing a child. It was used in Hebrew form in the passage from the Song of Songs in chapter ten. The root LD points to anything born, propagated or bred—an expansion of abundance born of division—including any confined aspects of family, lineage or race. The Unity we are talking about is not subject to such divisions: everything is always connected and in communion.

In verse four, the word *yakun* is based on the Semitic root (KN) for fixing, constituting or grounding something in a body. According to the Qur'an, it is the word that the Holy One spoke to create the cosmos (for instance, see Surah *Maryam*, 19:35, *kun fa-yakun*). The phrase *la-hu kufuw*, usually translated "none comparable" or "none like" also means that nothing is equal, on a par or equivalent. We may talk about Unity, the Universe Being, the One or even God-Goddess, but all these are only metaphors and symbols pointing to a reality that is beyond philosophy, theology, mysticism, metaphysics, spirituality and spiritual practice. No one owns it, no one can claim to completely understand it. But One knows One whenever eyes and ears are open.

6. Everyone Bows When the Friend Passes By.

This version is based on selections from the Odes of Sa'adi from a literal translation from the Persian by R. M. Rehder in James Kritzeck's collection (1964: 237).

7. The Visit and the Gift.

This version is based on the previous literal translations from the Persian by Florence Lederer (1922) and E.H. Whinfield (1880).

Chapter Thirteen

1. A New Name for the Universe Being - Genesis 2:4.

The Hebrew word *toledot,* usually translated "generations," can also mean origin, descent, lineage, family register or genealogy. From its double set of roots, it points to a sign, symbol, hieroglyph or story (ThO) that has been born and unfolds for the purpose of satisfying some desire or purpose (LDTh). The word *behibbare'am* is another form of the word *bara* with which this story began: to draw from the unknown into the known. It is related to the Arabic "Beautiful Name" *al-Bari.* The word *'asot,* usually translated "made," refers to establishing the depths, foundations, or founding principles of something, of moving toward an irresistible goal.

As discussed earlier, the mysterious word *yhwh* (or rendered as all vowels, IHU/OH) usually translated "Lord," is considered in the Jewish tradition to be the name too sacred to be pronounced. It is certainly nothing like the transcriptions *Jehovah* or *Yahweh* that Christians often use. As mentioned previously, it has many root derivations and mystical meanings, due to the fact that the roots interlace each other. The double root HH, indicates universal life, breath, soul and abstract being doubled in strength. As a verb this root could be translated "to be being." This root is preceded by the sound I pointing to a power that has manifested intelligible life as well as to a past which has been without boundary. The letter is related to the human hand, to the forefinger pointing. In the middle of the HH root is placed the Hebrew letter *waw (*or as commonly pronounced today, *vav*), combining the possibilities of the English o and u sounds. This is the sign of a universal link between being and nothingness, the eye and ear, the door that converts one mode of existence to another.

D'Olivet (1815) comments that the root HH is "found placed between a past without origin and a future without limit. This wonderful noun therefore signifies exactly, the-Being-who-is-who-was-and-who-will-be"(II: p.68). He also points out that, if what were meant to be pure vowel sounds were hardened into harsh forms of the consonants (as in something like Jehovah), the name would point to a calamity or unfortunate existence, not a blessing. He speculates that this may have been the origin of the prohibition on pronouncing this name.

I again owe to my friend Rabbi Arthur Waskow the interpretation that a soft sounding of the consonants without vowels most closely emulates the sound of one's own breath. So, as Rabbi Arthur has shared in some of the retreats we have co-led, the name cannot actually be "pronounced," because the most holy "name" is the sound of our own breath, linking us in remembrance to the breath of the Holy One.

2. The Power and Glory of Dark Matter - Isaiah 6:3.

In *weqara'* and *'amar,* we see more forms of the creative "saying" words we found in Genesis 1:3-4, the first carrying the meaning of engraving, the second of radiating something into existence. The word *qadosh* is another form of the word *qaddesh,* which was used to name the Sabbath day in Genesis 2:3. It is usually translated "holy," and also points to a central point, pivot, focus or motive upon which everything turns as well as to setting apart something for a specific purpose or preparing the ground for something to happen. An Aramaic form of the word (*netqadash*) is used in the second line of the Lord's Prayer. For the rendering of the "unnameable Name" *yhwh,* see note one above.

The word *tzeba'ot,* usually translated "hosts," is often associated with the movement of stars or angels. The roots point to something that leaves material limits behind, breaks the bounds of the past, and is clear and radiant (TzA) as it progresses and moves (BA) toward an unnameable future (Th).

In the last line, the word *melo',* usually translated "full," is related to the word we saw in the previous two verses: It is what satisfies all needs, is abundant, strong and pregnant. The word *kebodo,* usually translated "glory," can also mean weight, wealth, esteem or, in a more figurative sense, the soul. Its roots point to a centralized force that acts from the abyss of existence or from the inside of all beings with power, light and abundance. This "heavy glory" shines from the soul of all existence, according to this passage. Perhaps one could say that it is the transformed *choshekh* of Genesis 1:2 as it finds its place within the ongoing creation story.

3. O Breathing Life - Matthew 6:9-13 and Luke 11:2-4.

The word *abwun*, usually translated "father," can also mean birther, parent, father-mother or from its roots, the All (A) birthing (B) mystery (U) into form (N). The word *tzebyanakh* in line four, usually translated "will," can also mean heart's desire or confidence. It is related to the Aramaic *saba*, which Yeshua uses when he agrees to heal someone ("the willing passion of the One is coming through me"—an expression usually translated "I will").

In line six, the words *washbuwq...shbaqn*, usually translated "forgive," may also mean to untie, embrace with emptiness, or return to its original state. Matthew's version uses the word *chawbayn* as the object of this releasing, usually translated "debts." The word also means hidden past or stolen property. In saying the prayer Aramaic Christians today of most denominations traditionally add the alternate word from Luke's version to this line (*chtahayn*) This word, usually translated "sins," can also mean failures, mistakes, frustrated hopes or tangled threads.

Line seven uses the phrase *wla' ta'lan lnesyuwna'*, translated in the KJV as "lead us not into temptation." The Aramaic, however, says "and let us not enter forgetfulness." The word *nesyuwna'* can also mean being lost in superficial appearances or materialism, the image of forgetting the Source. In second part of the line, the KJV renders *'ela' patzan men bisha'* as "but deliver us from evil." As we have previously seen, the Semitic sense of *bisha'* means unripe action, that which is out of its proper time, or continued beyond the appropriate time. The word *patzan* also means to loosen the hold of, to free or to break the seal that binds one.

In the last line the word *teshbuwchta'*, usually translated "glory," can also mean song, especially the harmony of the stars as it was envisioned by the Native Middle Eastern tradition. The phrase *l'alam 'almiyn*, usually translated "forever," means literally "from gathering to gathering." All other words have been considered in some form elsewhere in these notes. For a more complete discussion of a prayer rich with meaning, please see my earlier work particularly *Prayers of the Cosmos* (1990), *Original Prayer* (2000) and *The Hidden Gospel* (1999).

4. A Blessing of Lucid Fire and Secret Grace - 1QS 2:2a-4a.

This blessing is a variation of the one in Numbers 6:24-26 (KJV): "May the Lord bless thee, and keep thee: may the Lord make his face shine upon thee, and be gracious unto thee: The Lord lift up his countenance upon thee, and give thee peace." I have retranslated it from the Hebrew transcription of the Qumran Sectarian Manuscript (1QS) done by Martin Abegg (1999-2007, Accordance).

In the first line, the word *barekkhah* is another form of the word for blessing we found in Genesis 1:22 and 1:28. It can be read as breathing with magnetism, helping a being to bow and surrender to its purpose in life. We have also seen the word *tob* previously—"goodness" seen as being ripe and ready to fulfill one's sacred purpose.

In the second line, the word *yshmorkha* means to protect or keep, as though with a sphere of light or fire. The word *r'wh*, another word for "evil" in Hebrew, means that which is abnormally crooked or brittle compared to its natural state. This is an image of the breath that cannot find its own natural channel due to inner rigidities and so expresses its action in neurotic ways.

In the third line, the word *libkhah* is another form of the word we previously encountered for "heart," the center of one's passion and energy. The word *sekhl* means understanding, consciousness, contemplation, meditation, intelligence or wisdom.

In line four, the word *yachonkhh* means to grace with or uncover what was hidden, especially a strength or virtue. The word *d'at* means knowledge, insight or any understanding of diversity and presence that satisfies a particular purpose. The word *'olamym* is the Hebrew form of the Aramaic word *alam*, which we encountered at the end of Yeshua's prayer. Its roots (ALM) refer to the gathering of anything—ages, times, conditions, levels. Here, and in many Hebrew prayers, it refers to the mysterious and ancient First Gathering—creation and the time before creation. It is often translated in a Platonic (but not Semitic) sense as "eternal."

In the last line, the word *chasadyw* (based on the word *chesed*) can mean love, kindness, benevolence, favor, mercy, grace or beauty. Here is yet another Semitic word for love. This love is a silent, secret action that sympathizes with another, that offers a place of shelter and refuge. The word *shlom* is another form of the word for peace, or happiness. Figuratively, it is the note that unites and harmonizes sounds that had previously been heard as dissonant. In Jewish mystical tradition, it also refers to the fullness of potential before creation, a pregnant rather than empty peace.

5. Road, Compass, Fuel - John 14:6.

The Aramaic word *'uwrcha'*, usually translated as "way," is related to the Aramaic *nuhra*, the light as well as the older Hebrew word *aor*. Here, Yeshua says that connecting the small self to the greater Self, using his atmosphere for support, provides a light that uncovers a path, shows a hidden possibility and reveals a practical way not previously known. The word *shrara'*, usually translated as "truth," points to a solution or liberation, the opening of a circle, something solid and in accordance with universal harmony, with the measured tempo of the song of the cosmos. *Shrara'* is similar to the sense of right direction we previously encountered in the Zoroastrian *Ashem Vohu* prayer in chapter four. The word *chaye'*, which we encountered in other forms many times, again reveals the life-force, animal or primal energy that pervades the universe and nature. For a translation of the larger context around this saying, and others in Yeshua's last talk with this disciples, see my 2006 book *Blessings of the Cosmos*.

6. The Open Road - Surah 5:48b.

This surah (whose name means "a table spread") contains toward the end an account of Jesus' disciples asking him to provide them with a table of food as a miracle, so that they might believe in him (perhaps a reference to the same story found in John 6, out of which the "I am the bread" saying comes). Much of the surah discusses relations between Jews, Christians and Muslims in the Medinan community. This was after the Muslims left Mecca having been asked by Medina to organize the city around the message of Islam, a journey called the *Hijra* in 622 C.E.

The word *ja`alnaa* (from *ja'ala*) can mean to create, establish or esteem. From its old Semitic root (GU/GE), it indicates an "organic" sense of establishing, that is, to give life to organs of the body or to give medicine. The word *shiratanwwa* comes from *shara'a* meaning to show the way to a watering place, or to establish a law or highway. It comes from the same Semitic root (ShR) that means to liberate or open a way to harmony, or to laws modeled on that harmony. We saw the Aramaic equivalent in the previous selection. According to some Islamic scholars, a *shiri'ah* shows the beginning of a way or a general direction, and a *minhaj* (the next word mentioned in the Surah) is a well-traveled road. *Nahaja* (the root of *minhaj*) can also mean to follow a track, to trace or to make a map. One Qur'anic translator,

Muhammad Asad (1980, in Accordance 2007), comments on the two words:

> The terms *shir'ah* and *minhaj* are more restricted in their meaning than the term *din*, which comprises not merely the laws relating to a particular religion but also the basic, unchanging spiritual truths which, according to the Qur'an, have been preached by every one of God's apostles, while the particular body of laws (*shir'ah* or *shari'ah*) promulgated through them, and the way of life (*minhaj*) recommended by them, varied in accordance with the exigencies of the time and of each community's cultural development. This "unity in diversity" is frequently stressed in the Qur'an.

The word *yabluwakum* comes from *bala*, to test, try, prove, experiment, honor, or bestow favor. Its ancient Semitic root is BL, to moisten or make the earth fertile. The word *fastabiqul* comes from *sabaqa*, to go before, advance, surpass, strive or race. The word *khayraat* comes from *khara*, to choose, prefer, select or earn wealth. Its ancient Semitic root ChY, refers to the embodiment of life energy in nature and in form. By another reading of the root as ChR it shows a central fire radiating heat. The word *fayunabbi* comes from *naba'a*, to inform, prophesy, give news. Its ancient Semitic root NB is used throughout Hebrew and Aramaic to indicate inspiration, prophesy and exaltation (for instance, the Hebrew *nebi* and Aramaic *nabiya*). Rendered literally, the roots mean to bring outside into form what inspiration has created within.

The word *kuntum* comes from the verb *kana*, to be, exist or happen in form. We saw another form of it in the discussion of Surah *al-Ikhlas* in the previous chapter. The word *takhtalifuun*, comes from the verb *khalafa*, to succeed, take the place of, remain behind, forfeit one's word, disagree or branch off. The Semitic root ChL makes sense of these disparate meanings with the image of something extending too far, distended toward a particular goal that causes it to break off from the main body of something, causing a wound.

7. A Song About a Journey.

This version is based on the first part of the literal translation of #36 in the collection by R.A. Nicholson (1898: 140-143).

8. Gaze Gently on These Blossoms.

This version is based on the previous literal translations from the Persian by Florence Lederer (1922) and E.H. Whinfield (1880).

Index of Source Threads

Genesis Threads (Hebrew)

Other Hebrew Threads

Ancient Middle Eastern Threads

Aramaic Gospel Threads

Dead Sea and Nag Hammadi Threads (Hebrew, Coptic)

Qur'an and Hadith Threads (Arabic)

Sufi Threads (Persian)

Index of Meditations by Type

Sound and Embodiment

Gratitude and Celebration

Simple Presence

Index to Front Matter, Appendix, Notes and Commentary

Bibliography

Primary Texts and Research Tools

Alim Islamic Software: Qur'an (Arabic version and translations by Asad, Malik, Pickthall, Yusuf Ali), Hadith (Abu-Dawood, Al-Bukhari, Al-Muwatta, Al-Tirmidhi, Fiq-us-Sunnah, Muslim) and other References. (2000). Silver Springs, MD: ISL Software. www.islsoftware.com. This excellent resource is now also available online at www.alim.org

The Concordance to the Peshitta Version of the Aramaic New Testament (1985). New Knoxville, OH: American Christian Press.

Greek New Testament (Nestle-Aland, 27th Edition, second printing) (1995). Grammcord Institute (electronic edition). (1993). Stuttgart: Deutsche Bibelgesellschaft.

A Hebrew and English Lexicon of the Old Testament (Abridged). (1997). Based on *A Hebrew and English Lexicon of the Old Testament* by F. Brown, S. R. Driver, and C. A. Briggs. Oxford: Clarendon Press, 1907. Digitized and abridged as a part of the Princeton Theological Seminary Hebrew Lexicon Project under the direction of Dr. J. M. Roberts. Vancouver, WA: Grammcord Institute.

A Biblical Aramaic Lexicon of the Old Testament (Abridged). (1999). Based upon the Biblical Aramaic section of "A Hebrew and English

Lexicon of the Old Testament," by F. Brown, S. R. Driver, and C. A. Briggs. Oxford: Clarendon Press, 1907. Edited by Dale M. Wheeler, Ph.D. Electronic text hypertexted and prepared by OakTree Software, Inc. Vancouver, WA: Grammcord Institute.

Hebrew Masoretic Text. (1994). Westminster Hebrew Morphology. Philadelphia, PA: Westminster Theological Seminary. Electronic Edition. Vancouver, WA: Grammcord Institute.

Syriac New Testament and Psalms. Based on the 1901 Oxford: Clarendon Press edition prepared by G.H. Gwilliam. Istanbul: Bible Society in Turkey.

Peshitta Syriac Bible. (1979). Syrian Patriarchate of Antioch and All the East. London: United Bible Societies.

Qumran Sectarian Manuscripts: A New English Translation. (1996). Based upon the book "The Dead Sea Scrolls: A New English Translation," edited by Michael O. Wise, Martin G. Abegg, Jr. and Edward M. Cook (New York: HarperCollins Publishers, 1996). Electronic edition used by permission of HarperCollins Publishers. Vancouver, WA: Grammcord Institute.

Qumran Sectarian Manuscripts: Qumran Text and Grammatical Tags. (1999). Martin G. Abegg, Jr. Electronic Edition. Vancouver, WA: Grammcord Institute.

Ali, Yusuf A., trans. (1938). *The Holy Qur'an: Text, Translation, Commentary.* Lahore: Sh. Muhammad Ashraf.

Asad, Muhammad, tran. (1980). *The Message of the Holy Qur'an.* Published online at www.alim.org and as part of the Alim Software above.

Budge, E.A.W. (1911a). *A Hieroglyphic Vocabulary to the Book of the Dead.* London: Kegan Paul, Trench, Trübner & Co.

D'Olivet, Fabre. (1815). *The Hebraic Tongue Restored.* Nayan Louise Redfield, trans. 1921 edition republished 1991. York Beach, ME: Samuel Weiser.

Elliger, K. and W. Rudolph, eds. (1966/67) *Biblia Hebraica Stuttgartensia* Stuttgart: Deutsche Bibelgesellschaft.

Falla, Terry C. (1991). *A Key to the Peshitta Gospels.* Volume 1*: Aleph-Dalath.* Leiden: E.J. Brill.

Feyerabend, Karl. (1955). *Langenscheidt's Hebrew-English Dictionary to the Old Testament.* Berlin and London: Methuen & Co.

Gibb, H.A.R. and J.H. Kramers. (2001). *Concise Encyclopedia of Islam.* Boston and Leiden: Brill Academic Publishers.

Jeffery, Arthur. (1937, 2009). *The Foreign Vocabulary of the Qur'an.* Piscataway, NJ: Gorgias Press.

Jennings, William. (1979). *Lexicon to the Syriac New Testament.* Knoxville, OH: American Christian Press.

Kiraz, George Anton. (1994). *Lexical Tools to the Syriac New Testament.* Sheffield: JSOT Press/Sheffield Academic Press.

Kutscher, E. Y. (1976). *Studies in Galilean Aramaic.* Ramat Gan: Bar-Ilan University.

Lamsa, George M. (1957). *The New Testament from the Ancient Eastern Text.* San Francisco: Harper & Row.

Lipinski, Edward. (1997). *Semitic Languages: Outline of a Comparative Grammar.* Leuven: Peeters.

Omar, Abdul Mannan. (2003). *The Dictionary of The Holy Qur'an.* Hockessin, DE: Noor Foundation.

Sells, Michael. (1999). *Approaching the Qur'an: The Early Revelations.* Ashland, OR: White Cloud Press.

Siddiqi, Abdul Hamid. (1976). *Sahih Muslim: Being Traditions of the Sayings and Doings of the Prophet Muhammad as Narrated by His Companions and Compiled Under the Title Al-Jami'-us-Sahih, Vols 1-IV.* Lahore: Sh. Muhammad Ashraf.

Smith, J. Payne, ed. (1903). *A Compendious Syriac Dictionary.* Oxford: Clarendon Press.

Smith, Richard. (1999). *A Concise Coptic-English Lexicon, Second Edition.* Atlanta: Society of Biblical Literature.

Sokoloff, Michael. (1990). *A Dictionary of Jewish Palestinian Aramaic of the Byzantine Period.* Ramat-Gan, Israel: Bar Ilan University Press.

Thomas, Robert L., ed. (1981). *New American Standard Exhaustive Concordance of the Bible: Hebrew-Aramaic Dictionary.* Electronic Edition. Vancouver, WA: Grammcord Institute.

————————. (1981). *New American Standard Exhaustive Concordance of the Bible: Greek Dictionary.* Electronic Edition. Vancouver, WA: Grammcord Institute.

Wacholder, Ben Zion and Abegg, Martin G. (1992). *A Preliminary Edition of the Unpublished Dead Sea Scrolls: The Hebrew and Aramaic Texts from Cave Four, Fascicle Two.* Washington, DC: Dead Sea Scroll Research Council, Biblical Archaeology Society.

Werblowsky, R. J. Zwi and Geoffrey Wigoder. (1997). *The Oxford Dictionary of the Jewish Religion.* New York and Oxford: Oxford University Press.

Whish, Henry F. (1883). Clavis Syriaca: A Key to the Ancient Syriac Version called "Peshitta" of the Four Holy Gospels. London: George Bell & Sons.

Other Resources Consulted

Barnstone, Wilis, ed. (1984). *The Other Bible.* San Francisco: Harper & Row.

Bergson, Henri. (1913). *Time and Free Will: An Essay on the Immediate Data of Consciousness.* Boulder: R. A Kessenger Publishing Co.

Berman, Morris. (2000). *Wandering God: A Study in Nomadic Spirituality.* Albany: State University of New York Press.

Berry, Thomas. (1988). *The Dream of the Earth.* San Francisco: Sierra Club Books.

——————————. (1999). *The Great Work: Our Way Into the Future.* New York. Bell Tower.

Black, Matthew. 1967. *An Aramaic Approach to the Gospels and Acts.* Oxford: Clarendon Press.

Boman, Thorlief. (1960). *Hebrew Thought Compared with Greek.* Philadelphia: Westminster.

Boyarin, Daniel. (2004). *Border Lines: The Partition of Judeo-Christianity.* Philadelphia: University of Pennsylvania Press.

Boyce, Mary. (1979). *Zoroastrians: Their Religious Beliefs and Practices.* London: Routledge & Kegan Paul.

Breasted, J.H. (1933). *The Dawn of Conscience.* New York: Charles Scribners Sons.

Brock, Sebastian. (1973). "Early Syrian Aceticism" in *Numen* XX, Fasc. I. Leiden: E.J. Brill.

Brock, Sebastian. (1975). "St. Issac of Ninevah and Syriac Spirituality" in *Sobornost* 7: 2.

Brock, Sebastian. (1987). "The Priesthood of the Baptised: Some Syriac Perspectives" in *Sobornost/Eastern Churches Review* 9:2.

Buber, Martin and Franz Rosenzweig. (1994). *Scripture and Translation.* Bloomington: Indiana University Press.

Budge, E.A.W. (1895). *The Book of the Dead: The Papyrus of Ani.* London: British Museum.

Budge, E.A.W. (1911b). *Osiris and the Egyptian Resurrection.* London: Medici Society, Ltd.

Budge, E.A.W., ed. (1923). *Facsimiles of Egyptian Hieratic Papyri in the British Museum, Second Series.* London: British Museum

Callender Jr., Dexter E. (2000). *Adam in Myth and History: Ancient Israelite Perspectives on the Primal Human.* Winona Lake, IN: Eisenbrauns.

Camp, Claudia. (1985). *Wisdom and the Feminine in the Book of Proverbs.* Decatur, GA: Almond.

Clarke, Isabel, ed. (2001). *Psychosis and Spirituality: Exploring the New Frontier.* London: Whurr Publishers.

Clarke, H. Wilberforce. (1974). *The Divan of Khwaja Shams-ud-Din Muhammad-i-Hafiz-i-Shirazi.* A reprint of the 1891 edition. London: Octagon Press.

Coward, Harold. (1988). *Sacred Word and Sacred Text: Scripture in World Religions.* Maryknoll, NY: Orbis Books.

——————————, ed. (2000). *Experiencing Scripture in World Religions.* Maryknoll, NY: Orbis Books.

Dawood, N.J., trans. (1956). *The Koran.* Harmondsworth: Penguin Books.

Dhalla, Dastur M. N. (1942). *Homage Unto Ahura Mazda.* Bombay: H.T. Anklesaria.

Douglas-Klotz, Neil. (1990). *Prayers of the Cosmos: Meditations on the Aramaic Words of Jesus.* San Francisco: HarperSanFrancisco.

——————. (1999). *The Hidden Gospel: Decoding the Spirituality of the Aramaic Jesus.* Wheaton, IL: Quest Books.

——————. (1997). The natural breath. Toward further dialogue between western somatic and eastern spiritual approaches to the body awareness of breathing. *Religious Studies and Theology* 16 (2), 64-79.

——————. (1999). Midrash and postmodern inquiry: suggestions toward a hermeneutics of indeterminacy. *Currents in Research: Biblical Studies* 7, 181-193. Sheffield: Sheffield Academic Press.

————————. (2000). Genesis Now: Midrashic Views of Bereshit Mysticism in Thomas and John. Paper presented at the Society of Biblical Literature Annual Meeting in the Thomas Traditions Section, Nashville, TN, November 21, 2000.

————————. (2000). *Original Prayer: Teachings and Meditations on the Aramaic Words of Jesus* (audio program). Boulder: Sounds True.

————————. (2002). Re-hearing Qur'an in open translation: ta'wil, postmodern inquiry and a hermeneutics of indeterminacy. Paper presented in the Arts, Literature and Religion Section of the American Academy of Religion Annual Meeting, Toronto, Ontario, Canada, November 23, 2002 on the theme of Hermeneutics.

————————. (2002). Beginning time: a new look at early Jewish/ Christian ritual time. *Cosmos* 18 (2002), 1-7. Edinburgh: University of Edinburgh.

————————. (2003). *The Genesis Meditations: A Shared Practice of Peace for Christians, Jews and Muslims.* Wheaton, IL: Quest Books.

————————. (2003) *The Healing Breath: Body-based Meditations on the Aramaic Beatitudes* (audio program). Boulder, CO: Sounds True.

————————. (2003). "Reading John in Bereshit Time: Semitic Constructions of Creation Mysticism in the Early Syriac Versions." Paper presented in a joint session of the Christian Apocrypha and Nag Hammadi and Gnosticism Sections of the Society of Biblical Literature Annual Meeting in Atlanta, Georgia, USA on November 24, 2003.

————————. (2005). *The Sufi Book of Life: 99 Pathways of the Heart for the Modern Dervish.* New York: Penguin.

————————. (2005). Ordinary and Extra-Ordinary Ways of Knowing in Islamic Mysticism. In *Ways of Knowing: Science and Mysticism Today*, ed. C. Clarke, in press. Exeter: Imprint Academic, 2005. [Based on separate papers given in the AAR Mysticism Group in 2001 and the AAR Arts, Literature and Religion Section in 2002.]

————————. (2006). *Blessings of the Cosmos:* Boulder: Sounds True.

————————. (2008). Languages of experience: the theory and practice of a general semantics Sufi. *Cosmos* 24 (2008), 89-103. Edinburgh: University of Edinburgh.

Douglas-Klotz, N. , A. Waskow and J. Chittister. (2006). *The Tent of Abraham: Stories of Hope and Peace for Jews, Christians and Muslims.* Boston: Beacon Press.

Drower, E.S., trans. (1959). *The Canonical Prayerbook of the Mandaeans.* Leiden: E.J. Brill.

Drower, E.S., trans. (1960). *The Thousand and Twelve Questions (Alf Trisar Suialia).* Berlin: Akademie-Verlag.

Drower, E.S. (1962). *The Mandaeans of Iraq and Iran.* Leiden: E.J. Brill.

Eisenman, Robert H. and Wise, Michael. (1992). *The Dead Sea Scrolls Uncovered.* Shaftesbury: Element Books Ltd.

Erman, Adolf. (1927). Aylward M. Blackman, trans. *The Literature of the Ancient Egyptians.* London: Methuen & Co.

Errico, Rocco A. and Michael J. Bazzi. (1989). *Classical Aramaic, Assyrian-Chaldean Dialect, Elementary Book I.* Irvine, CA: Noohra Foundation.

Fitzmyer, Joseph A. (1997). *The Semitic Background of the New Testament.* Grand Rapids, MI: Eerdmans and Livonia, MI: Dove Booksellers.

Fox, Everett. (1995). *The Five Books of Moses: Genesis, Exodus, Leviticus, Numbers, Deuteronomy.* New York: Schocken Books.

Fox, Matthew. (1986). *Original Blessing.* Santa Fe: Bear and Company.

Fox, Matthew. (1992). *Creation Spirituality.* San Francisco: Harper SanFrancisco.

Friedlander, Rabbi Albert H. (1984). *The Five Scrolls.* New York: Central Conference of American Rabbis.

Gadd, Cyril John. (1924). *Sumerian Reading Book.* Oxford: Clarendon Press.

Gaster, Theodor H. (1956). *The Dead Sea Scriptures.* Garden City, NY: Doubleday & Co.

Glatzer, Nahum N. (1967). *Language of the Faith.* New York: Schocken Books.

Hareven, Shulamith. (1995). *The Vocabulary of Peace: Life, Culture and Politics in the Middle East.* San Francisco: Mercury House.

Hirtenstein, Stephen. (1999). *The Unlimited Mercifier: The Spiritual Life and Thought of Ibn 'Arabi.* Oxford and Ashland, OR: Anqa Publishing and White Cloud Press.

Hixon, Lex. (2003). *Heart of the Qur'an: An Introduction to Islamic Spirituality.* Wheaton, IL: Theosophical Publishing House.

Horne, Charles F., ed. (1917). *The Sacred Books and Early Literature of the East, Vol. VII, Ancient Persia and Vol. VII, Medieval Persia.* New York: Parke, Austin, and Lipscomb.

Hornung, Erik. (1982). John Baines, tr. *Conceptions of God in Ancient Egypt: the One and the Many.* Ithaca, NY: Cornell University Press.

Jafarey, Ali A. (1988). *Fravarane: I Choose for Myself the Zoroastrian Religion.* Westminister: California Zoroastrian Center.

Kanagaraj, Jey J. (1998). *"Mysticism" in the Gospel of John.* Journal for the Study of the New Testament Supplement Series 158. Sheffield: Sheffield Academic Press.

Kaplan, Aryeh. (1990). *Sefer Yetzirah: The Book of Creation in Theory and Practice.* York Beach, ME: Samuel Weiser.

Kelber, Werner H. (1997). *The Oral and the Written Gospel: The Hermeneutics of Speaking and Writing in the Synoptic Tradition, Mark, Paul, and Q.* Bloomington: Indiana University Press.

Khan, Hazrat Inayat. (1978). *The Complete Sayings of Hazrat Inayat Khan.* New Lebanon, NY: Omega Publications.

Korzybski, Alfred (1933). *Science and Sanity: An Introduction to Non-Aristotelian Systems and General Semantics.* Englewood, NY: Institute of General Semantics.

Kritzeck, James. (1964). *Anthology of Islamic Literature.* New York: New American Library.

Lamsa, George M. (1933). *The Holy Bible from Ancient Eastern Manuscripts.* Philadelphia: A.J. Holman.

Lamsa, George M. (1939). *Gospel Light: Comments on the Teachings of Jesus from Aramaic and Unchanged Eastern Customs.* Philadelphia: A.J. Holman.

Lamsa, George M. (1979). *New Testament Origin.* San Antonio: Aramaic Bible Center.

Langdon, Stephen. (1913). *Babylonian Liturgies.* Paris: Librairie Paul Geuthner.

——————————. (1917). *Sumerian Liturgical Texts.* Philadelphia: University of Pennsylvania Museum.

Lategan, Bernard and Willem Vorster. (1985). *Text and Reality: Aspects of Reference in Biblical Texts.* Atlanta: Scholars Press.

Layton, Bentley. (1987). *The Gnostic Scriptures.* Garden City, NY: Doubleday.

Lederer, Florence. (1920). *The Secret Rose Garden of Sa'dduddin Mahmud Shabistari.* Lahore: Sh. Muhammed Ashraf.

Lewis, C.S. (1969). *The Best of C.S. Lewis.* New York: Iversen-Norman Associates.

MacRae, George W. (1979). "The Thunder, Perfect Mind" in Douglas M. Parrot and James Robinson. *Nag Hammadi Studies, Vol. 11: The Coptic Gnostic Library: Nag Hammadi Codices V,2-5 and VI with Papyrus Berolinensis 8502, 1 and 4.* Leiden: E.J. Brill.

McCrickland, Janet. (1990). *The Eclipse of the Sun.* Glastonbury: Gothic Image.

Muhaiyaddeen, M. R. Bawa. (1979). *Asma ul Husna.* Philadelphia: Fellowship Press.

————————. (1987). *Islam and World Peace: Explanations of a Sufi.* Philadelphia: Fellowship Press.

Nasr, Seyyed Hossain. (1968). *Man and Nature: The Spiritual Crisis in Modern Man.* London: Unwin.

————————. (1978). *An Introduction to Islamic Cosmological Doctrines.* London: Thames and Hudson.

Nicholson, R.A. (1898). *Selected Poems from the Divani Shamsi Tabriz.* Cambridge: Cambridge University Press.

——————————. (1921). *Translations of Eastern Poetry and Prose.* Cambridge: Cambridge University Press.

Pagels, Elaine. (1975). *The Gnostic Paul: Gnostic Exegesis of the Pauline Letters.* Philadelphia: Trinity Press.

———————-. (1979). *The Gnostic Gospels.* New York: Random House.

———————-. (1988). *Adam, Eve, and the Serpent.* New York: Random House.

———————-. (1995). *The Origin of Satan.* New York: Random House.

———————-. (1999). Exegesis of Genesis 1 in the Gospels of Thomas and John. *Journal of Biblical Literature* 118,3: 477-496.

Parrinder, Geoffrey. (1995). *Jesus in the Qur'an.* Oxford: Oneworld Publications.

Pasha, Johnson. (1969). *The Secret Garden.* A republication of the original 1903 edition. London: Octagon Press.

Pickthall, Muhammad Marmaduke. (1953). *The Meaning of the Glorious Koran.* New York: New American Library.

Pritchard, James B. (1955). *Ancient Near Eastern Texts Relating to the Old Testament.* Second Edition. New Jersey: Princeton University Press.

————————. (1958). *The Ancient Near East.* New Jersey: Princeton University Press.

Pritchard, James B., ed. (1969). *The Ancient Near East: Supplementary Texts and Pictures Relating to the Old Testament.* Princeton: Princeton University Press.

Quispel, Gilles. (1975). Jewish gnosis and Mandaean gnosticism. In J.-E. Menard, ed., *Les Textes de Nag Hammadi: Colloque du Centre d'Histoire des Religions* (Strassbourg, 23-25 Octobre 1974), NHS 7, Leiden: E. J. Brill, pp. 82-122.

Rihbany, Abraham. (1916). *The Syrian Christ.* Boston: Houghton Mifflin.

Robinson, James, ed. (1978). *The Nag Hammadi Library in English.* San Francisco: HarperSanFrancisco.

Robinson, Theodore H. (1962). *Paradigms and Exercises in Syriac Grammar.* Oxford: Clarendon Press.

Rogers, Robert William. (1912). *Cuneiform Parallels to the Old Testament.* London: Henry Frowde Oxford University Press.

Rothenberg, Jerome. (1968, 1985). *Technicians of the Sacred: A Range of Poetries from Africa, America, Asia, Europe & Oceania. Berkeley*: University of California Press.

Ruzer, Serge. (1997). Reflections of Genesis 1-2 in the Old Syriac Gospels. In Frishman, Judith and Lucas Van Rompay, eds. *The Book of Genesis in Jewish and Oriental Christian Interpretation.* Louvain: Peeters, pp. 91-102.

Schimmel, Annemarie. (1975). *Mystical Dimensions of Islam.* Chapel Hill: University of North Carolina Press.

—————————————— . (1992). *Islam: An Introduction.* Albany: State University of New York Press.

—————————————— . (1994). *Deciphering the Signs of God: A Phenomenological Approach to Islam.* Albany: State University of Islam Press.

Scholem, Gershom G. (1949). *Zohar, The Book of Splendor.* New York: Schocken Books.

Scholem, Gershom G. (1954). *Major Trends in Jewish Mysticism.* Third Edition. New York: Schocken Books.

Schonfield, Hugh J. (1957). *Secrets of the Dead Sea Scrolls: Studies Toward their Solution.* New York: Thomas Yoseloff, Inc.

Schroer, Silvia. (2000). *Wisdom Has Built Her House: Studies on the Figure of Sophia in the Bible.* Translated from the German by Linda Maloney and William McDonough. Collegeville, MN: The Liturgical Press.

Suhrawardi, Shahab-ud-din. (1979). *The 'Awarif-u'l-Ma'arif.* H. Wilberforce Clarke, trans. (a republication of the 1891 edition). Lahore, Pakistan: Sh. Muhammad Ashraf.

Swimme, Brian and Thomas Berry. (1992). *The Universe Story.* San Francisco: Harper SanFrancisco.

Thackston, Wheeler M. Thackston, Jr., trans. (1997). *Tales of the Prophets (Qisas al-anbiya) by Muhammad ibn Abd Allah al-Kisai.* Chicago, IL: Kazi Publications.

Vanderburgh, Frederick Augustus. (1908). *Sumerian Hymns.* New York: Columbia University Press.

Vermes, G. (1987). *The Dead Sea Scrolls in English.* London: Penguin Books Ltd.

Waskow, Arthur. (1982). *Seasons of Our Joy.* Boston: Beacon Press.

Whinfield, E.H. (1880). *The Gulistan of Shabistari.* London: Trubner.

Wilson, Epiphanius, ed. (1900). *Sacred Books of the East.* London: Colonial Press.

Zaehner, R.C. (1956). *The Teachings of the Magi.* New York. Oxford University Press.

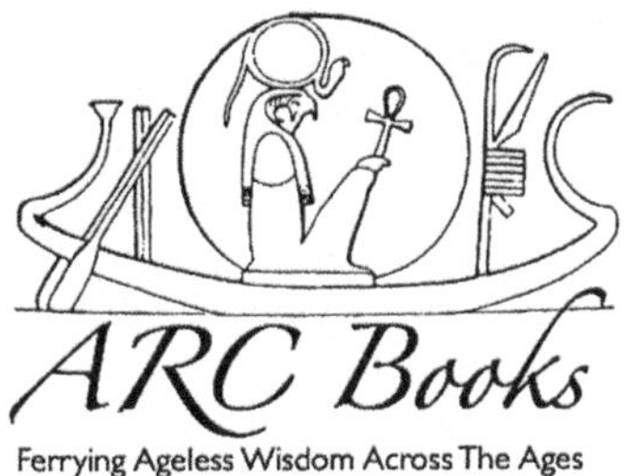

The Abwoon Resource Center (ARC), a project of Shalem Center, offers books, recordings, articles and information about workshops and retreats that support the work in this book. Its mailing address is 881 High Street, Suite 206, Worthington, OH 43085 USA.

The website of the Abwoon Resource Center (**www. abwoon.com**) includes a library archive of most of the articles by Neil Douglas-Klotz cited here, as well as podcasts of his talks and lectures, upcoming schedule internationally, and all published books and recordings.